KATRINA'S SECRETS

—*Storms after the Storm*—

C. RAY NAGIN

WITHDRAWN

ISBN: 146095971X
ISBN-13: 9781460959718
Library of Congress Control Number: 2011903367

TABLE OF CONTENTS

To my family: Seletha, Jeremy, Jarin, and Tianna whose love and support have never wavered.

This book is also dedicated to the wonderful, creative, and resilient people of New Orleans. May we never forget those who perished during Katrina or the struggles endured by the stranded in the Superdome, Convention Center, and on rooftops.

INTRODUCTION

———— ■ ————

I t was towards the end of my final term as mayor that I started to get significant encouragement to document what really happened after Hurricane Katrina devastated New Orleans and the Gulf Coast. This advice came from all types of people, within and outside the city. They all said I had an obligation to set the record straight and that this historic event should be recorded from my unique perspective, in my own words.

My initial focus after getting out of office was putting together a personal library on my two terms as mayor. It wasn't until after we had gathered documents, researched the internet, and interviewed key players, that I came to fully appreciate how amazing our comeback was. I also discovered how much inaccurate information there was about our experience.

Out of respect for those directly affected, I was inspired to write a forthright account of our many challenges, struggles, and triumphs.

Katrina's Secrets: Storms after the Storm provides a front-row seat that will take you on a historic journey that details critical decisions and controversial statements. Each chapter is based on a major event or a series of related events. As a result, the book flows thematically and in chronological order. This volume deals specifically with the immediate days before and thirty days after the storm hit. This period was so eventful and full of challenges that I could not cover everything we faced. Many devoted members of my administration are mentioned briefly, or not at all. I value their sacrifice and dedication, and I will be eternally grateful for their friendship and contributions.

This book series has three main goals. First, I hope to illustrate what it was like to be mayor of a city hit by a catastrophic event. I deal very honestly with race and class issues that were center stage just about every step of the way. I believe time will allow objective assessments on everything we did. Rational, non-emotional thinking will prevail, recovery momentum will continue, and historians will fairly compare similar recoveries. My sincere desire is that this book will serve as a resource for much needed changes to federal laws that govern our nation's future disaster responses.

Second, I write to give readers a perspective on the many complexities of disaster management, from total evacuation to planning and implementation to full recovery. Since this was unprecedented, we made our share of mistakes and I made many tough calls. Throughout the book, I set out the real-time, multi-layered decisions that built a firm foundation for our comeback. I address controversial adversaries and political forces that secretly conspired to slow down the recovery. Perhaps our experiences will prove useful for future decision makers who lead and manage a catastrophic disaster.

Third, I pray this account helps our nation become better prepared for major disasters. Since Hurricane Katrina, there have been almost four hundred major declared disasters in the U.S. alone. In fact, a person dies every eight minutes somewhere in the world from a disaster. Recent trends have shown natural disasters are often linked to man-made disasters. With Katrina, we experienced a hurricane and the failure of federally built levees; in Japan, an earthquake, tsunami, and man-made nuclear power plant failures occurred. Substantial dialogue is needed on preparedness, evacuations, response, and post-disaster resource deployment.

Katrina's Secrets: Storms after the Storm is based on my recollections, observations, and records. This account was confirmed with various documents, personal notes, interviews, news reports, and many other sources. I had two wonderful, talented individuals who worked with me on this project. The very capable Rebecca Mann helped with research, interviews, and the initial drafts. Terry Davis, who was with me almost every day right after the storm, provided initial edits and essential fact-checking. I could not have completed this work without them.

In the chapters that follow, I write about conflicts, what I did right, things I could have done better, and what I would do differently if I had a reset button.

Unfortunately, in life, there is no time machine that can take you back. After Katrina hit, I did my best with the resources and people I had to work with. All my life I had been looking for the ultimate challenge, and I finally found it being mayor of New Orleans at this time in history. It was still my honor and privilege to have served its great people.

I appreciate you giving me the opportunity to share my story.

CHAPTER ONE

RAINBOW STORMS

———————— ■ ————————

A secret is something kept hidden from others, known only to oneself or a select few. Nature has its own set of secrets—like a hurricane. They can be extremely deceptive. These storms often do not fully reveal their target until right before landfall. By this time it is often too late for many to get out of harm's way.

There has been much written and said about Hurricane Katrina and her impact on New Orleans. In fact, there have been as many as 56 million Internet search results via Google. Regrettably, there are way too many postings, televised reports, or news stories that do not represent what really happened. Unfortunately, these inaccuracies have been repeated over and over again. I know because I lived the Katrina experience.

There are many missing instances of behind-the-scenes power struggles, disaster capitalism moves, political antics, and character assassinations that have been skillfully shielded from the public—until now. These are Katrina's secrets. Some of the secrets, on the other hand, are very positive and quite inspiring. The very best secrets are the rainbows after the storms. This book presents more truth about what really happened before, during, and after August 29, 2005.

So how would you know when you are in the midst of being a major player as history is being created? You don't, because when you are in the moment, you are literally living second by second, hour by hour, day by day. It's only when the dust starts to settle and the sun permeates the darkness that you get to see the magnitude of what you have experienced, achieved, and survived.

It was destiny that I was mayor of New Orleans when Hurricane Katrina hit. At first I thought this may have been happenstance as I felt nothing could have prepared me for this miraculous journey. But in reality God had given me the skills, the temperament, and every ounce of determination that I needed. I didn't know it at the time, but now I do. If not for his grace and faith—and my love for my family and city—I could never have navigated the treacherous racial, economic, and political complications that arose.

There were surprisingly open talks by the city's old guard of socially reengineering the city. Some saw this disaster as a once-in-a-lifetime opportunity to create an environment that would lead to permanently displacing many of our citizens. I stood up and repeatedly said no to this evil plan. As a result I received relentless media floggings while being positioned as the main Katrina scapegoat.

My name is and forever will be associated with Hurricane Katrina. This storm devastated New Orleans and brought the city to the brink of extinction. She killed over eighteen hundred people throughout the Gulf coast and completely disrupted thousands upon thousands of lives. In my humble opinion, Katrina also exposed America's soft underbelly—issues of poverty, class, and race that are associated with most urban cities across the country. Unfortunately, New Orleans became the poster child of these social ills. This event immediately turned our misery into the ultimate reality TV show that mesmerized the world for months and years.

Nearly five years later, as the former mayor of New Orleans I feel more than ever that my story must be told. Secrets must be revealed, and the myths that have gained currency through repetition must be permanently discredited and abandoned.

One myth is that hurricanes and rainbows never appear at the same time in the same place. However, it has been recorded that on very rare occasions a spectacular rainbow can magically appear right after a devastating storm. While hurricanes can be stressful and very dangerous, rainbows are beautiful and are generally recognized as a sign that things are getting better.

Storms like Hurricane Katrina, which was the costliest in history with overall damage estimates exceeding $100 billion, normally produce powerful winds, torrential rain, high waves, and destructive storm surges. Hurricanes are among the most deadly forces in nature. As they make landfall they have also been known to spawn killer tornadoes. Although a hurricane's effect on people who live in coastal areas can be devastating, the irony is that they also serve a very useful purpose. They carry heat and energy away from the tropics and transport it toward more moderate climates. As a result, hurricanes help to maintain temperature equilibrium worldwide.

A strong hurricane can have a circular footprint of several hundred miles. Power rotates counterclockwise around its center, the eye of the storm. Inside the eye wall the sky is clear, free of clouds, and the winds are still. Move a half mile away from the eye and winds can gust above 150 miles per hour, causing the seas to become extremely violent.

A rainbow is a very different matter that often brings a smile to the face of the person who is lucky enough to see one. We have all had a certain fascination with rainbows. From the mythical tales of gold, wealth, and leprechauns, to the surreal pathway that bridges the earthly plane to the heavens, people throughout the ages have felt compelled to fantasize about its symbolism and significance. As if by design, as it stretches majestically across the sky, the appearance of a rainbow is almost instantaneous as though the intention is to surprise. Its transition of colors so magical, it holds court as though it always belonged there, then slowly fades back into the elements.

A rainbow can appear during the darkest of skies or the lightest of days. The most spectacular rainbow display happens just after it storms when half the sky is still dark as the storm clouds start to move on and the other half of the sky is clear with sunshine. The best angle to observe is a spot with clear skies where you are looking into the darkened background to marvel at a brilliant rainbow. Think about that—in order to see a radiant rainbow you must first go through the storm, and as the storm is leaving with the sky still half dark and half light you get to see it in its glory.

The city of New Orleans is a very special place. She is a city like no other. Positioned near the mouth of the Mississippi River, people come from all over the world to experience the music, food, culture, and our great people. New Orleans is the city where I was born. I grew up here, and I love every inch of her no matter the good, the bad, or the ugly.

This city is a lot like the conditions that create the most spectacular rainbow. She has her sunny side and contrasting dark side, both in constant play and struggle. Like a subliminal connection, it acts as a reminder of the links between good and evil that has both blessed and cursed this city. What most don't understand is what makes New Orleans so unique and cool is her gift of being a city of extremes that simultaneously combines elegance and wildness. To any observer this provides a wonderful, spellbinding day-to-day performance. However, if you were to look a little deeper, you would discover a city deeply divided economically with a long history of race and class conflicts. Most of the time this is kept as calm and as quiet as if you were in the eye of a hurricane.

The great thing is there's no other city in the world as charming, colorful, and eccentric as New Orleans. From the unlikeliest stretch of swampland rose the most likeable of cities. I like to describe it as an Afro-Euro-Caribbean city inside America. It's a wonderful concoction of creativity and flare that transcends the races—the French, Spanish, Irish, Italian, German, Asian, Caribbean islanders, American Indians, and especially African Americans. Like a siren call, this "sunny" side generates a steady flow of tourism and port activity, drawing people from all corners of the earth. This has sustained the city's economy and helped maintain our culture for almost three hundred years.

The spell of attraction and fascination that we cast, this lightness, cannot just be attributed to voodoo practice or ritual, but it comes down to our natural charm and our rich and elegant past. New Orleans is a melting pot, a living gumbo of specialness that no other city in the world can claim.

To truly understand New Orleans you need to walk the neighborhoods and experience its best asset, her people. I was raised in the inner city, in the Sixth and Seventh Ward where Creoles, whites, and blacks lived comfortably together. This checkerboard arrangement was replicated in many neighborhoods throughout the city.

The streets were and still are lined with grand old oak trees that complement the timber Creole cottages and shotgun houses. These neighborhoods were made up of mostly tradespeople—carpenters, bricklayers, seamstresses, plumbers, postal workers, and teachers. It was the type of community where if somebody's house was in need of repair or expansion, the owner would get the word out, cook a big pot of red beans and rice, and invite very willing neighbors over. Anybody who could swing a hammer came over to help on weekends. People would take turns helping each other. All you had to do was be nice, buy the supplies, and cook. Good people responded as they were confident that this type of act would be reciprocated for their home if needed. After the day's work was completed, everyone would eat, drink, and celebrate their collective accomplishment.

Most people in my neighborhood didn't have air-conditioning back then. So in the afternoon to escape the summer's stifling heat that started outside and then accumulated indoors, just about every-one would sit on their front porch in the evenings to cool down. There was usually one big window fan inside that worked overtime to blow hot air out of the house so you would have a better chance of sleeping comfortably at night. With so many people outside it gave you the op-portunity to really get to know and interact with your neighbors. The streets would be filled with a buzz of activity that would extend late into the evenings. Everybody looked out for one another. So if as a kid you did something wrong or did not give proper respect to an elder, your neighbors had permission to correct you and spank your butt, if necessary. If that happened, you could count on them calling your parents, and once you got home a repeat spanking was pretty much guaranteed.

My home was located close to the original settlement of the his-toric French Quarter in Tremé, the oldest black neighborhood in the nation. As a kid, I'd walk and ride my bike everywhere. With little effort

I could explore the area where our homegrown innovators Buddy Bolden and Jelly Roll Morton created the masterful art form of jazz that morphed into every style of music heard today. I'd walk through Congo Square, that magical place where hundreds of Africans, Indians, and others gathered on Sundays during slavery times to trade, sing, dance, and create music.

And if by chance it was early on a Saturday morning, then you were almost guaranteed to see a jazz funeral parade and second line. The band, with their deep beating drums, heavy dominating tuba, and lead trumpets would draw people from all around.

I slept in the front room of our shotgun house. I would hear the music in the distance and quickly jump out of bed, brush my teeth, wash my face, and quickly put on some clothes. I would wait on my front porch for the band (first line) with the horse-drawn casket slowly leading people (second line) of all races and ages.

At the start of the second line parade, the number of people following is normally small. But as the procession moves along, the numbers grow by leaps and bounds as more people come out of their homes to join in the tribute. The music is very somber at first to honor and mourn the dead. However, about midway through the music picks up its pace as everyone starts to celebrate the life of whomever passed to the by and by. The line continues to grow as we collect more people along the way, dancing for blocks and blocks and wiping away sweat with a handkerchief that doubles as a flag we wave above our head in rhythm with the beat.

When the band stopped playing it was your cue to leave, and everybody would go their own way, retreating back into their typical Saturday routine. The normal rhythms of the city would only be broken by passing fruit and vegetable vendors selling their wares in pickup trucks decorated as elaborately as an abstract canvas as they'd sing out, "I've got watermelons, red to the rind" to get people's attention while generating sales.

New Orleans has also had many a dark and stormy sky. Since its inception in 1718, this city battled against the elements, building and rebuilding on land that turned out to be mostly swamp. Against all odds, New Orleans grew out of the marsh, nestled between two massive bodies of water, the muddy Mississippi River and Lake Pontchartrain. The original settlers, the French, referred to the city as "Le Flottant" (the "Floating Land"), and to the English it was the "Wet Grave." It was an appropriate name when to this day you see mausoleums scattered throughout the city that are now tourist attractions and tend to be nearly as spectacular in architecture as the resident buildings that surround them. It's a city living almost on equal terms with the dead who are buried above ground.

Marie Laveau, the famous Queen of Voodoo, is buried in one of these, not far from Canal Street near downtown. Although she is no longer with us, the practice continues to be alive and well to this day. This unconventional faith dates back over two hundred years. The practice traveled to New Orleans with the slaves from Africa and the Caribbean. The slaves used it for protection from ailments and serious illnesses. Their power supposedly comes from those who have crossed over to the other side.

Although her name still conjures up fearful imagery of candlelit ceremonies with snakes and naked dancing in Congo Square while talking with the dead, Marie Laveau was not all what people presented her to be. She also had a very sunny side. In fact, Ms. Laveau was a strong community leader who often used her voodoo mystique to keep police and local politicians in line. She could be mysteriously effective for the greater good of needy citizens. Next time you visit New Orleans, I recommend you visit her gravesite and put your mark on her tomb for good luck. But be warned, although she is dead her energy is still strong, so we might find you later that night, dancing in a naked trance in Congo Square.

Most history books claim that New Orleans was "founded" by the French while ignoring the fact that Native American Indians were already living here. The location of the city was very strategic because she sat near the mouth of the Mississippi River with easy access to the Gulf of Mexico and the open seas.

Early settlers were constantly challenged as problems arose immediately and the area proved very tough to tame. One of the biggest challenges seemed to be that the Frenchmen who came over were apparently quite taken with the beautiful Indian women. Many deserted the settlement for the woods never to be heard from again. They were infected by love and/or malaria. So as the French continued to invest money and people into the settlement, problems continued to mount. To combat this, in the late seventeen hundreds the French solution was to empty their prisons and send prostitutes, thieves, hustlers, and con men here. *"Laissez les bon temps rouler"* in French means let the good times roll! The dark side and wildness of New Orleans started during this inception period and has continued in some form or another until today.

New Orleans soon became a thriving port city and also operated as the South's largest slave-trading center with twenty-five major slave-trading depots. Slavery is deeply intertwined in the DNA of New Orleans and is a major dark cloud that reigns over most of the city. Many Creoles and other blacks in the city bear reference to this past with French last names. These were attributed to their slave master's lustful and secret interracial love affairs, or rare mixed marriages. I too have French, African, and Native American ancestry and a number of French names in my family tree.

The Mardi Gras Indian tradition, where African Americans dress up in American Indian attire of elaborate beaded costumes to dance and sing Indian songs, evolved from the era of slavery. The intention was to pay homage to the Indians who helped free African Americans from slave masters.

So Every Mardi Gras morning in the inner-city neighborhoods of New Orleans, African American Indians come out with their "new suits" on. They meet up with their tribe to show off, dance, sing, drink, and take pictures with their adoring fans. Each new suit was worked on by the wearer for an entire year of painstaking hand-sewn detailed artwork.

Every Mardi Gras Indian tries to create the most elaborate, beautiful, and creative costume in order to win the title of "Prettiest Indian." Sometimes they would meet each other and these encounters would turn violent as they used it to settle scores while they postulated on who was the best. Over the years there was one Afro-Indian Big Chief, Tootie Montana, who year after year wore Indian suits that were heads and shoulders better than any others. He would consistently win the title and eventually changed the encounters by promoting peace over anger. He lived not too far from where I grew up. There is a must-see statue in Armstrong Park that honors the Big Chief. Don't miss it when you visit New Orleans as this sculpture garden also tells the story of how music and culture evolved from the Big Easy.

Music and culture runs deep in this city, in the sunny side of our DNA. Louis Armstrong, Mahalia Jackson, Fats Domino, Al Hurt, and the Neville Brothers are names that are as recognizable as the mighty Mississippi. The world knows us by our own indigenous art form, jazz. Music balances us. It heals us. It strengthens us. My good friend pianist Ellis Marsalis often says, "Music and culture are so prevalent in New Orleans that it oozes up from the streets and pavements."

The French Quarter has many pavements, and it is considered the city's ultimate residential and adult entertainment district. Seventy-eight square blocks of historical French and Spanish-infused buildings contain majestic two-story townhouses with steep roofs and elaborate iron lacework collage, grand chandeliers, and overgrown leafage that hang from balconies above. Shotgun houses as residences or those converted into bars and cafés break up the monotony of the two-story buildings. Gaslights and curved carriageways decorate the elegant aristocratic homes with cobblestone streets just hidden beneath a patchwork of asphalt that remind one of past days.

It is the home of Jackson Square and the magnificent St. Louis Cathedral, the oldest Catholic Cathedral in the United States that is still in use today. Extending from Esplanade Avenue to Canal Street, the majestic mansions are a contradiction to the twenty-four-hour Bourbon Street spectacular where wide-eyed tourists stroll up and down sipping "Hurricane" drinks from souvenir to-go cups. These drinks are sweet, deceptive, and very potent. They are made with two to three different types of rum, passion fruit syrup, and lime juice.

You will most likely see anything on Bourbon Street, from great live music, enticing half-naked women hanging out of shop doorways, and kids tap-dancing on the sidewalk for tips. To this day, the French Quarter is seen as a haven for debauchery and the unconventional. When referring to the French Quarter, Billy Graham once claimed that it's a place where he could feel the secret presence of Satan and other demons roaming the streets looking for willing victims. The French Quarter is full of sunny skies and many dark clouds. There is something for everyone here and then some.

Good food is also a major part of our culture. The sun definitely shines brightly in the kitchens of New Orleans. Monday is red beans and rice day, Wednesday is spaghetti and meatballs, and Friday is usually seafood. Sprinkled throughout the rest of the week you are guaranteed to find charbroiled oysters, fried shrimp po'boys, crawfish étoufée, muffuletta sandwiches, gumbo, jambalaya, fried chicken cooked in special butter oil, and of course, turtle soup. Desserts are to die for! Beignets, pralines, bread pudding, sweet potato cookies, and coffee with chicory are favorites of locals and visitors. And that's just for starters.

Eating is such a celebrated pastime that living in this city requires a structured exercise regime just to hold your weight gain to ten to fifteen pounds. Emeril's, Leah Chase, John Besh, Willie Mae, and K-Paul are local chefs who have gained international attention and provide inspiration for budding, up-and-coming chefs. We even put our own spin on Thanksgiving turkey by cooking it in a deep fryer. These tender, delicious birds are injected with special liquid seasoning and rubbed down with unique spices the night before it takes its dip in hot peanut oil.

Whether its restaurants like Little Dizzies, Ruth's Chris Steakhouse, Two Sisters, Galatoire's, Olivier's, or Commanders Palace, you are always guaranteed a great meal experience with authentic Nawlins flavor. And if by chance you need a quick cool down in the middle of one of our typical hot and humid summer days, "snowball" stands are only a few blocks away. They offer reasonably priced icy refreshments of finely shaved ice dripping in sweet distinctive syrups.

Each spring when the temperature is cooler, New Orleans Mardi Gras unleashes a world-famous rainbow that is arguably the best of them all. Over a two-week period people come from all over to have the time of their life. They dress up in costume and pretend they are someone else by letting their hair down—and I mean all the way down. When I was a young boy, many of the parades went through the historic French Quarter, and most of us viewed it from on the street. The Quarter is very narrow and the buildings are dense, so it was hard to see the parade floats until they were right upon you. The anticipation would build as the parades started approaching and people clamored to catch beads, trinkets, and cups. As kids my friends and I would jostle with each other to try and get up front for the best position knowing that Bach-Gorilla, one of the Krewe of Bacchus's signature floats, would soon be upon us to scare us into the next century.

Everything comes to a frantic, somewhat controlled frenzy on Mardi Gras day, Fat Tuesday, when at least a million people line the streets, twenty to thirty deep. Many dress in costumes to compete for colorful beads and Zulu coconuts. Mardi Gras day is the day when every unique aspect of New Orleans is on full display. The sunny side and dark side are fully represented by every kind of Mardi Gras mask known to man and woman. There are many secret fantasies being played out on this very special day.

Carnival balls are elaborate affairs that offer a very different experience than Mardi Gras parades. They are gatherings of the rich and not so rich who both delight in pretending they are royalty—kings, queens, dukes and princesses. Whether by choice or circumstance, high-class traditions and rich society values of the French were quickly adopted by New Orleanians during colonial times. Social standing became a top priority amongst the people.

After becoming mayor, I was fully exposed to this side of the Big Easy. I had been to several Zulu balls as they combined the elaborate royalty fantasy with a good old-fashioned, down-to-earth funk party. What I was not prepared for were some of the other balls.

For example, debutante balls such as the Young Men of Illinois Ball are also very popular. One of this annual event's purposes is to introduce young African American women into society. It is a black-tie event with all men dressed in tuxedos and top hats as they bow and dance with young ladies who curtsey and flaunt their flowing French gowns and fake diamond tiaras. A full orchestra plays classical music throughout the four-hour event. If you close your eyes you would think you were in Paris rubbing shoulders with European high society. But these are African Americans, the "talented tenth," the educated middle class as W. E. B Dubois called us, mimicking European culture better than white people.

I will never forget my very first Rex Ball as mayor. One hour into the pageantry the lightbulb went off for me as it relates to really understanding the depths and true psyche of my city. Rex is the so-called king of New Orleans Mardi Gras. The organization is private, historically all white males, and closed to all but the elite of the city, the "blue bloods." I sat there mesmerized! Everything was very formal. The exclusive Marine band performed with exquisite precision. All the men wore long tuxedo tails and gloves. The women were in long, beautiful evening gowns. All the military brass was there, generals and admirals from every branch of the REAL United States armed forces. The debutantes were introduced into society after having practiced their deep curtsey for many months prior. The king and queen of Rex with their very elaborate attire had already waltzed in and waved their wands at everyone who stood and applauded. Then all members and their significant others would go up to the throne after the king and queen sat down and take turns bowing to show their support and appreciation. This was a very serious affair, and there was absolutely no joking around.

All this ties in with another related tradition that occurs the day before on "Lundi Gras." On this day the secretly appointed Rex arrives by boat on the river to an evening event with thousands of people revving up the party and having a good time. At the appointed time the music temporarily stops, and the master of ceremonies reads a Rex proclamation asking the mayor to suspend all rules and laws and turn over all power to Rex effective then and the next day, Mardi Gras. In theory, if he complies then Mardi Gras happens. If not, the celebration would be called off. Talk about pressure. After the mayor says, "I concur," the crowd goes wild and then Rex addresses his royal subjects. Wow!

So we have the Rex Ball, a pageant that exudes New Orleans' fantasies by paying homage to a make-believe king and queen that is so far removed from the common activity of the street parades that the majority of the city's residents never even get to experience it. As a matter of fact, when African American mayors first got into office in the late 1970s, the old city hall, Gallier Hall, transformed for the most part to where black elected officials and their friends viewed parades and toasted the kings and queens of Mardi Gras, including Rex. The viewing stands there are mostly used by African Americans with other races also in attendance. In the next block at the Intercontinental Hotel, the queen of Rex sits and it is there that the "blue bloods," predominantly uptown whites, do the "Royal Mardi Gras toast" with the king and queen. The people on the streets are pretty oblivious to this twisted power play that tips Mardi Gras season into an underlying theme of social inequalities that has not changed much over time.

Interestingly, in 1991, a very brave woman, Councilperson Dorothy Mae Taylor, introduced an ordinance that required all social organizations, particularly Mardi Gras krewes like Rex, to certify publically that they do not discriminate and publish their membership roster. The ordinance became law. Needless to say, the power elites of the city were livid, and Mrs. Taylor was quickly demonized by their krewe brothers in local media and business. In protest, the nineteenth-century krewes Comus and Momus stopped parading. Most of the old-line krewes secretly filed suit in federal court claiming the ordinance was an unconstitutional infringement on their First Amendment rights of free association and was an unwarranted intrusion on the privacy of the groups. They won the lawsuit (5th Cir. 1995). The city tried to appeal, but the U.S. Supreme Court refused to hear the case.

So today it is still okay to have a private club in New Orleans that discriminates against people because of their race or gender. By the way, the official Mardi Gras colors are purple, gold, and green. Purple is supposed to signify "justice." Today some krewes have a token black or Jewish member or two, but this injustice remains as another dark cloud hanging over the city. Rex's record is also still intact that there has never been a person of color who has been its king or queen.

Mardi Gras day in New Orleans on the streets with the real people is an all-day ultimate rainbow spectacular! It is the "greatest free show on earth" celebrated with themed floats, marching bands, beads, king cakes, and a festive time to be had by all. Thousands of costumed people line the streets for hours in wait for hundreds of different parade floats, each with their own unique theme of satirical comedy or mythical fantasy.

There are at least four different Mardi Gras day experiences happening simultaneously in different parts of the city. Downtown is what everyone sees on TV with Zulu, Rex, and the truck parades. Then there are the exclusive viewing stands on St. Charles Avenue and at Gallier Hall. In the French Quarter it is basically an adults-only show with porn-like costumes that sometimes could even make hookers blush. In other areas away from downtown there are more family-oriented parades where very small children are the target market. In between the parades, children reclaim the streets by throwing balls, playing tag, or searching for fallen treasures. And finally, there is "Under the Bridge" where there is a main stage, DJs, live music, motivational speakers, hot wings, barbeque, lots of beer, and Mardi Gras Indians showing off their "new suits." Since the crowd is mostly African American here, the Zulu parade makes a special trip to that area just to hand out their exclusive Zulu coconuts and disband at their headquarters nearby.

Overall, Mardi Gras is a wonderful event where you are guaranteed a great time in spite of some race and class struggles that are as well hidden as the tears behind a clown-faced Mardi Gras mask. Most people on the streets don't care that many of the elegant Carnival balls have only token representation from other races or none at all. In fact, almost everyone has no knowledge that an ordinance that bans discrimination in Mardi Gras krewes was quietly challenged, overturned, and buried above ground. And on Mardi Gras day it is okay to pretend that we all are the same, and even though you can go anywhere in the city that you want to go, it is more likely you will end up watching parades in an area with people who look just like you and your momma's people. Anyone for a good old New Orleans Mardi Gras mask?

Race relations or the lack thereof with modern-day tensions relative to integration and power-sharing between the races went to another level in New Orleans in the 1960s. White flight to the suburbs kicked in big time. The Big Easy quickly became a majority black city politically while remaining whites fought aggressively to maintain economic and social power. To this day with the city being 62 percent African American there are still clubs whose members are exclusively the white business elite, that I cannot gain access to, even as mayor or former mayor. These clubs, like the Boston Club, the Louisiana Club, the Pickwick Club, and Stratford, are all social and economic development organizations that have direct ties and overlap with Mardi Gras krewes. They are the places where economic power congregates. The publisher and editor of the city's monopoly daily newspaper are members.

In the days before African Americans became mayors, it was automatic that the leader of the city had a VIP membership to another exclusive venue, the New Orleans Country Club. When Moon Landrieu was elected (a liberal white mayor who pushed for some equal rights) and Dutch Morial became the first African American mayor of the city in 1978, that automatic privilege was retracted. It's not surprising then that the former grand wizard of the Ku Klux Klan, David Duke, raised in the New Orleans area, came within a whisker of winning the seat of governor of Louisiana less than twenty years ago.

The civil rights movement in the 1960s posed a huge economic threat to the power players in New Orleans. During this period, across the nation, it was recorded that civil unrest was exploding in most urban centers. Why New Orleans didn't erupt like other cities in America is a question that we can only speculate on. The assassination of Martin Luther King Jr., only a couple of hundred miles north of New Orleans, was followed by an eerie silence that spread like wildfire as the city held its breath in anticipation of the repressed black population's retaliation. All that happened was a few incidents of minor looting and a few very crude firebombs thrown on commercial businesses. Compared to other cities, New Orleans was, well, the Big Easy, and relatively peaceful.

The majority of African Americans in New Orleans chose a peaceful protest after Dr. King's assassination. This generated enough attention that it enabled the elite blacks, mostly Creoles, to get together with the white power structure, and a secret agreement was quietly and quickly established. On the steps of city hall, Mayor Schiro and crew announced the end of the protests and in good faith appointed the city's first ever black mayoral aide, Mr. Philip Baptiste. In essence they announced, "We integrated, ya'll," and the city moved back into Mardi Gras mode where we all come together once a year and get intoxicated on fun to soothe our pain from the institutional effects of slavery and Jim Crow that lives on underneath our masks.

I took my first breath of life in 1956 at Charity Hospital, located in downtown New Orleans where most of the city's uninsured and poor were treated. It was also one of the country's leading hospitals for trauma admissions, treating many a victim of violence and gunshot wounds while providing an excellent training ground for interns and doctors across the nation. I grew up in a very loving and nurturing environment with both parents stressing education as the key to success in the future. My father held several different trade jobs such as bricklayer and truck mechanic but settled in as a skilled garment cutter at a local factory, Haspel Brothers. He worked there during the day and also moonlighted at night as a janitor at city hall. I would later run as mayor with a platform that included "cleaning up corruption" in government. The irony registered with some who knew that in the past my father had cleaned up city hall in a much different way. My mother was a homemaker for most of my youth, and she supplemented the family income by being a seamstress. Later she became a manager at one of the local restaurants.

My parents instilled in me that there is a God who is very real, and it has always been natural for me to pray and attend church on Sundays. I was raised Catholic, and in the next block from my home was Saint Peter Claver Church where I attended elementary school and was an alter server for many years. I was always a pretty good student who didn't have to work hard to make good grades. My real passion was sports. I learned to play most things by participating in pickup games daily in the neighborhood. As I started to play organized sports, I soon settled in on basketball and baseball. I captained both teams in high school, and my "southpaw curveball" earned me a baseball scholarship to Tuskegee Institute/University.

I arrived at Tuskegee not fully understanding its history and significance. Tuskegee was founded by Booker T. Washington in 1881 and is the place where Dr. George Washington Carver did most of his incredible scientific research with agriculture and the peanut. It is also the place where the Tuskegee Airmen were trained for their heroics during World War II. They never lost a bomber plane that they escorted into battle.

The environment on the "yard" of Tuskegee was not anti anything, but it was definitely pro black. It is a place where I fully learned about all the significant contributions that African Americans have made to our country and to the world. Tuskegee nurtured me into becoming an even prouder black man and taught me the importance of believing that I could compete anywhere in the world. History classes were primarily about inspiring black history that is not taught in the elementary or high schools in New Orleans or other places. Before the beginning of football games the entire student body would sing the normal national anthem and right after we would totally unite in spirit and voice to sing loudly the black national anthem "Lift Every Voice" with right fists clutched and raised high over our heads. Every time we did it I felt inspired to be an American and totally focused as a more enlightened black person.

I met some inspiring instructors and great people from around the world. This is where I was first exposed to members of the Nation of Islam. These brothers and sisters were so disciplined and focused. I loved college life. Since we were in a very small town, there was no Burger King or McDonald's, but instead we had Reed's Chicken Shack. If you happened to go there late at night and they had run out of raw chickens, which happened often, you could expect to wait an hour or so while they'd go out back to kill and pluck the feathers from farm-raised birds. But the wait was worth it as you'd be in for an extra treat of some awfully fresh fried chicken. This took "finger-licking good" to a whole new level!

I was always good at math and considered majoring in it but decided to pursue and obtained a degree in accounting. During the summers while in college I would drive to Detroit and work in a General Motors forging plant that made internal engine parts for cars. The money was very good, but the working conditions were brutal with red hot steel everywhere. After college I lived and worked around the country. I had a great experience in Los Angeles, came back to New Orleans, and later settled in Dallas. My true love was still in New Orleans, and I soon married my beautiful wife Seletha. We continued our careers and started a family in Dallas, but we both longed for the Big Easy and visited home whenever we could.

Most people who have lived, loved, or played in New Orleans know what Louis Armstrong meant when he sang, "Do you know what it means to miss New Orleans?" New Orleans is my home, but another driving force was that I had a wife who was raised here, and keeping New Orleanian women away from this city is next to impossible. It's nearly as difficult as removing Tabasco hot sauce from our cuisine.

In 1985 I returned to New Orleans and started working with Cox Communications as a controller on the accounting side. The company was in horrible shape. There was borderline fraud, and the books were such a mess with a balance sheet that did not balance. Even with a customer base of ninety thousand homes the company was losing money hand over fist and had deplorable relations with its customers and the city council. It was considered the black sheep in the Cox family. I love a challenge, so the opportunity to turn this business around was really exciting for me.

I learned every aspect of the business very quickly and was soon promoted to vice president/general manager of the New Orleans operation. We started fixing things on every front. To address our customer service issues and public relation problems I started a live cable call-in show. We invited all customers, but particularly the angry ones to call in, and I would address their problems on air. We would re-air the show multiple times over the course of the month. I believe I was the only cable general manager in the country who did this. We knew of one other person who tried it and cancelled his show after a very short period of time.

This show taught me how to turn negatives into positives. It also honed my skills on "romancing the camera" and effective communication with angry, frustrated people. We made improvements, kept talking positively, and before we knew it, our customer satisfaction surveys improved dramatically. The overall perceptions of Cox improved even though cable technology was still evolving with major reliability issues. It was not uncommon for it to go out in the middle of a movie or during a big heavyweight pay-per-view fight. Over time the technology got better, and we invested in significant amounts of employee customer service training. The live call-in shows became much easier as we successfully transformed the operation into one of the better performing in Cox.

Once the company was firmly back on track, I became restless and started to look around for other challenges. During this transition, in an effort to stay mentally sharp, I enrolled in the Tulane University executive MBA program and received an advanced business degree. I also felt the need to scratch an entrepreneurial itch and got involved in something very unique—professional ice hockey in New Orleans. I jumped at the opportunity with Cox's blessings. We initially had to overcome several major challenges. First, there had never been any ice rinks in the area. A new state-of-the-art arena would soon be under construction by the state that was designed to attract an NBA team. The new arena's potential attracted other interests from Tom Benson, owner of the NFL New Orleans Saints, and Rob Couhig, owner of the AAA New Orleans Zephyrs baseball team.

Our strategy was to beat them to market by setting up an ice rink in the city-owned Municipal Auditorium. Some of my partners had very close relationships with the city's top elected officials. We put together a business plan and raised the necessary capital. And amazingly an ice rink was built in a very unlikely place. This facility had been used for high school basketball games, concerts, and even was a temporary gambling casino for Harrah's. The finished hockey rink was very intimate with seating for four thousand. The fans fell in love with our team as we put on a very entertaining show from start to finish. The games were fast, exciting, and brutal with fights breaking out all over the ice at any time. We had established a professional ice hockey team, the New Orleans Brass, and our affiliation was with the then NHL world champions. This was an amazing feat since previously the city's fascination with ice was only for snowballs or cocktails with strong alcohol.

Once the new state arena was built, we publically competed against Mr. Benson and Mr. Couhig and won the rights to secure the lease in this new state-of-the-art, nineteen-thousand-seat arena. We played there and had a couple of successful years until the NBA Hornets moved to town. The state then terminated our lease as the power players never did like the idea of an African American majority-owned professional sports team playing in this building in the first place. The New Orleans Brass was forced to ceased operations.

In 2001, I settled back into my Cox duties, which had expanded to cover most aspects of telecommunications. My operation was still doing well, and we were pretty much on autopilot. I knew I needed a new challenge, something that would fully capture my imagination. I hoped this would be my ultimate challenge. Out of the corner of my eye I noticed the race for mayor of New Orleans was just starting. There were fourteen candidates, most of them career politicians. I starting hearing that many citizens were not excited or happy with this lineup; they wanted change. Since my Cox operations were regulated monopolies on the cable side, I interacted with top government officials regularly. I very clearly understood how governments worked. I knew the state of the city was not good. There was corruption, crime problems, public school failings, brain drain, blighted properties, and the economy was in a steep decline. As a result, most of our young people were leaving the city for opportunities in other places. The overall population was getting older and poorer.

Just like most citizens I was basically making the best of my time while consciously ignoring the declining state of my city. Instinctively, I knew we needed serious change but always depended upon someone else to push it through. One day I was reflecting on my attendance at the October 1995 Million Man March. I went to this march with some close friends to make a statement that strong black men could come together in solidarity. Our key objectives were to discuss self-help and self-defense against economic and social ills plaguing the African American community. We answered Minister Louis Farrakhan's call and were part of the two million black men who went to our nation's capital to show a more positive image to the world. At the end of the program everyone who was there pledged out loud that we would commit to a deeper responsibility and obligation to make our communities better. In other words, we were supposed to go home, get off of our butts, and go to work for the people. Maybe this was my time to make a bigger difference in my city. Should I run for mayor or stay at Cox was my question for the moment.

I walked around for days thinking about the possibilities of leading the charge to turn my city around. However, there were big questions to be answered. How would my family adjust? Was the city really ready for a change agent, a business candidate? What were the key themes that would connect with the public? I started having discussions with everyone who would engage with me on the city and what it needed. After the conversation, they would turn to me and say, "Maybe you should run." This started to resonate around town.

Then things culminated with two main incidents. First, when my two sons, Jeremy and Jarin, were both in high school, we were at home sitting around the dinner table one evening with them and some of their friends. We talked about the city and politics. I asked them what they were going to do when they graduated. To a person, every single one of them told me they believed they had to leave the city for better opportunities. They just did not see a future in New Orleans. It hit me hard as a father and a businessman that I owed it to my children and others to do everything in my power to ensure opportunities for our educated youth to stay and prosper in this city.

Later that week I went to have some work done on my favorite pair of shoes by my favorite shoe-shine man, and we ended up talking about the mayor's race. After we finished he turned to me, looked me straight in my eyes, and said, "You have to run." I went home in serious thought and later that night got on my knees and prayed for wisdom and guidance. Soon thereafter, after getting the okay from my family and getting buy-in from two of my best friends David White and Dr. Brenda Hatfield, I decided to enter politics.

I officially entered the race on the last day of qualifying. It was December of 2001, and the election was scheduled for February 2002. Most of the so-called political experts discounted my candidacy. They all thought I was a newcomer who entered the game way too late. What they didn't know at the time was our strategy was well thought out. We knew from studying past races that it wouldn't be long before the top candidates would start fighting each other. History said they would start to drag each other down. At the time I was consistently polling at just 3 percent. Our plan was to steadily gain momentum, and at the right moment when the fighting peaked we would con-nect with the voters, kind of run up the middle, and catch everyone by surprise. Our thinking was by the time we became a serious threat to win it would be too late for the major candidates to turn their attacks on me. This ended up playing out to perfection.

On election day, we surprised everyone as I ran first in the primary. My runoff opponent was Richard Pennington, one of the most popular police chiefs the city has ever had. He had major endorsements or support from the current mayor, District Attorney Harry Connick Sr., Congressman William Jefferson, and most of the city's political power structure. They were very confident, cocky, and tried all sorts of intimidation tactics. I was not impressed. They didn't understand that as the cable guy I was used to maintaining my cool in the face of pressure. There is nothing more frightening than a pissed-off cable customer whose HBO cut off in the middle of their favorite movie. They were cream puffs in comparison.

The televised debates were my favorites. Pennington would show up with a notebook or cue cards, and he'd read from them. This did not come across well. Since I knew my material well, I would look into the camera and speak directly to the citizens. I came across as knowledgeable and sincere.

In March of 2002 I won the seat for mayor with 59 percent of the vote, receiving 85 percent of the white vote and 40 percent of the black vote. This was a record-setting crossover vote for an African-American candidate. Historically, it is commonplace for black people to cross over and vote for white candidates, but for the most part, whites do not cross over and vote for black candidates. In analyzing the election results further, my vote was more about economics than race as I dominated any household that earned forty thousand dollars or more. However, this record crossover had an adverse effect on the black community and made some skeptical of me. There was a feeling among them that if that many white people voted for me, then something must be wrong with me and I would not work hard for their interests. It was also the first time in fifty years that a candidate with no political experience won the seat of mayor in New Orleans.

On May 3, 2002, I was inaugurated as the sixtieth mayor of the great city of New Orleans. The next day I was eager to roll out my plan for the city's transformation as I took my first step through the doors of city hall as mayor. The shining bold silver letters of my name and title decorated the entrance doors to the second-floor office where I would reside for the next four and hopefully eight years.

Within a couple of weeks, my executive staff, all of whom possessed strong business savvy backgrounds, and I cracked down hard on corruption. Our initial focus was on bribery, inflated contracts, and other fiscal waste. Soon there were major busts and media events with a large number of arrests and public firings. My private sector background, initially seen as a weakness when I entered the mayor's race, prepared me well for other things I was about to uncover. The city's finances were in a complete shambles. There were undeposited checks found stuffed in desk drawers, and we had a projected budget deficit in excess of $50 million. We entered city hall with just enough cash in the bank to run the city for two days. Some members of the outgoing administration had bragged that whoever followed them would find the cupboards bare. They were obviously serious about draining the city before they left as we barely found cupboards when we took office.

We also discovered millions of dollars in federal grant money guideline discrepancies and over $100 million in public projects backlogs. The U.S. Attorney and FBI were already looking into activities of the past administration, and we fully cooperated with them by abiding by the public records laws. Transparency in government was a key issue that I ran on. We were in the mode of cleaning things up quickly in hopes of freeing up cash for running the city. As a result, over eighty people were arrested on bribery, fraud, and malfeasance charges in connection with bribes relating to the city's auto inspection and taxi-licensing agencies. We discovered this practice was so commonplace that supervisors held training sessions for new employees on how to properly receive these "tips."

Most of those arrested were city workers who were escorted out of their homes in handcuffs early one morning. These actions sent a very loud and clear message that these types of activities would not be tolerated under my administration. In typical New Orleans fashion, many applauded our efforts while others thought it was way over the top. Getting rid of corruption and streamlining the procedures inside city hall wasn't my only focus. The next big hurdle was getting the city safely through the hurricane season, which started June 1. We got through the first couple of seasons in pretty good shape, but it was the one in 2005 that would change New Orleans and my life forever. During that hurricane season a very deceptive storm formed, Hurricane Katrina. Her impact resulted in my sincere desire to share with you this incredible story of devastation, desperation, tragedy, loss, death, greed, determination, faith, pride, unity, perseverance, and resiliency.

CHAPTER TWO

MANDATORY EVACUATION

———————■———————

W hen most people think of hurricane threats, they immediately envision heavy rains and dangerous high winds.
These are very serious and keep emergency preparedness
professionals awake at night, but there is another related, even more
menacing threat: storm surge. Many experts attribute the greatest loss
of life in a hurricane to storm surges. As the hurricane progresses, her
high winds push on the ocean's surface and cause a buildup of water
that turns into tremendous waves that grow as the storm intensifies.
As the hurricane makes landfall, the height of the surge can also be
magnified if it hits during high tide. Hurricane Katrina's storm surge
peaked at fifty feet when she was in the middle of the Gulf of Mexico.

New Orleans has a very unique topography that makes it even
more vulnerable to hurricanes and storm surges. As you may recall,
this area was primarily built upon swampland and marshes. Before
modern levees, the mighty Mississippi River would collect large de-
posits of soil and foliage as it forged across America, from Minnesota
to the mouth into the Gulf of Mexico. This river's sediment would finally flow to the low-lying areas throughout New Orleans to naturally
build up land height. So the closer you are to the river the higher the
ground. But as you move away from the river the land is lower due to
the lack of replenishment and natural subsidence. If you consider that
the city is almost surrounded by water, then you can envision a "bowl
effect" where much of the middle of the city is below sea level.

Early settlers quickly realized this dilemma and started to build levees near the water. These levees for the most part are large mounds of
dirt covered with grass stacked near the water's edge. These so-called

protective levees stretch for miles along the riverbank, canals, and lake. They can range from three to twenty feet high in certain places. So it can be a surreal feeling to visit New Orleans and be standing in the street or on a sidewalk in the French Quarter and look toward the river and see ships passing above your head in the distance. It's this very reason why hurricanes pose such an enormous threat to our city. As well as being extremely flat all around, New Orleans is America's largest city where half of its land lies perilously below sea level with some areas as low as ten to twelve feet below. The large bodies of water of the Mississippi River and Lake Pontchartrain cradle the city to create a bowl-shaped depression. So if a key levee is breached by powerful waves of water from a Category 5 hurricane storm surge, then water would quickly rush to the bottom of the bowl, filling the city to roof lines in some areas. A great irony about the current levee protection system is that while it now provides some protection from storm surge, the man-made efforts have affected the past benefits of the flowing river sediment which can now no longer replenish low-lying areas in the city, so its goodies just flow uselessly to the depths of the Gulf of Mexico.

To help further protect New Orleans from heavy rains and storm surges, in 1899 the State of Louisiana authorized the local Sewerage and Water Board to complete and implement a master drainage plan funded primarily by property taxes. Over a number of years the most extensive and complex drainage system ever built became a reality. This system consists of twenty-two strategically placed drainage pumping stations throughout the city that are manned twenty-four hours per day, seven days per week. Their combined pumping capacity is over 29 billion gallons per day, which is enough to empty ten square miles, fourteen feet deep every twenty-four hours. The flow rate, at over forty-five thousand cubic feet per second, is more than the flow rate of the Ohio River, the nation's fifth largest river. This system is also complemented by ninety miles of open canals and over ninety miles of subsurface canals connected to a complex array of oversized underground drainage pipes that relieve pressure by draining away excess water. Many of the subsurface canals are large enough to drive city buses through them.

The Sewerage and Water Board also constructed some of the initial man-made levees. After the flooding following Hurricane Betsy in 1965, Congress removed the responsibility for the local flood protection from the local levee and water boards and authorized the U.S. Army Corps of Engineers to do a major redesign and construct a levee and flood protection system for the maximum anticipated hurricane for the area at that time. The unfortunate nature of this order was the plan was to build to the last know disaster, and that was Betsy, or a Category 3 type storm.

Hurricane Betsy formed on August 27 and at her peak is tied as the second most intense storm ever. She was the first hurricane to cause over a billion dollars in damages, earning her the nickname "Billion-Dollar Betsy." This storm annihilated parts of the city, with a ten-foot storm surge that not only flooded low-lying areas but was also responsible for seventy-six deaths in Louisiana.

I was very young when Betsy hit, and like many other families in my neighborhood, we just couldn't afford to leave the city for an unplanned "vacation." So we rode out the storm and witnessed heavy rain, 110 mile per hour winds, and heard the roars of tornados. Initially there was minor street flooding, but eventually mass flooding from levee failures covered many areas of the city, particularly the Lower Ninth Ward. It took many days for the water levels to subside to where people could return to their flooded homes. Official reports claimed the levee failures were due to cheap construction and poor maintenance, but there are still persistent, widespread rumors that the levees were intentionally breached with dynamite by city officials as a way to relieve water pressure and potential flooding in the "more valued areas of the city," the French Quarter and Central Business District. To this day I can still remember looking out over the porch of my aunt's second-story home watching in awe as water devoured my neighborhood.

As noted above, the Corps of Engineers was supposed to design and construct a state-of-the-art hurricane protection system that could withstand a Category 3 storm. This project was still under construction when the city was hit by Hurricane Katrina some forty years later. The other unfortunate reality is the Corps of Engineers made very minor technological advances with levee construction over the years, the main one being concrete "I" walls built atop the earthen levees. This advance would prove to be ineffective during Hurricane Katrina as the power of storm surge was severely underestimated and routine maintenance was virtually nonexistent. Even with the amount of work and money invested into the levee and drainage system over years, the federal government will not be able to certify adequate protection against a Category 3 or higher hurricane until 2012 or beyond.

Another key element of our hurricane protection system dealt with our natural coastline, marshland, and barrier islands. In the past, these wetlands that surround the coast of Louisiana provided a buffer to the fierce storms that ravaged the state, slowing down their speed and strength. Every mile or two of wetlands absorbs one foot of approaching storm surge. In other words, five to ten more miles of marshland and barrier islands would have reduced Hurricane Katrina's New Orleans storm surge from twenty to fifteen feet, thus saving lives and property.

There are two major factors contributing to this land and safety loss: climate change and the oil and gas industry. Climate change is very real as the Gulf waters are getting warmer and warmer. We must all do our part to reduce our dependency on fossil fuel and reduce greenhouse emissions. The oil and gas industry in our area is both a blessing and a curse. This industry provides jobs, taxes, and corporate goodwill. It should be noted that the New Orleans area and the coast of Louisiana accounts for 18 percent of all U.S. oil production and 24 percent of all U.S. natural gas production. One-fourth of the entire nation's energy supply depends on support facilities in southern Louisiana. However, this industry has cut a checkerboard of open-water canals in the marshlands to allow supply boats and barges to efficiently service offshore oil and gas rigs. These pathways have weakened and accelerated the destruction of critical wetlands and coastline already damaged by climate change.

This loss of wetlands also affects other critical industries for our nation. New Orleans and other southern Louisiana ports are also first in the nation in total shipping tonnage. Over 500 million tons of water-borne cargo passes through Louisiana each year. We also have the most bountiful commercial fisheries, supplying 25 to 35 percent of the nation's total seafood catch. This should sound like an area where the nation would invest whatever it takes to protect these very vital national resources. The shame of it all is that at the current rate of coastal land loss in Louisiana, twenty-five to thirty-five square miles per year, nearly 640,000 more acres will be under water by 2050, an area nearly the size of Rhode Island.

During my first year as mayor in 2002, there were twelve storms that hurricane season. Only two made landfall in Louisiana. Both storms were Category 1 and scooted past New Orleans without major damage or loss of life. The fortunate thing about these events was we got to test our hurricane preparedness procedures and make improvements. The following year provided a reprieve; although there were sixteen hurricanes recorded, none made their way toward New Orleans.

In early September 2004, Hurricane Ivan, later renamed "Ivan the Terrible," was recorded as a Category 5 storm (the most intense category on the Saffir-Simpson scale) as it entered the warm waters in the Gulf of Mexico. This storm would become the tenth most intense Atlantic hurricane ever recorded, and at its peak it was the size of the state of Texas.

Once a hurricane enters the Gulf, we normally have seventy-two hours to prepare and/or evacuate the city and region. Early reports from the National Hurricane Center predicted that Ivan's center, the "eye," was headed for a direct hit on New Orleans. The potential for devastation and loss of life was high. I immediately declared a voluntary evacuation for the city and proceeded to take the necessary steps for emergency preparedness. Evacuations in our area are always very complicated as we coordinate with surrounding parishes to ensure everything is orderly so the interstate highways do not grind to a halt in gridlock. We had worked out a new phased regional evacuation plan where lower-lying cities leave first since they have to come through New Orleans to go north. After they finish exiting, at about fifty-plus hours from expected landfall, then the rest of the citizens of New Orleans hit the highways.

A major phase of our evacuation process is called "contraflow." This plan diverts the flow of traffic away from the southern region. In other words, all interstate lanes are rerouted to go away from the city. Therefore, once implemented there are no longer any incoming highway lanes. This was the first time that the plan was utilized, and although there were a few problems with the rollout, it was successful in that it did allow residents to move out of the city and region faster than expected. It was the largest evacuation recorded prior to Katrina, with an estimated seven hundred thousand people leaving the Greater New Orleans region. Our encouragement that each citizen have a personal evacuation plan that accounted for their entire family and any senior citizens in their neighborhood who may need assistance seemed to have paid off.

Of equal or larger concern are our citizens who do not have the financial resources to leave the city. My overriding motive was to balance all needs, protect every citizen, and minimize and/or prevent the loss of life if predictions proved true that Ivan would be a direct hit on New Orleans.

With the Ivan evacuation in full swing and between 60 to 70 percent of our citizens gone, it was now time to put a laser focus on those citizens who could not or would not leave. Unfortunately, over 28 percent of our citizens lived below the poverty line, and at least twelve thousand people relied on public transportation as their only form of transportation. We employed special emergency preparedness techniques for this segment of our population. We negotiated an emergency shelter of last resort in the Louisiana Superdome. This building could hold up to twenty-five thousand people and withstand winds of up to 150 miles per hour. The main sheltering area was also at least fifteen to twenty feet above street level. We were also able to provide National Guard troops who were stationed there for the duration, and they kept the peace quite effectively for the thousands who showed up.

Just like a wild animal, hurricanes have a tendency to be very unpredictable and can change direction quickly. After thousands had evacuated the city and the Superdome was safely and quietly secured, the storm changed direction at the last moment and passed within seventy miles of the mouth of Mississippi, barely missing New Orleans and veering to the north, making landfall east of Mobile Bay, Alabama. We dodged a big one!

I still stood firm on my decision to call the voluntary evacuation as the Sunday morning quarterbacks started to suggest we never should have evacuated in the first place. My retort that quieted them down was to suggest that if anybody had any doubts, then all they had to do was turn on the news to see what happened in Mobile and Pensacola. Eight people were killed, and thousands of homes and businesses were destroyed. Ivan cost the nation more than $14.2 billion in damages.

After Hurricane Ivan's close call to New Orleans, the Army Corps of Engineers approached Congress with a $4 million request to fund a preliminary study into providing better protection for the city and region. But the federal government was starting to feel the financial effects from the war in Iraq, and the request was rejected. They all knew that New Orleans could be adequately protected from a storm of this magnitude, but it would cost money, and unfortunately we were not a priority.

A senior Corps of Engineers official later claimed that "it's possible to protect New Orleans from a Category 5 hurricane...To do nothing is tantamount to negligence." Unfortunately, between 2001 and 2005, the Bush administration did not step up to the plate and reduced by 67 percent the Army Corps of Engineers' budget requests. For example, the Corps of Engineers requested $33.5 million for 2004 and 2005. Only $11.2 million was approved. These actions further left our city very vulnerable and with no real protection against a major hurricane.

In August of 2005, a seemingly inconspicuous storm formed over the southeastern Bahamas and erratically danced its way around the Atlantic Ocean as unpredictably as a forest fire rises and falls on the whim of the elements. Its performance and path switched between mild as a tropical storm, to a significant force as a Category 3, and then it weakened back to a Category 1 storm. This all happened within hours and was dizzying and remarkable at the same time.

By Tuesday, August 23, 2005, this deceptive storm appeared on the weather radar as Tropical Depression Twelve over the Bahamas. By Wednesday, it had strengthened to a tropical storm with gale-force winds of up to seventy-three miles per hour, just exceeding land's fastest animal, the cheetah's top speed. Over the next few days, the National Hurricane Center and our local weather stations monitored its direction, keeping us informed on her every move so that we could quickly implement a possible evacuation if needed.

Gaining in strength as the minutes ticked past, by Thursday, August 25, 2005, the storm was upgraded to Category 1, officially becoming the fifth hurricane for the season, and it veered west from the Atlantic Ocean heading for the Florida Panhandle. Named Katrina, which is a Greek name that means "pure" or "cleansing," this hurricane would soon enter the history books as the costliest, most destructive, and one of the five most deadly storms in U.S. history.

As soon as the hurricane entered the Gulf waters, my police and fire departments as well as the Sewerage and Water Board all began to initiate their updated hurricane preparation plan. We had done a lot of good work on our plan since Ivan, particularly with the Hotel Association. At one of our planning meetings with them we invited local weatherman David Bernard, who presented a computer simulation that showed floodwaters coming down Canal Street. We went on to explain to the Hotel Association members their responsibilities and liabilities if they didn't continue to feed and protect their guests. We stressed over and over that it was best that if a major storm was approaching that all hotel owners do everything in their power to help evacuate their guests out of the city.

That same Thursday morning I just happened to receive a very encouraging phone call. As mayor I had worked hard over the previous three years to transform the city's reputation in an effort to encourage and entice blue-chip investors to do business in New Orleans. One of these investors was none other than Donald Trump Sr. My assistant, Pat Smith, interrupted me in an early meeting with my executive staff to inform me that Mr. Trump was on the phone. "I think you really need to take this one," she said. I had spoken with him before, so I paused the meeting to take his call. "Mr. Mayor, this is Donald Trump," he said with his unmistakable New Yorker accent. He proceeded to explain to me that he'd been monitoring the progress and the property market in New Orleans over the last few years and was impressed with what he saw. "New Orleans is my next venture," he declared. "I want to build the Trump International Hotel and Tower in your city, and I have people all over the world who will buy my condos sight unseen once I break ground. I don't see any issues with selling these apartments and hotel rooms as your city suits my clientele perfectly." He finished his part of the conversation by saying that his clientele would love to have a place where they could come and really party, New Orleans style.

I thanked him for bringing his project to New Orleans, gave him my personal phone numbers, and pledged we would do everything in our power to make this a tremendous success. We both hung up the phone on a very high note. This was great news for the city. The Trump International Hotel and Tower would be a five-star, seventy-story structure with an estimated build cost of $400 million. The building would consist of 290 condos and 435 hotel units, a 126-foot spire, and a garage that could hold up to 715 spaces. It would become the tallest building in New Orleans and in the entire state of Louisiana. This type of investment would be perfect for our city and for Mr. Trump. He was broadening the Trump empire, and we would be able to leverage his activity to attract larger investments into the city. I immediately reflected back to when I decided to run for office, and this was exactly what I had envisioned. We were on a roll and I was feeling great, and a thought crossed my mind that nothing could stop us now. Then I snapped back to reality and remembered a storm was approaching.

Although I did not want to diminish this very positive news, I had to turn my focus back to preparing for the threat of a possible hurricane in the region. There is always a great deal of planning and execution that needs to be handled to ensure that we are as well prepared as possible. Coordination within the city and with surrounding cities/parishes and the state are absolutely essential to maintaining public safety. My initial calls were to the governor and the metropolitan parish leaders. Then it was a matter of running down a checklist internally. Who are the essential personnel who will remain behind to run the city? Do we have enough food and water for at least three days for the staff? Are we ready to implement our fleet plan where all city vehicles are fueled and stored securely? Are the city's buildings and equipment secured? Are transportation buses and other vehicles ready? Are our medical personnel ready for special needs citizens? Are backup generators full of fuel? Have we tested backup communications devices?

In addition to the internal issues, we were preparing for a potential emergency shelter for those that could not or would not leave the city. There were a number of issues that needed to be dealt with, and without my trusted chief administrative officer Dr. Brenda Hatfield and other key staff members, we would never have been as prepared as we were. However, in hindsight, I am not sure we could have totally prepared for what we were about to experience. No one in history has ever gone through anything like what was coming our way. No one!

At six thirty p.m., with winds of up to eighty miles per hour, Hurricane Katrina made her first touchdown in the United States, on the Florida Peninsula. Up to nine lives were lost as she moved through Hallandale Beach and then took a hard left, hugging the Florida coastline, and by early Friday morning she retreated into the waters in the Gulf of Mexico. Her journey across land had taken a toll on her strength, and at this point she was downgraded to a tropical storm. But all it took was one hour in the warm, regenerating waters in the

Gulf of Mexico and Katrina regained some of her strength, picked up speed, and once again became a hurricane. During the early hours on Friday morning when most of the city, besides Bourbon Street, was still sleeping, Katrina was once again a growing Category 1 storm.

I arrived at the office early as I wanted to get a heads-up from my staff on the status of our final preparations. I put another call in to the governor's office to coordinate our activity with theirs. Then there was the regular conference call with the National Weather Service, parish presidents, and emergency managers. We received expert updates on just about every aspect of the approaching storm: winds, speed, surge, tide conditions, probabilities on landfall, and predictions on how powerful the hurricane could become.

We also coordinated daily press conferences to keep citizens informed on the status of the storm and our preparations. These conference calls became regular morning and afternoon slots on my schedule. Once the early morning call was completed I would get in my car to travel to the local TV and radio stations for in-studio interviews to update our citizens.

These interviews also allowed me to have direct access to all of the lead TV station weatherpersons. They are an extremely talented group of professionals. We would share information and keep each other informed on the latest developments. Most had similar computer graphics and conclusions. However, there was one guy, Bruce Katz, a local weatherman for ABC26, who caught my attention as he proved to have a more in-depth analysis and used different techniques in making predictions. We connected intellectually, and he also had a great sense of humor. I began to rely on his storm assessment over the course of the next few days more than any other weatherperson in the area. Bruce was surprised that I knew something about the Loop Current conditions in the Gulf of Mexico. We spent lots of one-on-one time reviewing readings on water buoys that told us how warm waters were in specific locations in the Gulf. This information along with other data really brought home to both of us just how very serious this storm could be for everyone.

The Loop Current is one of the fastest warm ocean currents in the Gulf of Mexico and is responsible for dramatically escalating the force of hurricanes when the two collide. Flowing northward, the current is a clockwise recirculation of the warm Caribbean waters that flow through the Yucatan Channel that lies between Cuba and Mexico. Estimated to be around 125–190 miles wide, it can reach depths of up to three hundred feet of very warm water below the surface. This results in a feeding frenzy for any hurricane that passes over the current as the warm waters create a powerful energy surge that works to intensify the storm.

Normally, during the peak of hurricane season, the Gulf is often uniformly hot only at the surface. Outside of the Loop Current, these warm Gulf waters have no depth. As a storm churns through these shallow warm waters, cooler waters from below come to the surface that often weakens a hurricane's strength. But when such a storm passes over the Loop Current, the water can be eighty-five degrees or more and can be as deep as three hundred feet in that temperature range. This means that no matter how much a passing hurricane stirs things up, more warm water comes to the surface. For a hurricane, this is like throwing gasoline on an open fire.

After Hurricane Katrina crossed over Florida, she followed a path in the heart of the Loop Current. Over the next few days Katrina would peak, and at one point when she hit the warmest, deepest waters this hurricane went from a Category 3 to a Category 5 in just nine hours with winds as high as 175 miles per hour. With waves reported as tall as fifty feet, the doomsday fear was that the storm would come right up the mouth of the Mississippi River and completely wipe out the entire city. If the storm happened to take this worst-case scenario route, the powerful surge of wind and seawater against the natural flow of the river would cause water to overflow all levees and would result in severe flooding in every part of the city. If this were to happen, then thousands upon thousands would become homeless and the city would be totally shut down for a very long time.

Late Friday afternoon, the National Hurricane Center released a bulletin warning that New Orleans was now in the outer portions of the "cone of probability" for landfall. It was not long after that Governor Blanco declared a state of emergency for Louisiana, triggering an official request to FEMA to provide equipment and resources necessary to respond to the impacts of the emergency. This also allowed her the option to deploy the National Guard if needed. The next morning I signed a "Mayoral Proclamation of Hurricane Emergency" executive order for the city of New Orleans and immediately started sounding more alarms for our citizens to evacuate.

This executive order officially gave power to the police chief to take command and control of all law enforcement and military officers in the city. It also gave us the authority to immediately commandeer or utilize any private property; to direct and compel evacuation; to suspend or limit the sale of alcoholic beverages, firearms, explosives, and combustibles; to take all necessary steps to ensure that no looting or arson occurs; and it gave me the power to suspend any ordinance that was in effect. All these extraordinary measures were intended to ensure the public safety and welfare during this emergency. We were synced up with the state, fully engaged and ready to do battle!

Kathleen Blanco was born in and grew up in a small town near New Iberia, Louisiana, in the heart of Cajun country. This is a very small, intimate town with just one church and one school. Shortly after graduating from college Kathleen married Raymond Blanco, a football coach, and to this day just about everyone refers to him as "Coach." She started out as a schoolteacher and mother until she was appointed in 1984 to serve four years as Lafayette's representative in the Louisiana State Legislature. Coach was a true political junkie who continued to serve as her key political and campaign advisor. He helped her secure the state representative seat and all of her future political offices. Once her term as legislator was completed, Kathleen ran for and won the election for a six-year term as public service commissioner. Her next move was to run for and win the second highest state office, lieutenant governor, where she served two four-year terms. The culmination of her political career was a successful run for governor of the state of Louisiana in 2003. She came from behind in the polls in the last week and was the first woman in the history of Louisiana to take this post. She entered the governor's office without any meaningful executive level experience.

By five a.m. Saturday morning, August 27, 2005, Hurricane Katrina had strengthened to a Category 3 storm with winds of up to 125 miles per hour. Police, fire, EMS, and the Sewerage and Water Board put their staff on high alert. The Sewerage and Water Board ordered every pumping station to be manned twenty-four hours a day. All furloughs and vacations were canceled for all essential city personnel.

By ten a.m., a mandatory evacuation was called for the surrounding parishes—St. Charles, St. Tammany, Plaquemines, and low-lying areas in Jefferson—and a voluntary evacuation for the remaining Jefferson areas and St. Bernard Parish. In addition to the parishes' announcements, George W. Bush declared a federal state of emergency for Louisiana. In accordance with our regional evacuation plan, New Orleans along with surrounding areas of Jefferson and St. Charles parishes would be given formal voluntary evacuation orders around fifty hours from landfall. This phased approach ensures that additional cars moving into already congested roads would not create gridlock on the interstate highway system. We were moving unprecedented numbers of people out of southern Louisiana as the "contraflow" plan was working well. Traffic was understandably backed up but was also moving smoothly. We executed according to the plan timelines, and things worked well with evacuations throughout the region.

Inside city hall we continued to have regular meetings with all operations departments. Each department head would give update statuses as we reviewed our preparation checklists. We then reviewed the status of our shelter of last resort, the Superdome. We verified again that transportation, security, medicine, and food and water were in place. The legal department briefed us on legal implications for every step we had taken or anticipated taking. We felt we had everything covered, but we all continued to worry whether enough citizens had headed our warnings.

A further complicating factor was that Saturday turned out to be one of the most pleasant, beautiful days on record. There was not a cloud in the sky, and the sun was beaming, enticing people outdoors. With a slight breeze periodically blowing, the temperature was just perfect. The NFL New Orleans Saints were also scheduled to play a pre-season game, drawing large crowds and tailgaters into the city. People were out and about, walking and running in the parks, watching children's soccer games, and just enjoying this wonderful weather. However, I knew Mother Nature was being very deceptive. Just like a tsunami can fool uninformed innocent people who live near the coastline, hurricanes can be deceptive as well. As a moving vortex, the sheer force of the storm manages to secretly suck all bad weather into its periphery, revealing sunny skies and a beautiful cloudless day for the region about to be visited.

In spite of these distractions, many people had heard my calls to evacuate and were taking precautions by first securing their homes. They also followed the basic drill of buying bottled water and canned goods to last them for at least three days if needed. They fueled their cars, boarded up their windows with plywood, secured shutters, and removed patio furniture to secure places. Others had already left the city, and many were preparing to leave later that day or first thing Sunday. But for the most part, if you found yourself outside it just felt like another typical sunny day in New Orleans.

My gut was telling me that we needed to do another special outreach to provide a safety net to seniors and citizens who strictly relied on public transportation. We took another very important step by encouraging our faith-based community to reinforce evacuations through buddy systems within their congregations and surrounding neighborhoods. We sent a fax message, which was sent to all churches in New Orleans asking them to advise their congregations on Sunday of the imminent threat that Katrina had become. Kenya Smith, one of my most trusted assistants, busied himself taking the lead on this critical task. As luck would have it, we experienced technical issues with the fax machines and could not confirm fax deliveries. As if guided by a higher power, we also made personal telephone calls to pastors that day to ensure the message was delivered.

We were also coordinating with the Regional Transit Authority (RTA), a city-controlled agency that managed bus and streetcar services. They were a critical part of our emergency preparedness plan in that they were responsible for transporting people to the shelter of last resort, the Superdome. Once we verified that this facility was ready to take in evacuees, we double-checked strategic pickup points throughout the city where remaining citizens would go to be picked up by RTA buses. We had previously identified seventeen strategic locations throughout the city. The final phases of our pre-storm emergency preparedness procedures were in motion, and our sense was things were going well.

Our overriding fundamental strategy was to first evacuate as many people out of the city who had cars or could buy plane tickets. We also encouraged neighbors to look out for and support other neighbors, particularly our precious senior citizens. Citizens with medical or special needs were next for evacuation or special sheltering. And finally, for those who couldn't leave or wouldn't leave, we offered them free bus services.

We planned for food and water to sustain up to twenty-five thousand sheltered people for three days. After three days we were hopeful that between a state government with a $12 billion budget and the U.S. federal government that was the richest in the world that they both would find common ground to send the "cavalry" to rescue us. We would later learn the hard way that that fundamental assumption was somewhat flawed as it missed the point of whether there was political will at the top to do the right thing if hell or high water came our way.

Midday Saturday, Governor Blanco visited the region. With her was her husband, "Coach," and some of her key staff who came to meet with us in my office. We sat around my conference table and talked at length about the pending storm threat. During the middle part of the discussion the governor turned and looked me in the eyes and said, "Mayor, I'm getting everything in place that you need." It felt sincere and was reassuring to find that her manner and now actions were more supportive towards me than she had demonstrated since taking office. We moved to a regularly scheduled update conference call with parish leaders, regional emergency preparedness managers, and the National Weather Service. It seemed as though the governor and I were on the same page. In the middle of the conference call the governor stepped away to take a phone call from the White House.

Later that afternoon, after the governor and her team had left the city, I began to reflect back to the last governor's election and my approach to endorsing a candidate for that race. In the runoff I closely analyzed both candidate platforms, the Democrat Kathleen Blanco and the Republican Bobby Jindal. Their platforms were almost identical. This was consistent with a pattern I had studied over time that many Southern white Democrats normally vote and act like Republicans while somehow maintaining a façade of Democrat principles.

As I continued to study each candidate it hit me that I should send each one a letter to allow them the opportunity to put in writing what their priorities would be for New Orleans if they were elected governor of Louisiana in 2003. Two days later I got an elaborate, well thought out response from Bobby Jindal. Two weeks later, I finally received a very vague two-paragraph letter from Kathleen Blanco. I was very disappointed as deep down inside I wanted to support a fellow Democrat. However, I was mayor of a struggling city, and we needed more than party affiliations—we needed specific help. After sleeping on the contents of both letters, I knew exactly what I needed to do.

I ended up supporting Bobby Jindal. As a lifelong Democrat this was very cutting-edge for the South and extremely controversial. I believe in the principles of the Democratic Party, but when there is a close call between two candidates, I tend to go with the one who is best qualified and who I believe could be most effective.

Some of my key supporters and advisors were not very happy. I also called the Democratic U.S. senator, Mary Landrieu, who nearly hyperventilated when I informed her what I was doing. Next I called Kathleen Blanco, and she immediately became absolutely furious. She started ranting and raving about how could I do this and how terrible this was. I politely cut her off and told her I was planning to do a press conference soon after I hung up with her. She then shouted at me, "You are making a big mistake, and there will be hell to pay for you in the future" and hung up the phone abruptly.

We held the press conference, announced my endorsement, and the entire state was abuzz. With my support and others, the local daily newspaper the *Times Picayune*, and the current governor Mike Foster, Bobby Jindal became the solid frontrunner to become Louisiana's next governor. In fact, he was leading in most polls by twelve points the Monday before a Saturday election. He pulled me aside one-on-one that day while campaigning in New Orleans and asked me to be co-chair of his transition team. I looked him in the eye and told him very directly that he had not won yet and he needed to concentrate on effectively answering a very negative healthcare TV attack ad that had been running for over two weeks. I was very concerned that he had not answered the attack in the medium that it was presented in, TV. My overall message to him was that he needed to stay focused on being aggressive in the race and the transition would take care of itself. Unfortunately, he did not heed my warnings and ended up losing a very close race. He was stunned and humbled. He would not repeat the same mistake four year later when he succeeded in becoming governor of Louisiana.

Years later, Governor Blanco's words would come true in ways no one in their wildest dreams could have ever imagined. When Blanco said there would be hell to pay for me in the future—it was actually prophetic. It may not have been the hell that she was referring to, but it was still something completely unimaginable. Little did we know that Hurricane Katrina would unleash a hell on this city that was straight off the history pages of Kobe, Watts, New York after 9/11,

Sarajevo, or some other disaster or war-ravaged place. She ended up being in one of two key positions to make decisions that would either make my experience with Hurricane Katrina something that would be remembered as one of the ultimate in team-based emergency management or I would be left to fend for myself along with other poor souls still in the city after the worst man-made and natural disaster ever. Unfortunately, we were pretty much left to fend for ourselves in full payment for being in hell.

We ended up finishing Saturday feeling good that our emergency preparedness implementation work was going very well. Special needs patients were taken care of, seniors were buddying up with church members and neighbors, and the Superdome was staged, manned, and ready to accept needy citizens. The estimates were that we had set a record with approximately 80 percent of our citizens now voluntarily evacuated. In the past, a "successful" evacuation resulted in 60 to 70 percent having left the city.

Later that night, I took my family to dinner at a local restaurant called the Steak Knife. When Katrina first entered the Gulf, my wife bought airline tickets for the family to evacuate to Dallas first thing Sunday morning. Our personal evacuation plan was for them to stay there a few days and return to New Orleans the following week. So we were having a going away dinner of sorts. The restaurant was very busy and doing great business. Although most diners seemed to be enjoying their meal, many made their way to my table to ask advice on the pending hurricane threat. They all asked basically the same question: "Should we leave?" My obvious response every time was, "Yes, you must go!"

In the middle of the meal I received an urgent call from Governor Blanco, who implored me to call Max Mayfield, head of the National Hurricane Center. I called him right after hanging up with her. We quickly dispensed with the pleasantries and went straight to the matter at hand. His comments and analysis hit me like a ton of bricks and struck a note of fear in my heart for my city. I immediately lost my appetite.

It felt as though time had slowed down as Mr. Mayfield explained in detail just how dangerous this storm would be. "Mr. Mayor, this is going to be real big and real bad! In my thirty-plus years of experience in tracking hurricanes, I have never seen a storm or conditions like this. I am not sure what has been done, but you must get everyone out of the city as soon as you can!" I thanked him for the very frank advice, and he said good luck and hung up.

I stood in shock for a moment to collect my thoughts. This was such a strong jolt of reality. A few minutes earlier I was feeling really good about a record evacuation, and now we had to go even higher with very little time left. I took a couple of deep breaths to clear my head and think. My adrenaline was starting to flow, and I thought to myself, "Okay, what needs to be done first?"

Instinctively I knew what I must do; I needed to order a mandatory evacuation. This had never been done before in the city's almost three-hundred-year history. I picked up my cell phone and dialed Sherry Landry, our city attorney, and updated her. I told her that I didn't care what she had to do, but we had to implement a mandatory evacuation. I then proceeded to tell her that she and her team may have to work through the night to get the formal papers ready for my signature as I planned to sign them as soon as they finished. I next informed my chief administrative officer, Dr. Hatfield, and my communications director, Sally Forman, who started the process for setting up a major press conference to be held first thing in the morning.

Max Mayfield's predictions immediately became a terrifying reality. Over the course of that evening, Katrina intensified from a Category 4 to a Category 5 storm right after midnight. By seven a.m. the next morning her winds were peaking at 175 miles per hour. Hurricane Katrina was approximately 250 miles away from New Orleans and now had a predicted storm surge of twenty-five to thirty-five feet high once she made landfall.

This really felt like we were preparing for major battle. Unfortunately, our opponent was a monster storm of enormous proportions. This opponent was still very deceptive as she never really showed her full strength or intended target until the last possible moment. At first she was a tropical storm who became a hurricane and then back to a tropical storm and then a hurricane again. She went from a Category 3 to a Category 5 storm in just nine hours. On Thursday she was headed to Florida/Alabama, Friday she was supposed to hit Alabama/Mississippi, and then Saturday she was pointed toward Louisiana and maybe New Orleans. Then late Saturday night all the computer models confirmed where she really wanted to go all along—straight for us. This ultimate warrior was Mother Nature. Look out, New Orleans, Katrina was on the way, and she was looking to do some major cleansing.

After the six a.m. Sunday morning region-wide conference call with the state, the National Weather Service confirmed Hurricane Katrina's strength and direction. I signed the second executive order and was ready to announce the first ever citywide mandatory evacuation. At nine thirty a.m. on August 28, Governor Blanco, the city council, and members of my staff stood by my side for this historic press conference. The storm's potential impact was so overwhelming that I knew the people of the city and the region needed to hear my message very clearly, to take it very seriously, and most of all not panic. After the governor spoke and advised the public that if they didn't leave the city then they needed to write their social security number with permanent black ink pen on their arm so that they could later be identified if things turned bad, I took to the podium.

I looked into the cameras and gave my best, most sincere heartfelt appeal for everyone to leave. Many citizens from the city and region would approach me later and thank me for what they described as literally saving their lives with my sincerity during this press conference. They all said that before they saw me that morning they were thinking about staying and riding out the storm. Most of these families lived in areas where their homes were either flooded to the roof line or were totally destroyed.

I also announced that we were opening the Louisiana Superdome as a shelter of last resort. The citizens were informed that buses would be pre-staged throughout the city to transport people to the

Superdome. I then set forth a dusk to dawn curfew as Police Chief Edwin Compass spoke firmly that any amount of looting no matter how small would not be tolerated. I then took the microphone again and said, "Every person is hereby ordered to evacuate the city. We are facing a storm that most of us have long feared. I don't want to create panic, but I do want citizens to understand that this is very serious, and it is of the highest nature."

Hurricane Katrina was expected to make landfall in New Orleans very early Monday morning. Before the press conference ended I had one other special group to address, thirty thousand tourists, many of whom were still in town occupying hotel rooms. I asked them to immediately leave also. If they couldn't get out, then they should stay inside on third-floor or higher hotel rooms and move away from windows. The term "vertical evacuation" was used to ensure the message hit the intended targets.

I closed by advising citizens who planned to come to the Superdome for shelter that they should bring enough food, water, medicine (if needed), and supplies to last two to three days. No weapons or pets would be allowed in the Superdome. The press conference ended, and we mingled around after to make sure the reporters had all the fact straight. Many of them were also pretty shell-shocked, and you could see it in their eyes that they were frightened and quietly planning their own escapes in their heads.

We were now at the point of no turning back. This decision meant that the city would be totally shut down for at least a week. Financially, the state, the city, large and small businesses, hotels, and restaurants would lose valuable income. The federal government would also lose money as our port, airport, river, oil and gas, and seafood industries would also shut down. This interruption would have a significant impact on revenue and cost, now and into the future. The potential cost to the nation was verified as being at least a half billion dollars each day we were closed. However, the money really didn't matter as much now as public safety was our number one priority.

Not long after my press conference, the National Weather Service issued a bulletin that echoed Max Mayfield's comments to me from the night before. The bulletin stated very bluntly the following:

"PARTIAL TO COMPLETE WALL AND ROOF FAILURE IS EXPECTED. ALL WOOD FRAMED LOW RISING APARTMENT BUILDINGS WILL BE DESTROYED. CONCRETE BLOCK LOW RISE APARTMENTS WILL SUSTAIN MAJOR DAMAGE…INCLUDING SOME WALL AND ROOF FAILURE.

"HIGH-RISE OFFICE AND APARTMENT BUILDINGS WILL SWAY DANGEROUSLY…A FEW TO THE POINT OF TOTAL COLLAPSE. ALL WINDOWS WILL BLOW OUT.

"AIRBORNE DEBRIS WILL BE WIDESPREAD…AND MAY INCLUDE HEAVY ITEMS SUCH AS HOUSEHOLD APPLIANCES AND EVEN LIGHT VEHICLES. SPORT UTILITY VEHICLES AND LIGHT TRUCKS WILL BE MOVED. THE BLOWN DEBRIS WILL CREATE ADDITIONAL DESTRUCTION TO PERSONS…PETS…AND LIVESTOCK EXPOSED TO THE WINDS WILL FACE CERTAIN DEATH IF STRUCK."

Against all of our collective efforts to encourage people to leave, there were still about forty to fifty thousand citizens who decided to stay and ride out the storm for whatever reasons. Hurricane Ivan, changing direction at the last minute, had obviously lulled some into a false sense of security. Unfortunately, there's a long tradition in this region of people riding out storms in their homes, and there are even small groups who throw "Hurricane parties," stocking up on adult beverages and partying their way through the night.

And then there were those who just couldn't afford to evacuate. The three days away paying for hotels, fuel (if they have a car), and food was just too costly on a very tight budget or no budget at all. It should also be noted that Katrina was hitting at the end of the month, so many had not received their welfare or social security checks that normally arrive in the mail around the first of each month. These individuals had very few choices other than to ride out the storm or go to a shelter.

In my continuing efforts to get the attention of anyone who was still not taking this storm seriously, I stressed during my in-studio media interviews that if anyone was going to stay in their homes, they should make sure they had a sharp ax handy. This ax visual really got many people's attention. The wisdom of this advice was if waters rose suddenly and flooded the first floor of their homes, then they could quickly get into their attics. If the water kept rising, they could then hack their way out onto the roof for safety. As this visual took hold, the interstate highways experienced another surge of vehicles. More people were getting in their cars and exiting the region. To this day people still come up to me and smile and tell me the ax story helped them to finally decide to leave and they were glad they did.

Now it was time to hunker down for the main event, Hurricane Katrina, a Category 5 storm whose footprint at her peak almost covered the entire Gulf of Mexico. By Sunday we were finalizing all preparations. Marcia St. Martin, director of the Sewerage and Water Board, called the EPA and informed told them that we were preparing to open sewer valves to dewater the city of waste. Since wastewater carries a certain amount of disease, we accelerated treatments and dewatered the system. We informed the EPA that we had run out of time and needed to discharge untreated waste directly into the Mississippi River. We knew we could experience a total loss of power after the storm hit, so in order to avoid sewerage backing up in buildings and on the streets, which would have created the potential for serious diseases to break out, we discharged. This was a very wise move since a real secret success story was that we did not have any diseases develop in the city after the flooding occurred.

Sunday was also the day I took my family to the Louis Armstrong International Airport to board their flight to Dallas. The airport was packed, and I felt reassured that my evacuation message was working as witnessed by the number of people leaving the city on the highways and at the airport.

Before they left home, my daughter Tianna, six years old at the time, gave me some very special and specific instructions. She had gone to a friend's birthday party on Friday and received as a party favor a betta fish, sometimes called a Siamese fighting fish. She wanted to take the fish with her on the plane, but I told her I was not sure the fish would survive the flight. She said, "Okay, Daddy, you take Fishy! Make sure you take good care of him as I want to see him alive when I come back." So like a good father, I took this fish to my office and then my hotel room, feeding it in the wee hours of the morning and cleaning his water every few days. This was just what I needed with a major hurricane bearing down on my city, babysitting a pet fish.

After kissing and hugging my family goodbye, I left the airport to head back to city hall. By the time I arrived there, the RTA buses were going full speed ahead in collecting people from the designated checkpoints throughout the city and transporting them to the Superdome. This was the final phase of our emergency preparedness plan as the Superdome was our short-term shelter of last resort. We had warned people not to expect the comforts of home and that it could take some time to get inside as we would be doing screenings and registrations.

By noon, long lines were forming, and they were getting longer and longer. Five to six people wide, the lines wrapped around the Superdome. Some brought most of what they owned—TVs, chairs, garbage bags full of clothes, luggage, guns, knives, you name it.

Weapons were not allowed inside. Before anyone was allowed to enter the Superdome, they were advised that there were several large receptacles near the door where they could place weapons, no questions asked. The receptacles soon filled up, and we had to bring in more. Everyone who entered was also thoroughly search by the National Guard.

What was remarkable was that the people lining up for the Superdome were extremely patient. They were quiet, orderly, and calm. To maintain order inside, the New Orleans Police Department had full command along with the three hundred National Guardsmen who served at their direction. These law enforcement professionals did an outstanding job on intake, and they got even better as the challenges increased exponentially as the tough days to come brought out the very best in these brave men and women.

Another courageous group consisted of the city's health director, Dr. Kevin Stephens, our Emergency Management System (EMS) employees, and a dedicated volunteer staff who worked nonstop to separate incoming individuals with medical or other special needs from the crowd going into the Superdome. This medical team efficiently moved sick evacuees into a makeshift medical unit that they set up from scratch inside the NBA sports arena, which was connected to the Superdome by a short walkway.

On my way back from the airport I had noticed the beautiful skies of yesterday were now replaced with ugly, dark clouds. As the lines grew longer at the Superdome, the sky opened up a bit and my heart went out to each and every person who was now waiting in a light but steady rain. We did our best to expedite check-in and move as many people inside as quickly as we could. But by late afternoon, there will still long lines of people waiting to get in. Ten thousand people were already inside as the rain and winds had begun to pick up, soaking most of the unprotected people who stood toward the end of the line. Shortly thereafter, the medical staff became inundated with the high numbers of sick people who were coming in. We were already experiencing medical supply shortages, particularly with oxygen tanks.

RTA buses kept coming, full to capacity. Other citizens were also driving their cars to the Superdome and parking them as close as possible. Some even panicked and jumped out of their cars, leaving them half parked and unlocked. Still others were walking or taking a taxi to the Superdome. It was clear from their pace and body language that fear was setting in. The news reports on the radio and TV were heightening concerns as the size and magnitude of Hurricane Katrina was finally hitting home to unbelievers.

The medical staff back at the arena had already put in an urgent request to FEMA for at least a hundred oxygen canisters. They also estimated and ordered an additional three hundred canisters to be delivered right after the winds died down, hopefully for late Monday delivery. It is unfortunate that FEMA could not deliver on either request, and the medical unit in the arena would later have no choice but to resort to hand ventilators. This required Dr. Stephens to recruit those who could, close family and friends of the patients and volunteers, to just sit by the needy patient's side and pump these devices manually for as long as their muscles could stand.

Another press conference was scheduled at five p.m. where we continued to encourage citizens to evacuate. I normally took the lead as it seemed that more and more people in the region were now depending on our updates on Hurricane Katrina.

By late evening it was rewarding to verify that "contraflow" was moving over twenty thousand cars an hour out of the region. For the ultimate procrastinators, it was now a deadly race against time and Katrina. When the winds in the region exceeded thirty-five miles per hour, the highways would be closed and those super tardy late-goers would have to return to their homes or the Superdome.

By eight p.m. Sunday evening, the vast majority of the citizens of New Orleans and almost one million people in the metropolitan area had evacuated. A dusk to dawn curfew was being enforced. The Superdome had close to twenty thousand people inside, and we were still receiving late stragglers. Despite all our efforts to ensure people left the city or were in a safe shelter, there were still reports that another twenty thousand citizens still remained in their homes.

Police cars were still out in the neighborhoods with blue lights and loudspeakers on ordering people to leave the city. "There is a mandatory evacuation, and all citizens must leave New Orleans now," was blared out all over the city. Officers also alerted citizens to where the pickup locations were for the RTA buses. Some officers even brought people to the Superdome.

In retrospect, Sunday had been an extra-full and very exhausting day. We implemented key plans, held multiple conference calls, debated strategies, ensured loved ones were safe and secure, and executed at the highest levels possible the most complex evacuation ever attempted for an urban area. I'd met regularly with key staff members, agencies, airport executives, and Entergy—the local power company. I also participated in numerous conference calls and press conferences. We checked every detail and knew all there was to know about Hurricane Katrina.

Under the direction of Colonel Terry Ebbert, director of the City Emergency Management Office, the Emergency Operations Center (EOC) pre-ordered from FEMA 360,000 MREs (meals, ready to eat) and fifteen truckloads of bottled water to ensure that we could adequately feed and hydrate those citizens who came to our shelter. This request also included the urgent need for medical personnel and other related support. FEMA officials committed to us on several occasions that these supplies would arrive no later than Sunday night. However, as the storm got closer and stronger, we were increasingly concerned that these critical needs would not make it in time. This would prove to be one of many unfulfilled promises by FEMA and the federal government during this odyssey.

Eventually only forty thousand MREs showed up. We did not receive any additional medical personnel or other critical medical supplies before landfall. To top everything off, only five truckloads of water were delivered before the storm hit. My adrenaline was now elevated to a new high. I knew that you could live for many days with very little food, but a human being could only last a very short time without adequate water, especially in New Orleans during August when it is very hot and humid. Later that night, my thoughts turned to the one question that would continue to haunt us for months to come: "How could this be happening in America to American citizens?"

Somehow late that evening I managed to quietly slip away and go home to pick up more of Fishy's food, a couple days of clothes, and some toiletries. On my way home it hit me just how empty the city felt. There was no one out and about. In contrast, only twenty-four hours earlier happy, fun-loving New Orleanians were either outdoors enjoying pleasant weather, watching the Saints football game at the Superdome, or were at their favorite restaurant or live music club on or near Bourbon Street. The city was then abuzz and there was a beehive of activity everywhere. Now the sky was dark, the winds had picked up, and the rain was pelting down, signaling the pending arrival of Queen Katrina, the cleanser. The streets were eerily quiet, wet, and windy, and the streetlights only illuminated empty sidewalks and boarded-up houses. After leaving home with my overnight bag, I made some final appearances at several TV stations for live citizen updates and then returned to city hall to hunker down.

Once back, I settled into my office on the second floor of city hall. I planned to sleep on a leather couch. Sometime around midnight my staff started to get real nervous. They reminded me that city hall was built forty to fifty years earlier and was not wind rated for a Category 5 storm. In fact, the building was already starting to sway with the winds. Our backup plan was to move directly across the street to the Hyatt hotel, which was adjacent to the Superdome. My executive assistant, Pat Smith, had pre-booked enough rooms for myself and essential city hall personnel. This hotel was also strategic because our local power company, Entergy, had set up their EOC there as the main hotel building had adequate backup power and redundant, secure telephone lines. We discussed this as a team and decided we would move quickly.

Everyone was on board except for Colonel Terry Ebbert, the city's head of Homeland Security and director of the EOC. His argument was that there was no way to move all of our telecommunication equipment this quickly, and we could not set everything up without losing contact with the National Weather Service at this critical hour. He also promised that if the building became really unstable, then he would get everyone out and not risk lives. He was an ex-Marine who had gotten the Purple Heart award, so I looked him in the eyes and reluctantly said okay. I trusted him and his judgment, and I knew he would get his people out of harm's way if necessary.

The rest of us moved to the Hyatt, where I was given a suite on the twenty-seventh floor with a separate area large enough to hold private meetings. Since this was so high up, I also had a safer sleeping cot on the fourth floor in a common ballroom, which is where I laid my head down for a few hours as Katrina took her time pounding our city. The only one who enjoyed the suite on the twenty-seventh floor that first night was Fishy.

All you could hear outside were consistent, powerful wind gusts. Without warning, you would hear the roar of wind and then big items being blown around and banging into buildings or any unfortunate cars parked on the street. On the fourth floor of the Hyatt in the big conference center, which we used as a meeting, sleeping, and eating area, we all nervously congregated. Throughout the night people would also gravitate outside these rooms to a viewing ledge that was surrounded by a beautiful glass-covered atrium overhead. During the day this atrium provided a good view of the Superdome, Poydras Street, and city hall. On this night, however, all you could see was rain splattering against the windowpanes and various materials that had been blown free. The banging of loose items got louder and louder as the night progressed, almost as if Katrina were playing a large bass drum in her own second line band. It was very unnerving, and many walked around extremely scared as we wondered whether the National Weather Service's predictions that high-rise buildings could collapse would prove true, particularly the one where we were residing, the Hyatt hotel. Most chatted anxiously, putting on our best game faces while wondering inside where was the nearest exit if we had to suddenly run for it.

We all knew Katrina was coming closer and closer. And then, right after midnight, as the storm started to pass over the edges of the city, the winds became wilder, and items, really big ones, really started flying and banging into the atrium. We all looked at each other as the full reality of what we were dealing with was preventing anyone from getting sleepy. I kept reflecting on those who were in their one-story or two-story homes who decided not to heed my repeated warnings to leave. My continuous prayers were that they had at least heard my message about having an ax handy.

This would be a very long night. Whatever would happen next would be up to the forces of nature and a higher power. I said many prayers that night as I knew more than ever that we were all dependent on the grace of Almighty God. Tomorrow was coming, and as soon as the winds died down we would get a chance to see what

Katrina's definition of cleansing really was. "Tomorrow, tomorrow, the sun will come out tomorrow." That song had better be true for all of us left in New Orleans. We would definitely see, tomorrow.

CHAPTER THREE

DEVASTATED LEVEES

———■———

G od's grace was with us as Hurricane Katrina made landfall not as a Category 5 but as a Category 3 storm with winds of 125 instead of 175 miles per hour. However, although we may have been spared from total destruction, there was still Category 5 momentum from Katrina as she rose up out of the sea. Her Wonder Woman–like strength destroyed everything in her path as she made landfall on August 29, 2005, at 6:10 a.m. in three distinct places throughout Louisiana. Like a well-devised secret battle plan, this hurricane first hit with a force so hard that she completely obliterated the small, sleepy fishing village of Buras-Triumph, on the coastline of Louisiana. Katrina's winds stretched 120 miles from the center or "eye," which means this storm's entire footprint spanned at least 240 miles across. After moving over southeastern Louisiana and into the waters of Breton Sound, she made her third and final landfall across the Louisiana and Mississippi coastlines. Storm surge as high as thirty to thirty-five feet rolled through Plaquemines and then St. Bernard Parish, flooding and annihilating anything in its path. Next up was the Lower Ninth Ward and St. Tammany Parish, who were both hit simultaneously with continuous sledgehammers of mountainous waves of water.

By daybreak Hurricane Katrina was fulfilling her destiny by moving over the city with immense strength and power. The wind was screaming around the Hyatt hotel, louder and crazier than a wild banshee, roaring down the streets and around other buildings. It was a hollow and constant drone like sci-fi possessed Gods chanting ominous incantations. The raindrops were so large that they sounded like gunshots as they hit buildings, cars, and the ground. This scene could have been straight out of a movie, but it wasn't—this was our unfortunate reality. Over the course of the next several hours, some would meet their maker while others would live to tell tales of very close calls.

It felt so surreal. Large pieces of gravel and other debris were swept up by the force of the wind and discarded just as quickly. Most were pelted against shattering glass windows like packs of Mardi Gras beads or painted Zulu coconuts tossed into a sea of people, many who get hit in the face or head as penalty for not anticipating where these items are really going. Large pieces of metal, roofs, fences, and garbage cans were blown around like Frisbees as this storm danced on our city.

We were in the midst of the beginning of the culmination of almost a week of watching and waiting to see the true intentions of Hurricane Katrina. A military expert would later say that she was the perfect enemy. Katrina was extremely deceptive and camouflaged herself well. This storm was erratic and then precise, weak and powerful, slow and fast, and she was least and most destructive dependent upon what was analyzed. Once she was finally and fully revealed, it was way too late to do anything further to protect yourself.

Her destructive forces cut off all communications. She destroyed all major transportation routes out except one. She left many wounded, sick, and dead. Katrina ended up totally closing down an entire Gulf coast economy, shut down water and sewerage systems, interrupted the nation's oil and gas supply, closed airports and seaports, and rendered several million people homeless. Katrina was a very bad girl! She had never been to Bourbon Street and heard that we served an alcoholic drink called the "Hurricane," and she wanted one for the road.

As her outer edges reached land early Monday morning, Katrina's winds were peaking at 150 miles per hour. Her forward speed quickened to fifteen miles per hour. As she officially made landfall at 6:10 a.m., her wind speed was down to 125 miles per hour and she was moving around eighteen miles per hour, now in full sprint to get some libations on Bourbon Street. We were hunkered down as outside conditions were changing spectacularly. Katrina's winds and rain were starting to hit violently.

Around eight a.m., I'd just managed to wrap up another meeting when we moved to the atrium area on the fourth floor. Since it was a glass overhead structure, we went there often as this gave us the best sense of what was happening outside. As we'd stopped at the ledge in conversation, we noticed that the wind was gusting stronger than ever. Within minutes the hurricane had released a series of tornados that swept over the Superdome, moved down Poydras Street, and the strongest one was headed directly for our hotel. The noise was deafening. It sounded like a number of freight trains on course to collide with our building. We could clearly hear glass and windows starting to crack and explode as debris, loose rocks and other materials picked up by the winds pounded our safe haven from multiple directions. The sounds of exploding glass got louder and louder and closer and closer. Our natural impulse was to dive for the floor and cover our heads as some were showered with bits and pieces of very sharp glass as it sailed through the air. Without warning a huge piece of wood blew through the windows and wedged itself between some sleeping firefighters. What a rude awakening for them. For the moment the hurricane seemed to be right there with them in their room as they scrambled for safety.

Next thing we knew was all room windows on the north tower of the hotel were totally blown out. Curtains were left flapping inside and outside these rooms like ships' sails in the wind. Now totally exposed to the elements, rain and debris invaded these rooms and ruined all of the furniture and fixtures. Next up, an office building right next door was also stripped of most of its glass shell. This latest event lasted only a few minutes, but it felt like hours. Once the tornados finished their dirty work, we were not allowed the luxury of relaxing. Hurricane-force winds were getting stronger and stronger as the eye of the storm was moving closer and closer.

Anyone who was fortunate enough to have fallen asleep for three to four hours was now wide awake. We now know that in the midst of all of our excitement with tornados that our levees had started to breach from storm surge around nine a.m. and the "bowls" were starting to fill up. But it would take many hours for this information to be confirmed as we were still stuck inside by the fierce winds. Hurricane Katrina had taken her drink in New Orleans in a to-go cup, and now she had many other places to see.

To complete this briefing of the adventurous travels of Hurricane Katrina, by four p.m. that same day she was near Jackson, Mississippi, with winds of seventy-five miles per hour. She caused damage there as she still had a full head of steam trucking along at eighteen miles per hour. She then paid an unpleasant visit to Tennessee, through Kentucky, Ohio was next, and she finally dissipated at eleven p.m. in southeastern Canada. Before she gave up the ghost by dissipating into thin air, she caused roads in Quebec to be eroded by heavy rainfall, a not so nice going away present of sorts. What a girl, the bad girl who drank, strutted her stuff on Bourbon Street, and cleansed a path from the Gulf of Mexico all the way to Canada!

Now let's get back to the details of what was happening with us at the command center as Katrina was making landfall and moving toward New Orleans. Our team was still holed up in our building, and it was hard to get a real grasp of the situation outside; the sounds in the distance could only tell us so much. Telecommunication services were still functioning at this time, so phone calls and e-mails were flying throughout the night. I believe I may have gotten only two hours of sleep. After freshening up a bit, listening to voice mails, and answering well over a hundred e-mails, I started my official day with a five a.m. conference call with key staff.

I recalled Police Chief Eddie Compass and Colonel Terry Ebbert, director of Homeland Security and Emergency Preparedness for the city of New Orleans, being very vocal during this session. I could tell their adrenaline was flowing at a high level. They were both focused and commanded a good amount of respect as they directed very critical functions. They both had close ties with all the law enforcement offices throughout the state. Colonel Ebbert reported that winds were

peaking and Lake Pontchartrain water levels were already apprecia-
bly above normal. He was rightly concerned that if these lake waters
continued to rise before the storm actually got here, then surge could
cause severe overtopping and major flooding. He strongly advocated
that we monitor this matter very closely. Chief Compass was focused
on his men and women as he wanted to ensure that the officers,
vehicles, and equipment were secure and out of harm's way. We had
pre-positioned boats at the National Guard station in the Lower Ninth
Ward. He also reported that the city was very quiet with no incidents
of crime. Our citizens were either gone or in lockdown mode inside
their homes.

As soon as I'd finished that call I immediately dialed into the
standard six a.m. conference call with the National Weather Service,
state government officials, parish presidents, and emergency managers. Our focus was an update on Hurricane Katrina and to obtain
damage assessments on the coastal and metro New Orleans areas.
The initial reports were generally positive, and although the winds
were still strong, it was widely reported that we had just about
weathered the worst. My gut was telling me we were not out of
the woods yet. I knew that storm surge could still be an issue, both
from the forward direction of the hurricane and then from the counterclockwise natural rotation of the hurricane that could push massive amounts of water into the lake. My premonition that this lake
surge could overpower our drainage canals would later prove to be
accurate.

Trying to stay optimistic, I instructed my staff to start preparing for
debris removal once the storm had passed. Our goal was to accomplish as much as possible before citizens started to return to the city.
I tasked Dr. Brenda Hatfield, CAO, and Veronica White, our sanitation
director, to prepare a post-storm cleanup plan. We went through most
of the morning developing our priority list of things we would need
once the winds died down. We'd also prepared and submitted to
FEMA a very detailed list for more food, water, medical supplies, debris
removal equipment, and other required assistance.

Unfortunately, the majority of media outlets had jumped on the bandwagon with the hasty positive news that we had dodged a big bullet. They misread Katrina's intensity downgrade and forgot that she was a Category 5 storm long enough to produce massive storm surges. Reporters continued to speculate that the storm wasn't as bad as predicted, and many started to relax. But I couldn't calm down, not until it was verified that we were truly out of the woods.

Instinctively, I needed to see for myself that the city had fared well. Until I was outside, driving through the dry streets of my city, I couldn't wholeheartedly accept what they were saying. That ride outside would be hours away, as the winds were still too strong. The only thing we could accurately confirm was that the storm was still with us and her surge could still cause mass destruction. As long as any part of its 240-mile footprint was covering us, there was a strong possibility that it could also turn on a dime and push water over levees and into the lake to cause major flooding. The last time this type of flooding occurred was during Hurricane Betsy forty years ago. So we were long overdue.

As Katrina continued to pound the area, we commandeered the fourth-floor ballrooms in the Hyatt and set up a mini–city hall operation with meeting rooms and computer equipment. We were in regular communication with the EOC across the street in city hall. In addition, Entergy, the local power utility operator for New Orleans, worked out of this area as well. As a matter of fact, they originally identified and secured most of this space and were gracious in sharing critical resources. I seemed to have spent most of my morning either there or in my suite checking in with different departments throughout the city. Besides the EOC, police, and fire departments, I'd kept in constant touch with Entergy to monitor the city's power grid and with Marcia St. Martin, director of the Sewerage and Water Board.

Around ten a.m. Monday as the storm continued its march inland, it was surprising to me that our local media was still saying the worst was over. As quickly as the latest round of news was transmitted, the strong winds and storm surge started knocking TV and radio stations off the air. Most other forms of communication also went dark. That's when we started to have cell phone, e-mail, and BlackBerry message problems as cell towers were falling like dominos.

Hurricane Katrina's storm surge was feeling the effect of moving from open sea water that offered no resistance to now being over land. Storm surge of thirty to thirty-five feet when she hit the Louisiana coastline was now around twenty to twenty-five feet high near New Orleans East and the lower Ninth Ward. The big problem was the levees that had been built to Hurricane Betsy standards of a maximum height of fifteen feet forty years ago were now standing at only eight to twelve feet because of natural subsidence and a lack of maintenance. So when a twenty-foot wave hits a twelve-foot-high levee, there is bound to be severe overtopping and flooding. Later studies by the Army Corps of Engineers concluded that initially most of the levees held, but as water came over them the sheer force of the water dug holes on the backside that weakened the entire structure, which led to major breaches. This overtopping phenomenon is called scouring.

As the eye of the storm got closer, the more the surge waves pounded the levees, and soon there were multiple breaches. Unconfirmed reports started to come in that water was rising in a number of low-lying areas. In some cases the water supposedly rose as high as eighteen feet so quickly that people and pets drowned almost instantly. Thousands of other unsuspecting people who recognized the ferocious sound of the waves and were quick enough to beat the rising water were stranded in their attics or on their rooftops, totally frightened and pleading to the open sky to be rescued. We were still all pretty helpless at this stage as we really couldn't do anything but pray that the winds would die down quickly enough so that we could get out and start rescuing citizens. My sense was something very bad was unfolding. It was absolutely frustrating that we were stuck at the hotel for several more hours as the storm's high winds were still way too strong for us to send out our police, fire, and other emergency responders. We had to stay put and not risk any more lives.

Our 911 center was absolutely flooded with phone calls from frantic, hysterical people. These calls were directed to both police and fire lines. Hundreds and perhaps thousands of calls were coming in as the hours passed. Most of these "emergency" lines were jammed, and the ones that worked were full of desperate pleas for help. Deputy Chief Riley told me later that when he went into this area in NOPD headquarters to check on how the staff was doing he observed that just about every dispatcher and 911 operator was visibly shaken and crying out loud. He asked one of the dispatch supervisors what was going on, and she told him that words could not explain, he just had to listen for himself. So she handed him the headset, and he plugged in to listen to one of the dispatchers from the Fifth District, which serves the Ninth Ward. All he heard were people begging and screaming for help saying, "the water's rising," "the water's up to my neck," "my husband has been blown off the roof," and "my children are drowning." He struggled to fight back his own tears.

During one point in the 911 center, over six hundred calls came in twenty-three minutes from the Lower Ninth Ward and the New Orleans East area. We later learned that during roughly the same time water rose from zero to fourteen feet over a large portion of these two areas. The wind had created so much momentum and the water was moving so fast and so powerfully that many first floors took the meaning of "beachfront property" to a whole new level. Many people were forced to take an ax and chop through to their roofs, clinging to chimneys or exhaust vents.

There were also a few extremely unlucky citizens who were somehow on the streets, and as they heard and then saw a wave coming in the distance, their only option was to hurriedly climb to the top of the nearest full-grown tree. For the next hours or days their fate would be holding on for dear life while strong wind, rain, and waves whipped all around them, trying to pry them free and force them into the swelling waters below. In other areas the storm surge was so powerful, forming a wall of water nearly twenty feet high, that it lifted whole houses off their foundations and tossed them around like a mini version of a sinking Noah's ark. This water didn't discriminate—it devoured everything in its path as it passed through levees and raced to the low-lying areas in our bowls. These horrific conditions continued to drive calls in to our emergency phone lines.

We received these calls and had no way of helping the people on the other end of the phone line. All the phone operators could do was listen to the frantic voices, try to stay calm, and offer as much mental relief as they could. Many of our dispatchers would later tell me that they also prayed a lot. Some reached their limit and had to stop taking calls to recompose. Many of our phone operators would never be the same. Many of our citizens would never be the same. With hurricane-force winds still at a hundred miles per hour or more, we were still in for several more long hours of listening, waiting, planning, and praying that God's mercy was with us and the people stuck in the worst part of this storm would somehow survive.

They continued to receive call after call from people who were becoming increasingly more depressed and distraught, screaming, crying, and begging for rescue. "Send a boat, a plane, anything…just please save me." "I can't hold on any longer. I'm stuck in my attic and the water is up to my neck." "I have two young children, and we're on our roof, and the water is still rising." "My wife fell in some fast-moving water that was over her head. She can't swim. Please come quickly."

Our dispatchers kept trying to reassure the callers by saying help would come as soon as the winds died down. We couldn't send anybody out when winds were above fifty-five miles per hour. At sixty miles per hour the winds can overturn a vehicle. Many dispatchers also knew that some of the callers did not make it. One particular caller said the water was rising quickly as she yelled in the phone, "It's in my attic, in a one-story house." The phone call suddenly went dead. Then somewhere after that conversation, a radio communication from the Fifth District announced that they just saw the first body float past in the water.

Unfortunately, these were the ones who decided to ride out the storm in their homes. They would not leave the city or go to a shelter despite many spirited warnings. I am sure now in their individual moments of distress many questioned their decision to stay.

Unfortunately, it was too late to change their condition as destiny was now in control. I continued to pray earnestly.

By now, there were many unofficial reports streaming in that were hard to verify. The National Weather Service and parish presidents were also receiving conflicting reports about flooding in their areas. To ensure that we stayed on top of critical functions, I would also regularly check in with Dan Packer and Rod West of Entergy to understand the status of active power throughout the grid. Marcia St. Martin of the Sewerage and Water Board was also extremely helpful in keeping us abreast on the status of pumping stations. These pumping stations were a key line of defense for maintaining dry streets and homes in the city during normal conditions. She gave regular updates on our water and sewerage systems.

Marcia was particularly concerned because water pressure had suddenly declined to very low levels. She and Chief Engineer Joe Sullivan thought that a large tree had uprooted in City Park and broken a main pipe. Marcia kept an even closer eye on our self-generating power station that was our backup just in case Entergy experienced major power outages. The other key person for real-time information was Colonel Terry Ebbert, who was working almost nonstop to ensure we were doing everything we could do to minimize loss of life and property.

The most frightening unconfirmed report we received was that the Seventeenth Street Canal that feeds into Lakeview and Mid-City had a very large breach and this particular "bowl" was starting to fill up with water. New Orleans is actually made up of three bowls—one in the Lower Ninth Ward, another in New Orleans East, and the third is the Mid-City bowl, which was where we were, and it would be affected by a breach at the Seventeenth Street Canal. Many sections of Mid-City are below sea level. With water now supposedly streaming through the streets of Mid-City, it paved the way for a natural flow into the downtown area. The potential was there for severe flooding throughout the CBD with the exception of small areas closest to the river, the French Quarter, and the river side of Uptown. This scenario could cause a prolonged shutdown of all major businesses, every hospital, and all high-rise hotels. If the Seventeenth Street Canal had indeed been breached, then we were in a race against time to plug it before pumping stations would be totally overwhelmed. It felt like floodwater was assaulting us everywhere and ultimately trying to conquer this great city.

Our pumping system was designed to keep the city from flooding from a ten-year storm event, something that happens once every ten years. What we were dealing with at the moment was something much more powerful and deadly, a five-hundred-year flood event. Our drainage pumps were well built but were never designed to handle flooding like what we were getting ready to experience. We did everything we could do and then some to keep this equipment operational. These pumps were semi-automated and manned twenty-four hours per day. Our crews stayed to the bitter end. As a matter of fact, some of our staff was so dedicated that they put their lives at risk to keep these stations draining the city. They were determined to overcome this storm, and we eventually had to order some to leave to ensure their safety. Once the order was placed many felt a sense of defeat, as we all knew the water had won for now.

Before they left their post, many again went way beyond the call of duty. Moats were dug, inflatable levees were erected, and sandbags were stacked high. These brave employees tried everything. But the water was too deep, too fast, and too strong. To further illustrate their dedication, we almost permanently lost four employees who were stationed in the Lower Ninth Ward and New Orleans East. The water there rose so quickly that we barely got them out. The group of men on duty reported a wall of water coming through Station 5, forcing them to climb to the rafters. Pre-positioned inflatable rafts were a godsend that actually saved their lives.

Unfortunately for us, the identified bowls were filling up in just about every major section of the city. This would not stop until the water level in the city reached the same high water level in the lake. Once that happened, at least 80 percent of the city that is the birthplace of jazz would be submerged like the mythical Atlantis. My city was on its way to becoming a series of misery-filled swimming pools.

Later that evening, the winds finally diminished to levels where our first responders could leave their confines and fan out across the city. They got in dry vehicles that were safely stored pre-storm, commandeered boats and anything else that would float, and jumped into the water to rescue our people.

Unfortunately, the 911 calls were still coming in at very high levels, and phone operators were totally consumed with more traumatic calls for help. These very resilient operators were physically and mentally exhausted after having received thousands upon thousands of frantic, desperate calls. Luckily, our very old, 800 MHz police radio system seemed to hold up as it was not cut off by the many other cell towers that were knocked down by the wind and surge. Phone operators relied exclusively upon this system to communicate to our first responders exactly where help was needed. The police chief also used this radio system to constantly check in with his troops in different areas of the city to provide us with the best field data available. Since we had not had much of a chance to verify any of these reports firsthand, all we could do was trust our people, continue to monitor in real time, and make vital lifesaving decisions every minute from our command center.

All ten hospitals in the city were under severe stress, especially Charity Hospital where our uninsured, underinsured, and severe trauma patients go for medical care. Just like the Hyatt hotel, many of their windows were blown out and damaged, letting in the humid air, wind, and rain. As the downtown streets flooded, the electrical systems of just about every medical facility that was in basements or on the first floors lost power. This was demoralizing as a powerless hospital meant that medical equipment used to administer help to patients could no longer function. This condition forced nurses and doctors to utilize manual devices, like hand ventilators, for treating sick patients. We would later learn that a good number of doctors had left the city before the storm hit. However, many other brave doctors and nurses stayed behind and worked themselves to the brink of total exhaustion trying to keep people alive.

My sister Alana, who is a registered nurse, was on duty at one of these hospitals. She later told me stories about how they first had to move all occupied beds into the hallways so that they could keep better watch over the patients. They also had to carry some patients up several flights of stairs as they did not know how high the floodwaters would rise. The heat of the day made the sick even sicker, and many patients just did not survive.

I heard similar stories from doctors and nurses at other hospitals. It was extremely painful for those who had pledged an oath to heal the sick as many found themselves almost helpless during these extreme, surreal conditions. These brave nurses and doctors who stayed continued to do God's work. Many used creative treatments to comfort patients who were severely ill, scared with elevated pulses, body temperatures raised by the lack of air-conditioning and August humidity, and who were generally overwhelmed by Hurricane Katrina's dramatics.

The pace of rescue activity and challenges was now breathtaking and relentless. At one point we were in the EOC, powered by backup generators, when a very wet emergency rescuer entered the conference room and started showing us some fresh pictures from several flooded areas of the city. As the pictures were being passed around, we were all speechless at what we were seeing. Water was everywhere, and the flood lines were between six and eighteen feet high. Some homes had water to their roof line. Everyone in the room was awestruck as the reality of Katrina's devastation was now fully verified with enough evidence to convince even Judge Judy.

I had two executive protection officers who were with me during pre-storm times, Wondell Smith and Louis Martinez. As the reality of these images continued to sink in, I noticed a dramatic and sudden mood change in Wondell. He became unusually quiet, didn't look well, and was obviously distraught. This was a dark-brown-skinned man who was literally turning pale right in front of our eyes. I turned to him privately and said, "Wondell, are you alright?" He responded as he fought back tears, "That house right there in this picture is my dad's house." As he pointed to the picture, it was hard to recognize the house that was now standing in over nine feet of water, just below the gutters around the roof. He then turned and walked to the other side of the room to try to gather himself. For several minutes he did not say another word and just stared out the window in deep thought.

During my time in office I have noticed that police officers are very stoic in their duties. Here was Wondell knowing that his father and uncle were inside this house, possibly drowned or near drowning, but because he was assigned to protect me, he was willing to maintain discipline and his duty to his job. I walked over to him and looked him in the eyes and said, "What are you still doing here? You've got to go and get your dad." For a second he looked conflicted, but when he saw I was dead serious, he shook my hand, said thanks, and next thing I knew he bolted out the door.

Many hours would pass without hearing a word from him on how things were going. It was starting to get dark outside. Everyone was very concerned, and I was wondering whether I had made the right decision to let him go on this rescue mission. Then I thought about what I would do if my father was in the same predicament. Without a doubt, I would have gone to try to save him without approval from anyone.

What we didn't know at the time was Wondell had been exceedingly busy since he left us. As he departed the Hyatt a close friend, a sheriff's officer, joined him as they drove his car to the high-rise interstate and took the exit nearest his father's home. They veered on the off ramp to the water's edge. Luckily there was a boat nearby that they confiscated. After struggling to get the boat's motor going, they proceeded throughout the neighborhood and eventually made their way to Wondell's father's home.

Wondell later told us his heart was racing as they tied the boat to a post on the front porch. Next, he attempted several times to open the front door, to no avail. Noticing that the sun was starting to go down and time was not on his side, he moved forcefully to kick in the front door. He first waded through neck-deep waters in the living room. He found no one. Next he checked the bedroom and still came up empty. Finally he came to the kitchen as there was still enough light outside to not walk into or on something and break a leg or arm. The water was still rising as he moved into the kitchen and realized he had arrived just in the nick of time. An immediate sense of shock and relief came over him as he saw his dad alive, riding an upturned refrigerator with his disabled, buck-naked uncle, lying on his back and placed high on the kitchen counter. Wondell hugged and kissed his dad and uncle, who returned the affection.

It was now getting dark, so Wondell grabbed some clothes, put them on his uncle, picked him up, and carried him to the boat. His dad walked close behind with his hand resting firmly on his son's shoulder. Once everyone was back safely in the boat, Wondell took a deep breath, exhaled, and relaxed a bit. However, his mood quickly changed when the motor on the boat would not start. They tinkered and tinkered, and finally after over an hour the motor started. As they moved through the neighborhood, they could not resist rescuing other people along the way. His father's neighbors were taken one by one from being stranded on their roofs. Now that the boat was full, they started heading for the exit ramp where the car was parked.

In the next block, one of the rescued neighbors shouted, "You know what, Mrs. Jacques lives over there. I am sure she did not leave; we should check to see if she needs help." The sun was just about down at this point, and it had become dark outside. Seeing clearly was now a major challenge. All streetlights were either out or had been knocked down. It was also not safe to wade into the waters as they saw several snakes, and someone claimed to see the eyes of an alligator two hundred yards from the boat.

Wondell maneuvered the boat over to Mrs. Jacques' home and managed to climb onto the roof. There was no sign of anybody on the roof, so he yanked off the turban fan whose function is to keep the attic cool during summer months. As he looked down into the newly created hole and waited for his eyes to adjust to the darkness, he saw two eyes looking back at him. Mrs. Jacques, a fairly spicy old lady, was standing on her tippy-toes just keeping her mouth out of the water as it came up to her chin. After chopping a hole in the roof big enough to pull her out, the first thing she said to Wondell after being rescued was, "It's about time you guys came to get me." Everyone in the boat smiled, but they also knew she was scared, wet, cold, and exhausted. If they hadn't gotten to her when they did, she would surely have drowned just like so many of the unfortunate ones.

Wondell, his family, and his newfound friends arrived back at the Hyatt around eight p.m. It was a good thing he showed up when he did as I was ready to lead a search party to go find him. When he showed up carrying his uncle and walking with his father, we were relieved and thankful. God had answered our prayers once again. We would pray more and more as time went on as we were getting a steady flow of reports of despair and courage minute by minute.

You name it—it was happening in just about every area of the city. More breaches, high water almost everywhere, and families stranded in attics and on roofs. The stories that were being relayed were shocking and overwhelming. It seemed that the city was drowning, and fast. A man was in his home in New Orleans East when a fifteen-foot storm surge hit that area. He was downstairs in his kitchen fixing a meal when he heard the roar of the ocean. Next thing he knew the water hit his front door with such force that it blasted open. Water was up to his chest in an instant. All he could do was drop his sandwich and run up his stairs and into his attic. Luckily, he had pre-positioned an ax, and as soon as he cut a hole the water was hungrily trying to devour him. He barely made it onto his roof and moved quickly to the highest point as the water magically decided to leave him alone. The only thing he had in his possession was bottled water, a few candy bars, and his pistol. The pistol would later prove to be a lifesaver.

At nightfall he noticed two sets of eyes moving in the distance, which turned out to be huge, eight-foot alligators! Soon it became very dark with the only light being the moon. He panicked as he noticed the eyes were slowly coming closer and closer to where he was. He was wet, alone, and frightened. One set of eyes got too close for comfort, and he pulled out his pistol and shot several times, releasing most of his bullets and killing one of the gators. In all the commotion, he lost sight of the other gator. He spent the rest of the night and several other nights on the top of his roof, never sleeping, always on edge for the moment when the missing gator would surprise him from an unseen angle and try to eat him alive. Fortunately, after four days a helicopter came by and rescued him, but he would never be the same.

Then there was a gentleman in the Ninth Ward who had somehow climbed out of a window and onto his roof with his two young daughters. His house was completely flooded, and it seemed that the foundation wouldn't hold up against the force of the water, so he had to move to the house next door. There was water all around, but the house next door was only a couple of feet from his. Their best option was to jump from one rooftop to another. He jumped over and helped one of his young daughters successfully jump over also. As he was going back to get his other daughter, the first daughter panicked and tried to jump back, fell, and got caught up in the water and was swept away. Unfortunately, the father couldn't swim. He had no choice but to stay on the roof with the other daughter. What a tremendous burden he will have to carry for the rest of his life. As a father, I immediately felt his pain as I also have a young daughter. I can't even bring myself to think how that would have felt, for a father to watch his child drown right in front of his very eyes.

I heard story after story, each one as heartbreaking as the next. There were many people who climbed up trees to stay out of the water. There were multiple reports of snakes, alligators, and even sharks swimming in the murky waters. Others citizens were stuck in extreme heat in their attics without water or any means of escape. The heat along with the unknown of what was happening outside was enough to drive several people insane.

For those who didn't make it, their remains would stay floating in the waters, in attics, on interstate highways, or on the few dry sidewalks in the lucky parts of town for days. Most remained fully exposed and uncovered to anyone who passed by them. One of the many tough decisions I had to make was that with considerably more demands than resources, I had to order police, firemen, and other emergency responders to focus on rescue of the living. The dead would just have to wait for things to calm down.

About an hour or two after Wondell left, I somehow managed to quietly slip away to my suite on the twenty-seventh floor. Completely overwhelmed by the day's proceedings, I was determined that tomorrow, Tuesday, would be different, and I pushed aside any doubts so I could focus on critical next steps. I spent two hours alone thinking through the day's events, and I outlined in good detail our priorities for tomorrow and the coming days. As there was no manual to consult, I had to drum up all the management and technical strategies and skills that I had accumulated over the years. I knew I would be managing an unprecedented disaster that was unfolding all over my city, and with every passing minute things were quickly deteriorating. We needed a road map to get through this mess.

I quickly convinced myself that it was imperative that I stay calm, logical, and fairly unemotional. I knew that my business and now government background had prepared me well. Throughout life I'd always held a personal philosophy of regardless of the challenge or circumstance I would never get too high or too low, but would always try to stay on an even keel, evaluate the facts, and keep my emotions in check. I was now practicing what I had preached over the years.

During my business years, I had completed several emergency preparedness training courses, but I doubt there was anything out there that could have fully prepared me for the arrival of Hurricane Katrina. Maybe if I had gone and fought in an actual major war with an enemy as deceptive and as powerful as Katrina then I may have been experienced enough, but even that line of thinking could be easily challenged. This was virgin territory, a road that no one else had traveled.

At that moment I had very limited resources, problems everywhere, unverified information, unreliable communications, and water hazards growing in size and scope. This was not a time for a pity party. I had to figure this out, make some tough decisions, and prioritize very limited vital resources to be as effective as possible. Many lives depended upon me getting this right.

On a plain piece of paper I wrote the obvious: the first thing we would do was to turn our attention to the rescue of citizens in need. We would focus on the living and leave the dead bodies for another day. We had very limited manpower and a possible thirty thousand people stuck in many damaged, flooded areas of the city. One of my first orders Tuesday morning would be for first responders to focus solely on rescue. Every resource we had was to be focused on saving lives. We believed we had fifteen hundred police officers, five hundred firefighters, and three hundred National Guardsmen in the city and the Superdome. We needed more resources, but this was all we had, so we had to do the best we could.

The next step after all were rescued would be to completely evacuate everyone out. Patching up the levees and dewatering the city would be the next priority. In reality, we worked on these first steps simultaneously. Next, we would recover the dead, identify who they were, and arrange for respectable funerals. Debris removal would be next up as there were many downed trees and damaged and collapsed houses in the streets and on certain properties. Once the debris and hazards were removed, only then could we safely start a phased repopulation process.

The water, sewerage, and drainage systems would have to be restarted or rebuilt. With repopulation proceeding, we would immediately start the planning stages for rebuilding. After adding a few more key elements, I had a complete plan outlined on this one page, front and back, that I would slightly enhanced over the coming days. This list traveled with me in all future meetings. Anytime I'd talk to FEMA, my staff, the media, or others about how we would recover, I'd referred back to my list. I was able to keep track of this document for several weeks until one day I could not find it. I looked everywhere with no luck. It is a good thing I had memorized it word for word.

My suspicion is someone close to me took it as a piece of memorabilia to use for a future book that they secretly planned to write later. God bless them.

In the solitude of my very hot hotel room, I wrapped up my thoughts, folded my one-page action plan, and went down to the fourth floor to meet Wondell and his boat crew. It was good to see him safe and sound. Later that night sometime after nine p.m., Louis, who is part of my executive protection team, came in the room and told me there was a FEMA guy asking to meet with me. It was Marty Bahamonde, the only FEMA representative pre-deployed to the city of New Orleans. He entered the room followed by several members of my executive staff. He had bunkered down with Colonel Ebbert in the EOC since Saturday, two days before, but this was our first real substantive conversation. Marty was no newcomer to disasters and explained to me his history working on recovery missions around the world. He was particularly experienced in natural disasters such as hurricanes. Marty had also worked in Iran where they successfully helped to restore a key city there following a catastrophic earthquake, which resulted in thirty thousand deaths.

Marty gave us eyewitness accounts of just about everything we had been hearing. He expressed to us in no uncertain terms that things were extremely bad in the city and region. Marty also shared with me that he had a premonition before Katrina hit, and over the course of the last several days he had been sending e-mails to his boss Michael Brown, director of FEMA. He was also constantly contacting various other FEMA and Homeland Security representatives asking for help, more supplies, and more troops on the ground. He also told them about the horrors that were unfolding, but he received little to no response. This lack of reaction left him perplexed and frustrated. He felt the FEMA executives just did not get the magnitude of what was happening in New Orleans, or else they just did not care.

As I sat at the table, Marty positioned himself directly across from me with my staff filling in the other empty chairs. He had a very serious and sad look on his face. When he first entered the room, we made eye contact and I could tell that this conversation would be life-changing as my city was in deep, deep trouble.

As he continued to detail for us what had really happened, I was struck at how straightforward he was. Later on I appreciated how honest he was because most of the FEMA representatives that we dealt with wouldn't come out and tell it to you straight. I later learned that all FEMA representatives go through extensive training on how to deal with people in disasters. The federal government's policy is obviously, "Don't ever tell people how bad it is up front."

But Marty Bahamonde was different in a good way. He wasn't interested in sugarcoating reality. He would prove himself over time as actually the most honest of all the FEMA people that we encountered. He had his game face on and immediately started laying everything out. No one else in the room spoke as we all listened as if E. F. Hutton was talking. He explained that earlier that afternoon at around five p.m., he had managed to convince a Coast Guard pilot to take him up in a helicopter so that he could survey the damage. The winds were still really strong, so they could only stay up for about fifteen to twenty-five minutes at a time. He was the first to confirm many of the reports I'd heard throughout the day. His particular focus was the damage to our city that started with the levees breaching at the Industrial Canal.

He discussed the huge barge he'd seen that had not been properly tied down before the storm which had broken free from its mooring to crash through the levee. It was now floating wildly through the streets. Waves of water preceded and pushed this barge with such force that whole houses were either crushed or lifted off their foundations. The entire Lower Ninth Ward was totally flooded.

Marty also informed us that New Orleans East and St. Bernard Parish were also under water. He described in great detail the destruction that the water was causing. He also mentioned there was another breach at the Seventeenth Street Canal, but he wasn't sure the extent of the damage.

He then almost knocked me off my seat when he said major sections of the Interstate 10 twin span bridges were gone and there was no way to escape to the east. The storm surge had literally picked up whole concrete panels that weighed tons and threw them into the deep lake water.

He also emphasized that the bowls were filling up and that there was still the potential for more levee and canal breaches. It looked to him like 70 percent of the city was now under water. He had already seen dead bodies floating around town. Everything that came out of his mouth was now moving in slow motion. I drifted into my subconscious for a moment and thought to myself, "Why me, Lord?"

After Marty finished his briefing on Katrina's realities, I pulled out my priority list that I had completed earlier and started to discuss our needs with him. Besides our action plan, we also had a detailed list of commodities and equipment needs for FEMA to quickly fulfill. Marty was impressed and complimented us on it. He told me that this was one of the best initial action plans he had ever seen presented by a city after a disaster. He said, "Most politicians wouldn't be thinking in these terms. This is very unusual for a political leader to give me a list with specific actions like this." Marty suggested that I immediately let the state know our priorities so that they could task FEMA to action. This was precisely my intention for crafting the plan earlier, and I put in a call to the governor. Unfortunately, she was not available at that time.

In between more scenes from this verbal horror movie, we asked Marty more questions. He answered all of our inquires patiently and also advised us that he'd already put in a number of calls to FEMA headquarters requesting for them to send immediate help to sandbag and repair the levee breaches. Like a six-shooter on his hip, he reached for his cellphone to put in another call to them so he could get a response, anything to update us on FEMA's actions. But unfortunately he could not get an answer. They were just not responsive and didn't seem interested in really helping. Later in a congressional hearing over FEMA's lack of response to disaster relief for Katrina in those initial days, a number of e-mail transcripts were presented. They depicted Michael Brown and other FEMA executives as cavalier, careless, completely disengaged, and in way over their heads.

Marty started wrapping things up by telling me that this would be a long road in the future as the average time FEMA stayed after a normal disaster was ten years, a full decade. After he said that, I realized that Katrina was proving to be anything but normal, so we would probably have them for decades. Before he left, I asked him how soon we could begin evacuating the more than twenty-five thousand people who were in the Superdome out of the city. We immediately needed at least 750 buses to be sent to the city to take them out. Later when the Convention Center filled up, the buses needed grew by another 500, bringing the total need to 1,250 buses.

Marty once again tried to get somebody on the phone at FEMA headquarters who could provide much-needed resources and honest answers. But once again he had no luck. He then said as we were concluding the meeting, "Look, this is much worse than what you guys have been hearing. Basically, all is lost." He continued by saying because of the severe widespread flooding, transportation into and out of the city could only go through the west as all other roads were now impassable and under water. To make matters worse, more and more water was seeping into the city because of the levee breaks. He also verified that thousands and thousands of people were stranded on roofs. This corresponded with the 911 calls that we'd been inundated with. He informed us of other people who were floating on rafts, plastic tubs, or walking in chest- and neck-high water. Marty finally finished his briefing, we thanked him, and he left with his head down and shoulders sagging like the Katrina-whipped puppies we all were.

More and more citizens were escaping rising waters by heading downtown. They were still coming to the Superdome for shelter, and it was already near capacity. Without any real options, citizens were being forced out of their homes from the wind and rising waters to brave the elements and head for safer, higher ground downtown.

I started getting reports that the Superdome was maxed out, and if the current streams of people continued, we would hit the thirty thousand mark shortly. The National Guard troops who had primary responsibility for maintaining order in the Superdome estimated we would run out of space before morning. So earlier that day we brainstormed options as it relates to other facilities that were high and dry that could be quickly utilized as a second shelter of last resort. We needed a building that could hold thousands of people, and we quickly concluded our best option was the Morial Convention Center. What made it attractive was it was on a major boulevard downtown. It also had several hundred thousand square feet of open space. This building was also next to the river, it was high and dry, and it was about a mile and a half from the Superdome.

The police chief informed me we had a problem in that the doors were locked and we did not have keys. Since we had the emergency powers to confiscate buildings, I ordered him to open the building by any means necessary. He fully complied, and we were in business.

Our sheltering backup plan was to officially open this facility as another shelter early Tuesday morning and divert the stream of people coming from the floodwaters to it. Unfortunately, there was no way we could screen these desperate folks, so we would have to take whoever came, the good, the bad, the ugly, and the armed. Therefore, since this plan was communicated through our EOC, we fully expected the federal and state government to now move a lot quicker. The stakes were so much higher with more people being mixed in with some who were also severely stressed out and potentially fully armed.

The other interesting factor was helicopters were dropping off rescued citizens from other flooded parishes into the city. The downtown hotels were all shutting down, and some tourists were now walking to the Convention Center looking for shelter. Unfortunately, Marty was still trying to no avail to get someone in FEMA or Homeland Security to act effectively. He was still walking around fairly depressed with his head held down in shame for his boss's insensitivity.

The lack of response also could have been attributable to the fact that communication with the outside world was becoming less reliable as wind and water damage fully manifested itself. There was now little to no cell phone coverage. Most of my staff had BlackBerries, so we relied upon PIN message because they were secure, encrypted e-mails. They were also fast and point-to-point, from the sending device directly to the receiving one without having to go through a server. However, we soon realized that PINs were not being delivered in a timely manner, and most were being lost in the ether.

It had gotten to the point where my BlackBerry had little to no calls or e-mails during most of the day. It was only around three a.m. that some connection would happen where I would receive maybe two out of every ten messages. My most reliable method for keeping in touch with the outside world was a small windup radio that my wife gave me before she evacuated to Dallas, Texas. The windup feature generated power to the radio once the batteries went dead. At first I'd laughed at the gesture, but I took it at her insistence. Now I was so grateful for her wisdom and foresight. That radio was the only way we received current news reports and heard all the untruths that were being told in Baton Rouge and Washington.

The next thing that required an immediate decision was Marty's account that the Seventeenth Street Canal had also been breached. He did not know how big it was, but we were starting to hear more and more that floodwaters were headed downtown. Everything that we had learned and verified thus far seemed to hang around our necks like a noose. There was no denying it. Marty was scared. As I looked around, I noticed the same fear in my staff's eyes as they saw similar fear in mine. It was decision time, and I knew what I had to do.

I immediately informed everyone in the hotel and most in the EOC that first thing tomorrow morning they needed to leave the city. We would only keep a very small skeleton crew of administrators. The only exceptions were first responders or experts specifically selected by myself or Colonel Ebbert. There was huge risk and uncertainty every-where. Would any more levees breach? How high would the water get? How long before power, water, and sewerage would stop func-tioning? Had the Superdome exceeded capacity? How long would the people tolerate not having enough food and water? How would we handle fires? What crisis would happen next?

I pushed hard for most to leave. I also implored them to quickly spread the word. We also alerted the Hyatt management that they would have to make arrangements to get their guests out, fast. We announced this to all who were on the fourth floor where cots were still set up for people to sleep in the ballrooms. Many people had moved to this area because of the unsafe wind conditions related to the hurricane and tornados. We also had some of our police officers and fire fighters sleeping in separate ballrooms on the same floor. As the reality of what we were announcing sunk in, anxiety levels started to go up, and I mean really high. Some were just stunned, and others were in a state of borderline panic. The hotel staff was working feverously working on transportation options. I had never seen so many people run up to their rooms and pack their bags so quickly in my entire life.

After this announcement, I returned back upstairs to my room as I needed some time alone to digest all the information that Marty and others had just downloaded. I first went into the bathroom to check on Fishy and topped up his fish tank with a half-empty bottle of water. He was fine, completely content and oblivious to what was happening outside his world, a small bowl. I then went back to my bed and tried to put a call in to my wife, Seletha. A conversation with her would be great and would help me mentally escape for a moment and allow me to get her perspective on how this was unfolding. The phones were so irregular that I didn't get through, so I lay down on my bed and stared up at the ceiling. It was now nightfall in a completely dark city. Because of the high, gusty winds, we were forced to wait once again until morning. I tried to drift off to sleep, but there was just too much going through my mind. The morning had started so positively. After the initial press reports, we'd thought we'd dodged the bullet. And then things went progressively downhill from there.

I must have dozed off from sheer exhaustion as I was awakened around two a.m. by a call from my wife. I could tell from her voice that she was very concerned about me and the city. However, her words were positive and reassuring. Having been married for almost twenty-four years, she knew me well and spent most of the time let-ting me know that she and our children, Jeremy, Jarin, and Tianna, were doing well. She asked me about the city, and I explained to her from a macro standpoint what was going on and what we were doing about it. Seletha was astute enough to not ask me too many questions about the disaster. She allowed me to focus on her and the kids as she knew I needed a brief break from the Katrina madness. The phone connection then started to fade in and out, so we ended the call with both of us saying "I love you," and then the signal was totally lost. I tried to drift back to sleep but couldn't, anxious about what would unfold in the next few hours. I had to continue to insist that everyone must leave immediately—everyone!

Colonel Ebbert had mentioned to me earlier that he was going to try and arrange a helicopter ride for me the next morning so that I could see the failed federally built levees and the resulting devastation for myself. As I lay there, I became even more anxious as I had never ridden in a Black Hawk before, and I was growing more impatient to take to the sky so that I had a full perspective on what needed to be done next to save New Orleans.

Meanwhile, around the same time that night, Deputy Chief Riley and another officer were out patrolling various parts of the city. There was a rumor going around that a tidal wave was headed for the city. As they were driving around in a very tall, high-water vehicle, they started to notice water in areas where earlier that day there was none. They next observed some water near the Superdome. As they headed back to police headquarters, the water around them got so high that they could not drive any further. They radioed for assistance, and an officer came to get them in a boat less than a mile away.

It was pitch black and difficult to see your hand in front of your face. The only light was from flashlights. As their boat moved past the nearby prison, Deputy Chief Riley could tell from certain landmarks that the water was rising and must have been about eight feet deep. This depth was verified a few minutes later when they guided the boat right up to the elevated landing at police headquarters. It just happened to be eight feet high. Deputy Chief Riley knew that things were getting much worse and tomorrow would challenge us all like nothing we had ever faced. Unfortunately, his instincts were right on and then some.

CHAPTER FOUR

HELIPORT PHOTO OP

By daybreak, the rhythm of New Orleans was no longer the swagger of a jazz masterpiece but now seemed to be analogous to that of a phonographic record or CD playing at the wrong speed. Vibrant neighborhoods and the central business district were now all pictures of absence and despair. The sounds of happy people and the greatest music in the world were replaced with moans and pleadings for relief from rooftops, interstates, and the Superdome. The smell of our own unique Creole and soul food cooking coming from warm, intimate, loving family kitchens and restaurants that once filled the air was now replaced with a stench of stagnant water mixed with multiple toxins, death, and decay. Corpses were scattered throughout the city, on the interstate, on sidewalks, and floating in water. All appeared to be contorted and bloated into some unnatural look and form. Some floated slowly in place as if saying they were not ready to leave this life or their homes. And still others lay in isolation, untouched and for the time being unaccounted for. As a matter of fact, all of them were currently unaccounted for.

Military helicopters decorated the sky, replacing the normal majestic soaring of our native birds. There were no signs of hawks, sparrows, robins, ducks, or pelicans. Not even a single butterfly could be seen floating around anywhere.

Since it was early morning, activity levels inside the Superdome were just starting to stir as many tired, hungry, and thirsty individuals made their way toward exit doors, walking in an instinctive zombie-like daze toward fresh air. They were also anxious to take in the latest scenes outside in hopes that conditions had improved to the point where they would be released. Any sign, any signal of hope would have generated a cheer normally reserved for a New Orleans Saints game against our intense rival, the Atlanta Falcons. Unfortunately, all that awaited them outside were images that would ignite feelings of overwhelming hopelessness, anguish, and more fear of the unknown that was unfolding right in front of our eyes. They were in Katrina's prison as the National Guard presence that lined the temporary retaining fences reminded them that they were confined. Their world of movement was limited to inside the Superdome, outside only on the second-floor plaza area around the Superdome, and the adjoining bridge to the Hyatt and shopping center.

I was already starting to have a hard time keeping track of what day it was. So much had been happening all at once that I had to be reminded by my security team that it was Tuesday, August 30, 2005. As we exited the Hyatt, someone pointed out in the distance the oily, brackish, discolored water that was starting to stealthily creep into downtown. I later learned that a strong trickle began around midnight the night before, smothering the concrete on the streets and sidewalks, swallowing it up, block by block. This was another aspect of Hurricane Katrina's secret and deceptive nature that was unfolding without much fanfare. There had been no tidal wave or big rush and no alarming sound to warn us of this furtive invasion. Over the course of the last eight or so hours, the water had slowly but steadily moved our way. Just that morning, within the time it took me to finish my first bottle of water, Poydras Street that runs between the Hyatt hotel and city hall went from a thin layer of floodwater to being between two to three feet deep. The Superdome now appeared like a huge floating buoy, an island all to itself.

I was very concerned that possibly every chemical known to man was circulating in these floodwaters. It was now mixed with various kinds of fuel, oil, pesticides, fertilizers, poisons, garbage, urine, feces, deceased humans, and dead animals. It was a gumbo of filth. As I surveyed this highly seasoned broth, it hit me like a twenty-foot hurricane surge that the potential for the entire city to flood was now a very real possibility. As the lake continued to empty more and more water into the streets, there was no way to really know whether downtown and the French Quarter would end up with five or fifteen feet of water. This very real threat solidified beyond a shadow of a doubt that our number one priority was still to get as many people out of the city as soon as possible before the only remaining exit route was cut off by expanding floodwaters.

It was shortly after daybreak when I first received confirmation from Marcia St. Martin at the Sewerage and Water Board that the Seventeenth Street Canal had been breached. She also told me the hole was rapidly expanding. She went on to say some of her engineers had managed to go up in a helicopter as the sun was coming up to survey storm-related damages. A key objective for them was to determine if there were any areas where lake levels were low enough for us to create new man-made breaches so that the flow of the floodwaters could be reversed. Unfortunately, none were found. They were also on the lookout for freshwater leaks bubbling up from the floodwaters so we could begin to map all broken water lines.

Right after they landed, Marcia called me to give me a full briefing as floodwaters were now racing faster and faster downtown. After she finished I asked her, "Are you absolutely sure? Do you fully understand what this means?" Her response was, "Yes, unfortunately I clearly understand we are in serious trouble." I was just not totally ready to believe the truth that was ringing in my ears. The reality was the Seventeenth Street Canal's breach was at least two hundred feet long. It could grow as water was flowing like a waterfall from Lake Pontchartrain into New Orleans neighborhoods such as Lakeview, Mid-City, and now downtown.

Mrs. St. Martin also tried to get me to focus on our power station in Carrollton. If it became overwhelmed by floodwaters and went down, then all systems—water, sewer, and drainage—would simultaneously shut down. I heard her but didn't really fully comprehend the magnitude of what she was saying. Maybe I had already reached my daily limit of bad news. We finished the conversation as she provided me with a final status on which pumping stations were still working and how many were down. I asked her to keep me informed as things developed as she possessed some of our most accurate, real-time information. I closed by reminding her once again that whatever happened to make sure we kept our employees as safe as we could under the circumstances. She assured me she would.

We were now at the point where every hour, sometimes every minute there was some life-threatening calamity that was being reported. This disaster was definitely not for the faint of heart!

Within the hour Marcia was calling back. This time she took the opportunity to update me on a call she had received from Aaron Broussard, president of Jefferson Parish, regarding Hoey's Cut. We had our largest pumping station there, Pump Station Number 6, which helped to drain many sections of New Orleans and parts of Jefferson Parish through a water merging canal called Hoey's Cut.

The significance of this particular drainage system was due to the fact that the city of New Orleans was built long before Jefferson Parish. As Jefferson Parish developed, they realized that they did not have drainage capabilities in new areas and experienced major flooding every time it rained hard. Since the Sewerage and Water Board already had a drainage system in place with extra capacity, a deal was cut for us to provide pumping services for Jefferson Parish on a cost-reimbursement fee basis. For many years we simultaneously drained about seventy-five thousand acres of Orleans Parish and twenty-five thousand acres of Jefferson Parish. It was a win-win relationship where all excess rainwater merged into the Seventeenth Street Canal for Pump Station 6 to drain it all into the lake.

Marcia went on to inform me that President Broussard requested that the dam on the Jefferson Parish side of Hoey's Cut be lowered and cemented shut to provide additional protection for Jefferson in case of storm surge from Lake Pontchartrain. Our problem was that if this expected surge were to happen, the engineering design was for both canals to accept the water pressure equally so neither would collapse. However, if one side was closed off, then that would put additional pressure on the open side and almost ensure collapse. Marcia's instincts were to tell Jefferson Parish no, and I confirmed that with a firm "Hell no!"

We would later learn that our neighbors in Jefferson Parish were playing games all along, trying to get somebody, anyone on our side to say yes to this destructive request. Apparently before they put the call in to Marcia, they had asked the Sewerage and Water Board Operations Team to close Hoey's Cut. The Operations Team said no. They then asked Mr. Joe Sullivan, the board's chief engineer, for permission to close Hoey's Cut, and he too said no.

It was apparent that public pressure was building over there as officials in Jefferson Parish made several major mistakes in their preparation for Katrina's arrival. First, they had done a relatively poor job of maintaining the integrity on their side of the canal and their floodgates, so water was seeping through any opening that it could find. They then wanted to be able to close Hoey's Cut so that they could prevent any more flooding from lake surge and floodwaters from Orleans Parish getting into the canal. But more importantly, it also put them in position to execute a very devious and detrimental temporary pump plan. What we didn't know at the time was that they planned to quickly bring in temporary pumps connected to large, flexible pipes that were draped over their side of the Seventeenth Street Canal. This equipment was secretly provided by Shaw Industries after the storm hit.

So long gone were the days when the two parishes worked cooperatively to jointly build Hoey's Cut to protect each other. Now, post-Katrina the word "team" seemed to be replaced with a big fat "I" on the Jefferson side.

After our second phone conversation concluded, Marcia called President Broussard back to let him know the final official answer was no. Unfortunately, in the middle of the night Jefferson Parish clandestinely blocked their side of Hoey's Cut anyway. To add insult to injury, they later pumped their floodwaters into a breached canal, further flooding our citizens who were stuck in attics and rooftops. A parish official was reported to say in one of their secret meetings, "So what, they are already flooded anyway. Who cares?" It seems as though besides being incredibly callous and insensitive, some of the Jefferson Parish leadership were also overreacting to another very poor decision made by the parish president to evacuate all of its pump station operators on Saturday, before Katrina hit. This left them with pump stations that could not be turned on at all as heavy rains and storm surged attacked high-end homes in very exclusive areas of the parish.

They were implementing the parish's so-called secret "doomsday" plan. The doomsday scenario happened, and now we know that their plan was to save lives and property only for the good people of Jefferson Parish and to hell with anyone else. Katrina was still bringing out the best and the worst in people, even elected officials who are sworn to serve the public interest. Equally as amazing is the fact that we would later turn this information over to *60 Minutes*, the top local TV station, and the local newspaper. All of them unfortunately looked the other way by accepting the lame excuse from Jefferson Parish that the doomsday plan was only implemented for a relatively short period of time.

Back at the EOC and the Superdome, stress and tension levels went to all-time highs as very visible rising water was now in many previously dry areas. People everywhere were past anxious because no one really knew what would happen next. Would the water levels ever stop rising? When would we run out of food and water? What if the levees on the river started to breach? Was this the end of the world? I couldn't help but notice this mass fear and paranoia. I saw it in everyone's eyes. It forced me to dig down deep internally and keep my game face on even though I was a bit scared myself. I used every psychological technique in the book that I had learned over the years to get as many people as possible to calm down. My body language, every movement and mannerism, was being watched by all. I was in a fishbowl of sorts; I was beginning to know exactly how "Fishy" felt every day.

At this point, Deputy Chief Riley and others were still at police headquarters as water had started making its way inside. Several dispatchers who were going to the snack machine on the first floor around four thirty that morning had noticed water was about three feet high inside and rising. They immediately ran back upstairs, screaming and crying uncontrollably. Deputy Chief Riley surveyed the emerging conditions and called for an evacuation of the building. He then requested the SWAT team come to rescue them in their zodiac boats. Around 150 people, including recruits, cops, dispatchers, and some family members, were evacuated to a nearby high-rise bridge.

All communications were down with the exception of one active channel on the radio system, which was a mutual "A" channel that was utilized by everyone in the region. The big problem was there were so many people on this one channel that it was next to impossible to carry out a timely urgent conversation. Basically all you could do was just listen to the calamities.

Police headquarters personnel and critical equipment were now high and dry on the Broad Street Overpass. Almost immediately they were confronted with another crisis as Criminal Sheriff Marlin Gusman was close by, on the other side of the overpass with several hundred prisoners and only eight or so sheriff's deputies. Sheriff Gusman was desperately requesting backup and help. The prison had lost all power, and the prisoners started panicking, rioting, and setting fires. Unfortunately, most of his other sheriff's deputies evacuated before the storm or hurriedly left during the chaos as the disaster unfolded.

Deputy Chief Riley informed Sheriff Gusman that his best option for additional manpower was the Louisiana Department of Corrections. He strongly suggested the sheriff contact them immediately as NOPD was overloaded with major escalating challenges. During this time looting was increasing on Canal Street and downtown, officers were stranded, and some were even stuck in a hospital. NOPD just didn't have extra resources to help him at that time.

The thing that Deputy Chief Riley did do was to order a captain and four recruits to the roof of police headquarters. He told them to take a corner of the roof to provide cover for the sheriff and defend the building. There were a significant amount of automatic weapons and ammunition inside that could not fall into the hands of violent criminals.

This type of flooding was a first for the city of New Orleans. Never before had we seen these depths over such a large footprint. For example, Xavier University, the premier place that trains more African American doctors and pharmacists than any other university in the country, had six to eight feet of water. The president of the university, Dr. Norman Francis, had managed to get through to us and was pleading for help. It turned out that Dr. Francis, his key staff members, and some college students were stranded in their main administration building. The good news was they were safe for the time being, but the bad news was they would have to wait until we rescued other citizens who were more at risk, still trapped in attics or on roofs.

I was also preoccupied with evacuating hotels and getting all but a skeleton crew from my staff out of the hotel and EOC; they needed to be in vehicles on the road toward Baton Rouge. The waters were flowing faster, and the levels were getting deeper and deeper. The one exit route from the Hyatt to the interstate now had a foot of water on it. If they waited too much longer, these hardheaded, super-dedicated staffers would have to swim out and then pray for the best.

Earlier that morning, I BlackBerry PINed my executive staff and asked them to meet me in the fourth-floor ballroom at the Hyatt. We had a very short meeting as my message was very direct and simple: "The Seventeenth Street Canal has also been breached; all the bowls are filling quickly. There is only one escape route left, and most of you must leave right now." I instructed my chief administrative officer, Dr. Brenda Hatfield, to take most of the essential personnel with her to Baton Rouge and set up the Continuity of Operations office, a remote city hall that could operate for months and perhaps at least a year if needed. Once the meeting wrapped up, we all hugged and the departing scattered hurriedly to pack their belongings and retrieve escape vehicles. Time was not on our side as the one remaining escape route now had two feet of rising water on it.

My next move was to send Terry Davis over to the EOC in city hall to advise Colonel Ebbert to evacuate most of the staff there. The plan was to move the EOC and resume operations in the Hyatt main ballroom. It was very clear that the water would soon flood the basement of city hall where most of the electrical equipment was housed. We were sure that city hall would soon be without power as its backup generators were also very old and unreliable. The Hyatt, on the other hand, had excellent backup generators thanks to Entergy. The only unknown for the Hyatt was how to get more diesel fuel once the initial supply was exhausted. With the city government and Entergy soon to be fully co-located, we would work in partnership to get this critical task completed in a timely manner.

Colonel Ebbert was initially resistant and somewhat stubborn about moving this operation. He was so focused on the ever-unfolding crises of Hurricane Katrina that he did not see clearly the benefits of doing this at this time. My backup plan was to wait twenty minutes and send Sally Forman over to give Terry support in making the case. If the tag-team approach did not work, I would go over myself for a one-on-one meeting.

The great thing about Colonel Ebbert was that he was totally focused on the enemy, Katrina, and losing was not an option. He had not slept much since the storm first hit the Louisiana coast. He was also somewhat comfortable being hunkered down in city hall. The man is a very good taskmaster who was focused on the immediate challenges and clearly understood every angle of what currently confronted us every minute of every day. Colonel Ebbert also had great contacts, especially with Homeland Security and FEMA in Washington DC. He was on regularly scheduled conference calls with high-ranking officials at both the federal and state level. But like the rest of us, he was equally flabbergasted by the obvious lack of sufficient response from higher levels of government. The combination of a lack of sleep, nonstop crisis management, and now the prospects of moving his whole operation had him agitated, disappointed, and frustrated.

The key was to get him to see that the disaster had rapidly grown beyond the square footage and technical capabilities of what the fifty-year-old city hall building could handle. We would need a lot more space, many outside experts, room for very large multidisciplinary task forces, and tons of sophisticated telecommunications equipment for managing rescue, dewatering, dead body retrieval, debris removal, and long-term recovery. Besides, most of us were already operating out of the Hyatt, which had easier access to the heliport, so it just made more sense to have all critical operations under one roof.

Colonel Ebbert came around as I knew he would, and the EOC started packing for the move across the street. It took them almost two days to fully settle in at the ballroom. Eventually our EOC grew so large that the initial occupied space had to be expanded by removing dividing panels that created the maximum square footage possible in the main ballroom of the Hyatt. Regular power would soon shut down in the entire city, and the Hyatt eventually ran on backup generator power. Our biggest concern here was if the floodwaters got higher than these four floors, then all bets would be off as everything would be lost.

Around eight a.m., I had a brief meeting at the Hyatt with Marty Bahamonde, the lone FEMA representative. He informed us that Governor Blanco, Louisiana Senators Mary Landrieu and David Vitter, and his boss Michael Brown were scheduled to arrive by helicopter later that morning, around ten a.m. Upon hearing this, I delayed my initial helicopter tour of the city and planned to meet this entourage at the Superdome heliport. This area had been amazingly set up as an efficient, multi-helicopter flight operation by the Coast Guard.

It was somewhat reassuring for me to know that these top government officials would now get a chance to see firsthand the devastation so that they could better understand our needs. Hopefully the result would be immediate follow-up and delivery of much-needed equipment, supplies, and buses. As we waited for our high-level visitors, we kept a very close eye on water levels around the Superdome and the Hyatt. Every minute that passed the water became deeper and its coverage wider.

As we waited, I observed several of my key staff, other city workers, and hotel guests were all racing to locate their vehicles so they could get out of the city. Fortunately for us, my staff had pre-parked most city vehicles in nearby high-rise parking lots. Since they were now fairly frightened and under stress, the process of tracking down these vehicles took a lot longer than it should have. Others in the hotel were also exceedingly disoriented as they ran around trying to get their belongings together. We heard many shouts of, "I'm coming, hold on," "Did you see my overnight bag?" "I'll just need to get my pillow," or "I need to find my eyeglasses."

As you can imagine, some people were really having a tough time dealing with the chaos and the thought that more floodwater was rapidly moving our way. As a result, we had real drama in the Hyatt. For example, a former city councilman, Lambert Boissier, was hyperventilating and his wife was in tears as they could not find his much-needed medicine. Pat Smith, my executive assistant, was found outside sitting on the sidewalk, holding her grandbaby, crying and smoking cigarette after cigarette. She is normally a really strong person, but this was just too much for her. Renee Gill Pratt, another councilmember at the time, wanted to stay behind and keep her elderly mother with us. I finally convinced her that it was best to take her mother to Baton Rouge where there were functioning health care facilities.

Finally, there was another major political challenge—councilmember Jackie Clarkson, who had served the city for many, many years. Many of us loved Jackie, even if some considered her extremely high maintenance. I knew she really wanted to stay around but I worried that it was primarily for potential prestige due to an absolute love for being in front of a microphone or TV camera. She loved the spotlight almost as much as she liked being catered too. I immediately concluded that there would be no way that I could effectively concentrate on the many tasks confronting us if she stayed behind.

So I devised a sly strategy to persuade her to leave the city and head to Baton Rouge. Holding her arm as I spoke to her, I said, "Jackie, I need someone with your expertise to be able to deal with the governor and to speak directly for me. I need you to go to Baton Rouge to be my spokesperson." She looked at me smiling and nodding. I knew it was working. Then I said, "Jackie, you have a very good relationship with the governor. You are also one of the few people who truly understand what is needed in the city. We really need you in Baton Rouge telling them exactly what to do." She was melting and said, "Oh really—you are right, I'll do it!" She bought it hook, line, and sinker. I was enormously relieved. With a huge grin on her face, she packed up her belongings and marched out the door with her head and Southern belle big hairdo held high. She was about to embark on an important mission. Now I was freer to fully focus on leading the city through this ever-unfolding crisis. By the way, Jackie ended up doing a fine job in Baton Rouge after all. It was definitely the right call.

Along with my staff, hotel guests from all over downtown were also being evacuated. There were about thirty thousand tourists in town before Katrina hit, and the potential liability for their continued well-being was too much for our hotel management groups to continue to risk. Most of these visitors were put in vans or buses and taken to the airport via the only escape route. One by one, the hotels started to close down as most were running out of food, water, and power.

Many of these tourists obviously had better connections than the people in the Superdome and managed to secure a cozy seat on special commercial flights out of Louis Armstrong Airport. We would later learn that the military also flew in all sorts of planes to take them and some of our neighbors in the suburbs out of the area. These fortunate souls never had to wait around for FEMA buses. They never experienced extreme thirst from not having enough water to drink, eating MREs, or smelling toxic water or untreated human excrement in their nostrils for days. Good for them as I wouldn't wish what we experienced on my worst enemy.

With everything else that was unfolding, I was always mindful that there could be up to twenty thousand people still in their homes who did not leave before Katrina hit. With more and more discouraging news being consistently reported, we all worried that many more were being lost in the flooding waters as time continued to march forward. So we made the decision that I should make one last media push to urge people to get out if they could. We thought we had time to make a quick appearance on the WWL TV station, the last one left on the air. It was located in the French Quarter, and we believed I could rush over there before meeting with the governor and crew. So Wondell and Louis grabbed "Big Daddy," and we headed over there.

Big Daddy was one of my assigned city-owned vehicles, a large, impressive black Ford SUV Explorer. My daughter Tianna absolutely loved this truck, especially when we went over big bumps in the road. She would sit in the very back seats and jump up in time when we hit one and just laugh out loud as if she were on a rollercoaster ride at an amusement park. She actually named the vehicle Big Daddy and wanted to ride in it every time we went somewhere as a family. I was thankful that Tianna was safely in Texas with my wife as I was sure she would not have enjoyed this ride after a hurricane as powerful as Katrina had hit the Big Easy.

On our way over to WWL, we were forced to maneuver around lots of storm debris. The water levels in the streets were also getting higher, so we drove on the highest part of the street near the neutral ground. Luckily, in preparation for the storm Wondell and Louis had attached our flood-proof exhaust pipe on Big Daddy. This pipe attached with bolts to the regular exhaust pipe and curved up ninety degrees all the way up the rear of the vehicle. This add-on feature allowed us to go through deeper water without it backing up in the engine. It was great that they had the foresight that now allowed us to get through the waters in our path as we headed for the TV station.

As we arrived, the remaining news personnel were already packing up to leave town. They too had recently found out about the Seventeenth Street Canal breach and had seen water flooding the downtown area. With their suitcases and grocery bags packed and in hand, they were pretty much heading out the door as we entered. There would be no TV interview today at this station or any other station. Getting back in Big Daddy, we rode around the city for a few minutes until the high water forced us to head back to the Hyatt and the command center.

As soon as we hit the doors we could sense that anxiety levels were off the charts in the Hyatt. Some had left, but others were still in panic mode and basically stuck in neutral. Fortunately, in fairly short order we managed to get most of them in their cars and driving north. However, we were now down to the toughest cases. A very extreme one was one of our press secretaries, Tami. She was not originally from New Orleans and didn't say a single word after my briefing earlier that day. She froze up, and the look on her face with her poked-out eyes full of fear showed that she was not handling the stress well at all. We eventually calmed her down enough to get her moving. Unfortunately, her fears made her somewhat clumsy and disorganized, so it took her longer than usual to pack and get her stuff together. I finally walked up to her and said, "Young lady, you have to leave right now, or you will be stuck here for many days or perhaps months." That got her going and eventually into the escape van. Dr. Hatfield told me later that Tami did not start speaking again until after they arrived in Baton Rouge.

It wasn't until around nine thirty a.m. that Dr. Hatfield and about fifteen to twenty other staffers piled into vans and cars and left the hotel headed for the only exit route. I am sure they were also fearful for the city, friends, and colleagues they were leaving behind. By this stage the water had gotten so high that they could only drive in the street for one block. Dr. Hatfield later told me that they tried to go out from the Hyatt towards the direction of the post office, but the water was so high that they couldn't make it through. So Mike Boudy, her executive protection person who was driving the car, swung the vehicle around, avoiding the debris and glass that was everywhere, and was forced to drive on the sidewalk to get through the water. When they got to Poydras Street, it got really scary as water was coming into the seating area of the SUV. She thought that they all were going to drown. Mike drove as fast as he could and made it to Loyola Avenue. They barely made it to the entrance ramp of the Crescent City Connection Bridge that took them to Highway 90 and then into Baton Rouge.

Once there, they were amazed that there were cars and people everywhere. Evacuees were all over Baton Rouge, and all the hotel rooms were taken. Thankfully, there was little to no storm damage up there. Restaurants, grocery stores, and shopping malls were packed. Officer Boudy dropped Dr. Hatfield off at her son's house and then took Tami to the airport where her father had somehow arranged for her to fly home to Houston, Texas. This experience was all she could handle, and Tami didn't come back to the city for quite some time.

After Dr. Hatfield got a bit settled in Baton Rouge, a friend picked her up and took her to the governor's emergency operation center. State Senator Cleo Fields was there and had earlier conveyed to me how surprised he was at how dazed and overwhelmed the governor and her staff had been prior to and as the storm was hitting Louisiana. Now my chief administrative officer, Dr. Hatfield, would witness this with her own eyes.

Cleo had called me late Sunday evening and told me that he had just left the State's Office of Emergency Preparedness in Baton Rouge and he sensed an intense air of panic in the room. He had gone in to see what preparations were underway prior to the storm hitting. His assessment was that the state was accepting and preparing for the worst instead of preparing to prevent the worst. Amazingly, they had already ordered four thousand body bags.

On Tuesday, Dr. Hatfield noted that the governor and her staff all seemed disengaged and were walking around baffled. However, when the cameras came around, they perked up to look the part by wearing brand-new yellow raincoats that had never been wet or dirty. Dr. Hatfield desperately tried to get key state personnel to better understand that New Orleans was severely flooding and conditions there were horrific. They didn't really seem to comprehend or care much. She then went up to the governor and stated firmly, "New Orleans is flooding." The governor looked up and just gave her a blank stare. Next she turned to the governor's chief of staff, Andy Kopplin, and told him the same thing. He too looked at her with a blank stare that quickly turned to a frown. She couldn't convince any of them to understand and help. Dr. Hatfield tried over and over to remind them that she had just left the city and floodwater was coming in from at least three different directions. All these state officials did was to stay busy preparing for the next televised updates. Their yellow raincoats needed some more artificial wear and tear.

Back in the city at ground zero, it was now time to refocus on rescue efforts. More and more reports streamed in of people frantically needing help. It was crazy and made sense at the same time. Police, fire, and EMS fanned out all over the city. They were working together to rescue as many stranded citizens and victims as possible. They managed to secure their own personal boats and to confiscate any other vessel that could float.

To further complicate matters, fires started breaking out spontaneously. Most were caused by broken gas lines and looters. Many broken gas lines flared up out of the water with huge flames that created an eerie, unbelievable scene. Despite all the extremely dangerous conditions—the flooded streets, fires, low/no water pressure, debris, downed power lines, looters, frightened citizens, and a general lack of communication—these brave police, fire, and EMS professionals answered the call without hesitation.

Because of multiple water main breaks and pump stations going offline, falling like dominoes, there was not enough water pressure for fighting fires. The New Orleans Fire Department under the direction of Chief Charles Parent once again performed above the call of duty. They became extremely creative in fighting the many fires that were exploding minute by minute. They reverted to rural fire-fighting techniques where firefighters dropped hoses and drafted the floodwater out of the streets to get water flowing on these fires. A few days later, more resources arrived as military and out-of-town teams of helicopters started dropping water scooped out of the Mississippi River. This was the first time in New Orleans history that helicopters were used to fight fires.

We now know there were three major areas of levee breaks due to Hurricane Katrina. The first break caused massive flooding in the lower Ninth Ward, Arabi, Chalmette, Meraux, and New Orleans East. The source of the flooding there was due to three breaches and overtopping of the levees along the conjoining Industrial Canal, Intracoastal Waterway, and the Mississippi River Gulf Outlet (MRGO). The next major break was in the levee walls of the Seventeenth Street Canal, which flooded the Lakeview, City Park, and Mid-City areas. The final breaks were really a pair at the London Avenue Canal that caused major flooding of the Lake Vista, Gentilly, and Elysian Fields corridors. If you total up all the major and minor levee breaks throughout the city, it would come to around fifty.

With over 80 percent of the city now flooded, calls and screams for help on rooftops and in attics were coming much faster than our manpower could handle. In spite of this unfortunate certainty, our first responders were magnificent! NOPD's Special Operations Division and other police officers who had boating skills and boats were some of the first people in the water rescuing trapped citizens. They started as soon as the winds died down below tropical force, around four p.m. Monday afternoon. Rescues continued for several days and throughout the night with flashlights. The only limiting factor we had was not enough boats, and this could have been averted.

Deputy Chief Riley would later brief me that just before Katrina hit, he asked a young lieutenant in a meeting in Dr. Hatfield's office for more boats from the National Guard. The officer later confirmed that he forwarded the request to his superiors, but it was secretly denied. The reasoning was that they would have boats pre-positioned at Jackson Barracks. Riley explained to them the reason to disseminate the boats to NOPD was so that they could launch rescue operations from eight different locations throughout the city. He ended up being absolutely right because Jackson Barracks is less than a mile from the Industrial Street Canal in the Lower Ninth Ward. It was completely destroyed by the storm surge, so all those pre-positioned boats were either totally unusable or lost.

In spite of this loss, first responders found a way to get things done. Firefighters alone documented over eighteen thousand water rescues. A total of over thirty-five thousand ambulatory and non-ambulatory evacuees were then transported to Louis Armstrong International Airport with the brave assistance of many heroic Coast Guard helicopter pilots. Others were simply helped off their roofs and brought to the high ground of the highway overpasses or to the Superdome and Convention Center. Many people rescued from the water spent hours and even days waiting at these "temporary" locations in the canicular heat of August. They were down from roofs and out of floodwaters, but their new reality was unsanitary conditions and little to no food, water, shelter, security, or information.

There were also a few city workers, relatives, certain VIPs, and religious leaders who were in need of rescue. They were calling any number that worked. Our offices and cell phone numbers were being constantly called, and occasionally one of these individuals would get through. They would be very insistent as they were used to getting immediate responses to their requests.

I had an uncle, my father's brother, who somehow got through to me and left a rather pleading voice mail message: "Hey nephew, you have to come get me." Unfortunately, I could never connect with him as phone service continued to digress rapidly. Even if I could have, I most likely would have told him the same thing I told others: "We will try to get to you soon, but we do not have the resources to come right now. Your best bet is to try to walk, float, or swim to the elevated interstate, if you can." Unfortunately, I never got the chance to talk to him during these chaotic times. Fortunately my uncle made it to the interstate and was later flown out and ended up in Phoenix, Arizona. He lived there for three years and then moved back to New Orleans. I later found out that a cousin on my father's side drowned during the flooding. This hurt a lot among the other pain I felt daily.

There were also a few essential city employees who had problems following directions. As part of our emergency preparedness plan we identified those who were supposed to hunker down with us in the EOC or at our backup command center. One of these essential personnel was our director of Parks and Parkways, Ann McDonald. She is somewhat of a free spirit and can be stubborn at times. So before the storm, we specifically reminded her that she was to bunker down at city hall with the rest of us. We knew from experience that much foliage would fall after the storm passed, and she was our resident expert on trees and green space. Amazingly, at the last second she decided to ride out the storm at her home in Gentilly. After the flooding started, we received a number of desperate calls from her that she was stranded on her roof. When I first heard about this problem, it was hard for me to come to grips that we really needed to rescue her. We sent a rescue team to get her and some of her neighbors. She would later receive a hug from me and a very stern one-on-one coaching session with Dr. Hatfield to ensure she never pulled that kind of stunt again.

Floodwater rescues in this particular urban city had many extraordinary, rare challenges. The floodwaters washed in all types of swamp animals and other foreign creatures. For example, in nearby parts of Louisiana, there are many different types of snakes. Some are venomous, like the rattlesnake or coral snake, but most of them nonvenomous such as the brown snake or crawfish snake. To most urban dwellers, a snake is a snake and swimming with one is not our idea of a good time. There were also alligators, and we heard many reports that several sharks were seen feasting on a drowned animal or two. We were never able to verify these shark tales that primarily came from New Orleans East.

Smaller pest like cockroaches, termites, lizards, rats, and mice were either floating in a whirlpool of muck or competing for dry ground with humans. The swamp flies and mosquitoes were relatively nonexistent the first day or two after the storm. After that they exploded in population. It was a bug smorgasbord, an all-you-can-eat buffet as a feeding frenzy ensued on the readily accessible bodies that were in trees, hanging on roofs, on interstates, and sitting in boats being rescued or rescuing. It was truly astounding how quickly the city had become a torturous hell and a titanic struggle for survival.

To make matters even tougher, by nine a.m. that same morning the temperature was already around ninety-eight degrees. It was hot, African hot. And with so much water around, the humidity level was above 100 percent. As we struggled to get our command center moved and continued to manage this unprecedented disaster and rescue operation, there was less and less air-conditioning inside city hall and the Hyatt. The humid outside air soon became the same air inside. At the Superdome, more people moved outside just to get fresh air as the funk of human excrement and unwashed bodies was overpowering. The Superdome did have a few holes in its roof, and most of the white covering on the roof was shredded and blowing in the wind. It looked like a mound of rice floating in a bowl of gumbo that was a sea of rancid water and debris. The sun was now baking everything, especially people and the floodwater.

Most at the Superdome had not had enough drinking water. Of course, we were still waiting on FEMA's deliveries. As these exhausted, dirty, thirsty people stood outside, their need to drink was worsened by the sun and seeing all the floodwater surrounding them below. Of course, none of what they saw below was drinkable. It was like another added layer of torture. To make matters worse, the MREs that we had received on Sunday were quickly running out, and there was no sign of any more food coming. A very small FEMA medical team had arrived at the Superdome, but they were nowhere near the amount of staff needed to administer help and relief to the thousands of people who were struggling with illnesses, fatigue, and stress, and some were slowly slipping away.

Dr. Stephens, the city's health director, and his staff were miracle workers. With little to no sleep, they spent most of their time going back and forth between the arena and the Superdome treating as many patients as possible. There was another growing medical crisis facing us. Medical supplies and medicines were at dangerously low levels, and there were no assurances that we would receive refills anytime soon. We were now in full understanding that FEMA had consistently not delivered on several key promises, so any new ones we heard from this point on were met with extreme skepticism.

I looked at my watch and noticed it was time to move from the Hyatt to the heliport. We jumped in Big Daddy, which was now operating like an off-road vehicle that could almost float. Once again we took to the sidewalk to make it through the deep waters on Poydras Street and then successfully climbed the elevated ramp to the heliport on the other side of the Superdome. What we saw next was extremely impressive.

Just about all of the flat area that traditionally had been used for parking or as open space to herd large crowds into the building had now been converted into a major airport operation by the military. Most of the entire deck area was now full of helicopters, and they were all perfectly aligned. Aviation experts used big white Xs to mark up spaces for at least thirty helicopters. There was a separate takeoff and landing area where traffic controllers who were on foot would wave their colorful wands to guide the pilots in. Every ten minutes or so, a helicopter would take off or land, bringing people who had just been rescued into the Superdome or the arena.

The Coast Guard pilots were masterful. Those pilots bravely flew and flew and flew. I am sure they continually exceeded the maximum amount of hours that they could be in the air during a twenty-four-hour period. They were so dedicated and determined to rescue as many people as possible as long as there was daylight out there. They normally did not rest between flights. The focus was in their eyes, in their body language, and in their handshake when you met them. I was so proud of them and all the other people who were working overtime to save lives. I watched many men, women, and children come off of those helicopters after being rescued with smiles on their faces as their feet finally hit solid ground. They knew that they were out of danger and safe for the moment.

The meeting with the governor and her entourage was scheduled to be in the waiting area of the heliport. This area was inside the administration operation building that was nothing more than a double-wide trailer. The structure was there before the storm and somehow survived without any damage. This building would become a very familiar place for me in the days and weeks to come. After my meeting that day, I would fly over the city in a Black Hawk helicopter to survey the devastation. Colonel Ebbert, with his high-level contacts, had arranged for one to be available for this mission. I would later have one available to go up once and sometimes twice per day to survey progress with rescue, repair, and recovery.

After taking in the high activity levels of this very precise heliport operation, I quickly walked over to the administration office, walked up a short flight of stairs, and went inside. There were several heliport administrators there directing air traffic over the radio. I saw Marty Bahamonde sitting down on a rather comfortable looking sofa as he was patiently waiting. The governor, the two senators, and Undersecretary Michael Brown had not arrived yet, but I overheard over the radio that they were fifteen minutes from touchdown. I spent a little time with Marty reviewing the most immediate challenges, and it wasn't long before the governor's group was landing outside. I looked out the window and noted that they were traveling in style, in a relatively new corporate-type helicopter that the state had recently purchased.

As they entered the building, we stood up and shook hands with everyone. We then sat down and engaged in some small talk about how we were doing, how many people were in the Superdome, and how high the water downtown was. I recall how scripted they all sounded. It also jumped out at me how fresh they all looked; their clothes were all neat and pressed, and even the men looked like they had just gone to the barber and had some light makeup on. I looked around at the group I brought to the meeting and had to admit to myself that we all looked pretty shabby.

I then started to think with envy that they would have probably had a warm shower earlier that morning. They most likely had a big breakfast with freshly squeezed orange juice and hot coffee. In contrast, all we had for breakfast was a granola bar and bottled water. Because of the stress and food shortages, we only had a chance to eat one real meal per day. Besides a granola bar or a piece of overripe fruit in the morning, the only meal I could stomach was a late evening dinner. The pace of activity and the intensity of challenges had my adrenaline pumping from before sunup to well after sundown. This really worked to suppress my appetite. Jenny Craig would have been proud.

I regained my focus as the meeting turned to discussing matters of immediate importance. We started off by talking about security. I immediately pressed for more National Guard troops to be deployed to the area. The governor nodded with a very nervous look about her. I was not sure what it meant at the time, but I later put it together that she was having great difficulties making decisions. She told us she already requested more Guardsmen, but we told her we had not seen them yet. I also think she thought I would embarrass her and ask her why the Louisiana State Police left right after the contraflow evacuations and the storm hit. However, I didn't bring it up because I needed help for my city, and if she wanted to she could more than offset this with National Guard troops.

Amazingly, three months earlier I had toured the local National Guard headquarters down at the parish line in the Lower Ninth Ward. At that time, I was briefed by Adjutant General Bennett Landreneau, who was appointed by the governor and in charge of the National Guard for the entire state. He confidently told me that in the event of a disaster or significant emergency, the governor could order the deployment of fifteen hundred National Guard troops, and he could deliver them within twenty-four hours. So I was sitting in this meeting recalling this briefing from Adjutant General Landreneau and wondering where all the troops were. We desperately needed more support as we only had three hundred Guardsmen securing the Superdome.

Since the governor did not make a firm commitment, my instincts had me wondering what was really going on in this meeting.

The two senators spoke up and asked a few questions about conditions in the city, and they asked what other needs we had. Marty spoke passionately about what he was trying to get out of FEMA headquarters. I then pulled out my trusty one-page action plan and covered each item with them. They basically nodded their heads a lot and said, "Okay, thank you very much." I kept waiting for them to discuss the arrival of supplies and other help, but they never committed. It hit me that they were just going through the motions, halfheartedly acting as though they were interested in what was going on, but in reality there was no sense of urgency or real seriousness about helping us.

So after a few more minutes, a silent alarm went off and the meeting abruptly ended. The governor stood up first and said, "Well, that's enough for now, we're leaving. We need to get up in our helicopter for a complete tour of the city so we can see more." At this point all of my instincts were telling me something very strange was going on here. There was clearly some unspoken ulterior motive. Astonishingly, they were just leaving without making any commitments for helping people, citizens of Louisiana and American who were greatly suffering.

As they stood up, I started to scan the entire room to take it all in. Now the real picture was becoming clearer. This was one big photo op! There was a video camera crew with a still photographer snapping away like his finger was having an epileptic fit. Both had been filming the entire time. There was a professional producer with them as well. I'm not sure if it was a TV station or a documentary crew, but it was very clear that they wanted this visit well documented. There was also a person with an Associated Press credential around his neck. Then there were several young ladies taking copious notes.

Michael Brown, the head of FEMA, didn't say much of anything during the meeting. In fact, he blended so much into the background that it was only later, through e-mail transcripts from congressional testimony hearings, that I recalled his presence that day.

After they returned to Baton Rouge later that day, they continued to hold press conferences every couple of hours. It was now obvious that the main purpose of the heliport meeting was so they could return and say, "We've met with the mayor, we've surveyed the situation, and it's not a bad as people think it is. We've got troops on the ground, so it's all under control." That's basically what they kept saying. It was these types of untruths and manipulation that caused me to get upset and blow my cool later that week on a call to Garland Robinette's show on WWL radio. My verbal blast out to the world was mainly due to these officials spinning the truth, and it was past time for everyone in power to "get your asses moving to New Orleans." I was intensely disappointed that people of this stature and level of responsibility would come down to this calamity, see people suffering, and go back and say with a straight face that things were not that bad.

What upset me the most was that we were seriously running out of food, water, and other critical supplies, and this group was putting on a dog and pony show. I should not have been surprised as I had heard this nonsense before. Before this meeting, I chalked it up to ignorance because they had not yet come down to the flood zone. But now they had visited, seen for themselves, and there was no excuse for what was being said. To make matters worse, the three highest ranking political leaders in the state of Louisiana were right next to the Superdome and didn't even go over and talk to the suffering people, let alone go inside it. They didn't bother to speak with anyone other than Marty, Colonel Ebbert, and myself, and then as fast as they arrived, they left, with nothing to give us but more frustration, bad feelings, and disappointment. Little did we know, but this would be just one more chapter in a series of major disillusionments with higher levels of government.

Right after the governor's group left, I sat back on the comfortable sofa that I first saw Marty on and closed my eyes to shut everything out so that I could clear my head and refocus on rescue and recovery. After a few moments in solitude, I felt a little better and walked out of the administration building to hop in my ride to the sky. It was now time to see for myself how extensive the damage was that Katrina had wrought.

CHAPTER FIVE

HELICOPTER TEARS

By the time I reached my assigned helicopter, my heart was racing and my skin was tingling in anticipation of this devastation tour. Going up for my first helicopter ride post-Katrina was something I was both looking forward to and dreading at the same time. I really didn't know what to expect or what I was getting ready to see. I shook hands with the pilot and copilot and climbed into a middle seat of a massive Black Hawk. My two executive protection guys, Wondell and Louis, who were both over six feet tall, struggled to squeeze in the rear seats behind me. The copilot turned around to give us instructions on how to properly fasten our seat belts and put on our sound-suppression ear guards and microphone. He also offered us extra earplugs just in case we needed them. As we were strapping in, the helicopter blades began to slowly turn as the engines started up. Deep in my thoughts, I started to mentally drift back to the New Orleans I knew growing up. Within a minute or two the engines and blades were fully revved up. I checked my earmuffs as the engine noise was extremely loud. Within seconds we were airborne as the pilot gracefully lifted the helicopter off the ground.

As the chopper was rising, I looked out at the Superdome as I reminisced back to when this facility was first constructed. I thought about all the Saints games that I'd watched over the years. Some games were exhilarating, but most were so terrible that many fans put bags over their heads so it wouldn't be so obvious that they were Saints fans. It got so bad that instead of calling the team "Saints," we called them "Aints." Now the place where these games were held was just a concrete tent of wretchedness.

As we flew higher, I looked down on the multicolored mass of thousands and thousands of people who decorated the outside of the Superdome, consuming the space between the buildings and barricades. I could see the National Guardsmen strategically spaced with timed patrols, making sure that nobody left the site. I wondered to myself where would they go if they did manage to escape?

In pretty short order we were high above the Superdome. Most of the bright white panels from the roof of the Superdome had been ripped off by the winds, revealing a surface that looked like spilled burnt coffee. Then my jaw just dropped as I turned and looked out. From every possible angle, all I saw was water. There was water where dry streets used to be. There was water to the roof lines of homes, there was water in high school football stadiums, and there was water as far as the eye could see! The elevated interstate highways were full of people. Some were still making their way out of the floodwater, moving closer to the Superdome or just trying to walk out of the city. These highways were also covered in trash and debris.

As we slowly hovered over the Superdome, the pilot spoke to me through the electronics in the earmuffs I was wearing and asked me what I wanted to see. My quick, firm answer was, "Everything."

As the Black Hawk helicopter started its forward motion, the wind could be felt as the cabin where we sat was open to the air and sound that flowed all around us. I pressed the voice activation button and instructed the pilot that I would first like to see the Seventeenth Street Canal break, then we should go to Gentilly and the City Park area, to Pontchartrain Park, New Orleans East, the Lower Ninth Ward, and finally along the river to see Tremé and the French Quarter. He said okay, and off we went, beginning on a quest that I will never forget for the rest of my life.

As we were flying toward Lakeview, I was constantly looking out of the left and right sides of the helicopter. We were moving at a moderate pace, so I could really take in the full effect of what I was seeing. The neighborhoods and streets that I had ridden my bicycle on as a kid were no longer visible—they were all under water. I also saw the tops of flooded houses where friends and relatives lived that made me wonder if they had gotten out in time, or worse still, if they had drowned. Next we flew over a baseball field where I had played many games during my elementary and high school years. As a matter of fact, I pitched my first no-hitter in one of the parks we flew over. Now it had eight feet of water covering everything from first base to home plate.

It wasn't long before we started to fly over the Lakeview neighborhood. Lakeview is a very upscale community that is slightly mixed but predominantly white. Homes are very expensive in this area. In the distance I saw the Steak Knife restaurant where just three nights before I had enjoyed a family going away dinner and received the shocking Hurricane Katrina briefing from Max Mayfield of the National Hurricane Center. And in the distance was the Seventeenth Street Canal where I felt more of a desperate urge to see how bad this breach really was.

We passed over houses that were almost completely covered by the water. Some roofs from high in the air looked like floating frosted flakes in a breakfast bowl as people dotted very limited dry spaces. Some had taken bricks or parts of their roof to spell out "rescue me" or "help me" in very large letters across a major section on their roofs. Others joined in pairs to wave big white sheets with messages written in big, bold letters. And some just waved their arms with any strength they had left in hopes that we would take them to a safer place.

Even though we were high in the air, I could still see the stress and strain on their faces. I remember even at the heights we were I could see clearly see in their eyes the pain and suffering each one was going through. Even over the sound of the helicopter's propeller I could hear them yelling for help. My eyes welled up with water, and a tear or two rolled down my cheek. I thought to myself, *This can't be real. Not in this city! Not in this country!* We even tried dropping water bottles down to some but gave up as the wind was still too strong, and many bottles landed in the murky waters below, never to be consumed by humans.

As we were flying, our pilot and copilot were radioing to Coast Guard helicopters exactly where stranded people were. It was a matter of minutes before I started to see these magnificent mechanical birds with winches attached to a secure seat picking up distressed individuals.

The Coast Guard pilots were so skilled that my eyes soon became glued on one particular rescue in process. The rescue helicopter was right near a major power line, and the pilot was holding the helicopter steady enough so the electronic winch could lift a three-hundred-pound lady to safety. The winds would gust unexpectedly, but the pilot deftly held the helicopter in place so it wouldn't get tangled up in the power lines. The helicopter engine strained a bit, but the lady ended up safely inside. As soon as she became secure, she looked out in our direction and gave me a thumbs-up with a great big smile on her face.

Within seconds we were circling the Seventeenth Street Canal breach. I could see right below us a huge gash at least the size of two or three street blocks along the concrete wall. Since the wall was atop an earthen levee, the water was still flowing from the lake into the canal and then into the streets. The waterfall effect further added to the depth of water in this neighborhood. This once very beautiful, affluent neighborhood was now virtually hidden under water. Also in the distance was a marina where every boat had either sunk in place or was pushed into a concrete cove where all that was left was a big pile of splintered wood, twisted aluminum, and shredded sails. To think that only a few days ago all of these beautiful, majestic boats had decorated the surface of the lake, but now they were splintered about like large matchsticks.

I signaled to the pilot that it was time to move on to Gentilly and the City Park area. Our helicopter immediately responded, turned, and proceeded toward our next destination. Within a minute or two I recalled that I needed to see something else on the way. Greg Meffert, the city's chief technology officer, had asked me to check on his boat that was moored at a different marina near Lakefront Airport. Before I went up, he said to me, "Man, you have to check and see how my boat made out." He told me that he and his captain had done some specially tied knot on it that would allow the boat to rise and fall with the storm surge. Since this was his new "toy," he seemed to be more concerned about it than his own house, which was located not too far from this marina.

Greg was one of my most talented and effective executive team members. He had made some money during the dot-com days and absolutely loved a good challenge. When I first arrived in office, the city government's technology was extremely antiquated. For example, the main data system used cartridges that were like eight track tapes to store critical city data. There was a just started, dormant Web site with severely outdated information on it. I even had a red-colored rotary phone on my desk in the mayor's office that was supposedly used during emergency situations. It had no dialing capabilities and was like a real modern-day Bat phone.

Within a year or two, Greg had Microsoft and Dell partnering with us to develop unique, cutting-edge software. We replaced all mainframe processors and properly backed up all data offsite. Our phone system used the latest IP equipment. And our Web site was soon to become ranked among the best in the nation. Greg and his team also worked miracles right after Katrina in creatively figuring out communication systems that were invaluable as we managed this crisis.

Unfortunately, toward the end of my second term, the U.S. Attorney brought multiple felony charges against him and his wife for an alleged kickback scheme. The charges related to some innovative crime fighting surveillance cameras that were invented in New Orleans. Greg had started a company with a friend of his and sold this new technology to other cities. Unfortunately, he was still working for the city at the time. The feds claimed that he used his influence at city hall to get these contracts and was improperly compensated through the use of that company's credit card.

Part of the intrigue of his charges was that his partner was the actual owner of the boat I was checking. It was not really owned by Greg after all as the sales paperwork never went through post-Katrina.

One of his big problems was Greg had a strong tendency toward braggadocio, with a capital B. So just about everything he did would quickly become general public knowledge.

In November 2010, he reluctantly pleaded guilty to only two charges. All counts against his wife were dropped as Greg agreed to fully cooperate with the government. I wish him and his family the best.

From the marina we then flew over Gentilly and City Park. At one point I looked out in the distance and saw my neighborhood. I could see the top of my home and that there was water everywhere, so I didn't ask the pilot to fly directly over because I just didn't want to know the extent of the damage yet. I just thought all was lost and my home was not spared. I would later learn that my house and about forty around it were indeed spared since we were on a relatively high ridge, eight feet above sea level. Although my home had severe roof damage, thank God it had no flooding.

Looking out of the other side of the helicopter I could see our twelve-hundred-acre City Park, which is the second largest green space park in America. Every acre was under water. We next flew over Tad Gormley track and field football stadium. This facility is where I had attended many high school and college football games as well major track and field events. The water was so deep that half the stadium seats were covered. As I continued to scan the area, there was another nearby stadium, Pan American, that looked as though three-fourths of its seats were covered with floodwater.

As we flew on we saw many other people on roofs and on the upper-floor balconies of various apartment complexes. They waved at us vigorously, and many had written, "Save Us" on cardboard or white sheets. We could not stop but radioed in their locations and continued on. The frightening thing was that floodwater was still flowing in through the levee breaches we saw out in the distance, so there was no way of really knowing how much higher the water would get. From there the chopper's engines revved up again, and we continued north through Gentilly heading toward Pontchartrain Park.

Pontchartrain Park is the first African American residential subdivision in the United States. It has been home to many prominent black New Orleanians such as Grammy Award winner musician Terence Blanchard and award winning actor Wendell Pierce. Over five thousand homes were flooded to the roof line. I even saw the rooftop of my Aunt Mona's home. I gave thanks that my aunt and cousins had taken my advice and left the city before Hurricane Katrina hit. As a matter of fact, this community had done very well in evacuating as there were very few of their neighbors stuck on roofs.

One of the great centerpieces of the Pontchartrain Park community is the Joe Bartholomew Municipal Golf Course. Joe Bartholomew was born August 1, 1885. He was an African American golf course designer who was way ahead of his time. Joe became a caddie at age seven at the segregated Audubon Golf Course in uptown New Orleans. He was a self-taught golfer who was later sent to New York to learn golf course design. He ended up building many courses throughout New Orleans. The Metairie Golf Club and City Park Number 1 and 2 were all courses that he built. However, he was not allowed to hit one golf ball on any of them because of segregation laws. He also received little to no salary for his incredible work.

Joe's masterpiece was the golf course named after him in Pontchartrain Park. This course had the best drainage system in the region. It could rain cats and dogs and once it stopped within less than an hour this course would be playable. As we flew over it I recalled that this was one of the golf courses where I had learned to play the game and had completed many rounds there over the years. I'd also have to say that nearly every significant black professional golfer in the United States had played there at some point in time. This great golf course was now no longer visible to the naked eye. It was completely covered in eight to ten feet of water and was essentially destroyed. The sound of golf balls being struck with the call of "fore" would not be heard there for quite some time.

From there we headed to New Orleans East and could see more people on their roofs, water levels of extreme heights, and floating dead bodies. We also saw many ignited gas lines coming out of the floodwater just like we saw in Lakeview and Gentilly. If you used a little imagination, they looked like burning SOS flags waving in the wind. Through my microphone, I asked the pilot to slow down as I tried to locate familiar landmarks. My brother-in-law Cedric, friends, business-people, doctors, and religious leaders lived in a gated golf course community out here called Eastover. It was difficult trying to locate the homes that I visited many times, or even the layout of the golf course that I had often played on. The water levels were the highest I had seen thus far. There were also very large fish that would pop to the surface periodically. It was hard to tell if they were sharks, porpoises, or perhaps a small whale.

The last thing I was curious about in the east were several large commercial assets, such as the Folgers manufacturing plant, Michoud shuttle tank plant, and the Lakeforest Plaza shopping mall. As we flew over them, I was a little relieved that all but the shopping mall was in decent shape with some wind damage and relatively modest flooding.

We had three more areas to see before we headed back to the heliport: the twin spans over Lake Pontchartrain, the Lower Ninth Ward, and the Tremé/French Quarter areas. Soon we were over the open water of the lake. I could tell how high the water levels were as I processed how this would have looked pre-Katrina. I could also see for myself that the storm surge had picked up parts of the 5.4 mile long I-10 Twin Span connecting New Orleans to Slidell, and it had discarded large concrete panels by throwing them to the bottom of the lake. All that was left was an eerie gap-toothed smile of scattered concrete roadway that was once a major route into and out of the city. It was breathtaking to now see another manifestation of just how truly powerful this storm was. It was very clear that no one would be driving in this direction anytime soon. Basically there was no way to evacuate the city to the east. At this point I was feeling pretty defeated. I had seen enough and signaled for us to move on.

Within minutes I could see in the distance the Lower Ninth Ward and her levee breaches. As we headed over the Industrial Canal, we came up front and personal with the breach in the Lower Ninth Ward levee near Claiborne Avenue, where a loosely tied barge had burst through the levee wall. Water from the Mississippi River had toppled the levee near the Holy Cross School site, entirely consuming that neighborhood. As our helicopter slowed down and circled, I could see homes completely covered in water over their roofs! There were homes that had been lifted from their foundations and moved to a totally different part of this community. Other homes collapsed from the pressure and all that was left was splintered wood. Mind-bogglingly, there were cars and some refrigerators lodged in treetops. Very desperate, scared people were on their second-floor roofs screaming for help at the top of their lungs, and there were also those who didn't make it, more floating dead bodies. I hit my call button and asked the pilot to radio the Coast Guard and request that they immediately send more resources to the Lower Nine. Surprisingly, I did not see any rescue operations underway.

Although disturbing, my eyes were now automatically trained to notice the floating dead—men, women, children, and pets. The memory of my grandmother who had passed several year earlier was triggered as I saw several elderly ladies floating face down, engulfed by their flowing "comfort" dresses that had fanned out around their bodies like deflated hot air balloons. These same eyes of mine instantly filled up again with tears. This great neighborhood of elegance and wildness lay before us, a watery wasteland. This was the very proud neighborhood where Fats Domino lived. As a child I had frequently come here to visit many dear friends. I knew it well.

Unfortunately, I also recalled a dark side to the Lower Ninth Ward, one with more than its fair share of poverty, crime, AIDS, and drug activity. As we passed over Desire Street, the full magnitude of everything I had seen this day on this dreadful flyover sunk into my psyche.

I struggled to hold back tears, but I just couldn't and they started to flow. As the chopper continued to move over the area, I felt a continual stream of tears rolling down my cheeks. Not wanting to look back at my executive protection, I knew that they too were struggling with emotions. We were all very silent during this phase of our helicopter ride of devastation.

For a few minutes I allowed myself to feel and express all the pain and sorrow of my city. I felt and silently wept for our suffering citizens—the ones at the Superdome, those on the interstate, people on roofs, and any who were trapped in attics. Then I forced myself to snap back and somewhat regained control of my emotions. At that moment I was starting to believe that the FEMA guy may just be right. The city was totally destroyed and lost. "In a single day and night of misfortune," just as Plato had described Atlantis, it appeared New Orleans had met the same fate as that fabled city.

After a few minutes my emotions were pretty much under control. However, my heart continued to sink as I came to the realization that my beloved home, New Orleans, now 80 percent under water, may be permanently damaged. As I surveyed more telling scenes below, trying hard to digest the images that I was more accustomed to seeing in connection to war or third-world countries, my mind once again drifted back to my childhood days of exploring the city as a young teenager. The city of jazz, Creole food, Super Bowls, Sugar Bowls, second line music, the Essence Festival, the Jazz & Heritage Festival, and Mardi Gras was now almost barren and drenched. There were no rhythms of exhilaration and joy. Her elegance and mystique now all seemed real only in my memory.

As a deep sense of depression covered me, negative thoughts started to flow like the mighty Mississippi River. As I attempted to stay balanced and somewhat optimistic, my subconscious would snap back at me with thoughts that no matter how well we attempted to rebuild this city that many called "the Big Easy," her cultural identity could be gone forever, swept up and swallowed whole by inconsiderate floodwater. I thought, "My God, this is the worst possible scenario."

At that moment, I just couldn't see how we were going to rebuild the uniqueness of what we had after seeing this amount of devastation.

I then closed my eyes, took a deep breath, sighed, and with a wounded heart told the pilot to fly along slowly near the river so I could see what happened to Tremé and the French Quarter. These two areas were the essence of the historic and unique nature of New Orleans, and they just happened to be built on the highest elevated land. In my mind this was the last bastion of hope for a very remote chance at recapturing some type of future renaissance of the Big Easy. If this area was also under water and severely damaged, then the federal government would need immediate plans to house nearly five hundred thousand permanent evacuees.

The helicopter made a turn and started following the path of the mighty, muddy Mississippi. I instantly thought of my good friend Carol Bebel, who always reminds me that the riverside is where we lay down our burdens to rest. These words couldn't be more significant than now. Just when I had given up hope, we came upon the Marigny, then Tremé, and soon the French Quarter. The Marigny and Tremé both looked good with moderate wind damage and very minor flooding. The French Quarter was in even better shape. She was intact and unharmed. No flooding and no major damage could be seen from my sky view.

As we continued along the river, we slowly came upon the world-famous Jackson Square. I couldn't believe my eyes! I almost knocked my earmuffs off as I hurriedly ordered the pilot to stop. Time slowed down as we hovered in place right near the riverbanks. I could feel my heart beating fast as I slowly panned out the right side of the helicopter to get the best view as I took my time to fully absorb this moment. My peripheral vision was enhanced ten-fold, and I noticed for the first time that the sun was shining and a rainbow was in the background.

Jackson Square looked like a 3-D postcard! The park surrounding Jackson's statue appeared freshly manicured. The Pontalba apartments perfectly outlined the entire frame of this visual picture. The cathedral looked ideal and angelic. The steeple's highest, sharpest point seemed to reach out and touch the blue skies. The white paint on the church was pure, radiant, and brilliant. It was as if time had stood still. Here we were viewing the keys that symbolize what makes New Orleans so unique. Her historical assets, the very buildings that have been around for almost three hundred years, were virtually untouched and preserved.

A warm feeling came over me, and instead of tears on my face I was now smiling inside and out. Our wonderful street names started racing through my mind. Names like Hope, Desire, Pleasure, and Humanity seemed to resonate strongly, more so than ever before. After all that we had lost, the city's cultural jewels still remained. In that moment I knew that we were going to be okay. I knew we would rebuild stronger and better. I felt energy and determination rush back into my body. We were going to get through this. I knew this was a sign from God himself. Amen!

On the way back to our starting point, we flew around the Hyatt to observe all the damage from the tornadoes. Windows were blown out in a significant number of rooms at the hotel, at the adjourning shopping center, and at the office tower. As we were landing back at the heliport, I couldn't help but notice that the water had risen so high that we would have to leave Big Daddy where it was parked. The exhaust pipe extension wouldn't help at all now that the water was well above the level of the car's hood. I thanked the pilots, and we started walking back toward the command center.

As we walked around the barricades of the Superdome back to the shopping center entrance that led to the hotel, it gave me the opportunity to stop and talk to the people who were sheltered there. They were anxious and confused, and most were complaining about how uncomfortable they were. They also complained about not knowing what was going on, about not having enough food and water, and about the extreme lack of sanitary conditions. I had a young man approach me with a very young baby who was extremely lethargic. He said the baby had not had any milk formula in two days, and they had run out of diapers. He then opened the baby's mouth and pointed out how white and bumpy his tongue was. He tried to hand me the baby and said, "Here, you take him because I'm afraid with the heat and unsanitary conditions inside that he'll die if he doesn't get milk and water." As any compassionate human would, internally I struggled with this request. Naturally wanting to ease the baby's suffering, but I knew I could not do that. I had to think of all the people in the city who needed saving. I politely resisted taking his child and attempted to reason with him. We discussed the conditions in the city, and I assured him that FEMA was working on getting some formula and diapers for the babies. He backed down and thanked me for listening and for whatever I could do.

Next an elderly man limped over to me and sobbed, saying, "Just find me a quiet place to lie down and die because I can't take any more of this." I tried to calm him down but couldn't as he just turned and limped away the same way he came. My heart was heavy again as I watched these good people suffering needlessly. I couldn't help but wonder out loud again, "Are we in America? Are we not Americans?"

The next day after another flyover to observe rescue progress and what repair work was performed on the levee breaches, I was again walking around the Superdome talking to evacuees as Doug Thornton, the manager of the Superdome, came up to me and said I needed to come inside to get an update on the severe challenges they were now facing inside. As a matter of fact, he said there was an imminent crisis that I needed to be aware of. He was extremely concerned about the current state of the building. Key panels had been blown off the roof on Monday during Katrina's wrath, and there were large holes overhead and lots of water was leaking into the building. All toilets were totally backed up, and human excrement was everywhere.

Doug's biggest, most immediate headache was flooding in the basement where the electrical and mechanical equipment was located. If the floodwaters got any higher, then the backup power generators would fail and all power in the building would end. This would mean a totally dark building at nightfall with more than twenty-five thousand hot, frustrated, and angry people in it. He took us on a tour of the building, and we saw where his staff was sleeping on the floor and on couches. I again saw the holes in the roof. As we walked around, I noticed that inside the smell was so overpowering. I will never forget that stench that left a permanent mark inside my nostrils.

We then went down to the basement to check out the electrical room. There were many maintenance workers and supervisors working feverishly. Doug pointed out that they were building and reinforcing a dam to try and keep the water out of the system. They had been doing battle with this problem nonstop for at least two days. Although they were very creative and had fought the good fight, it was clear to all of us that it was just a short matter of time before the water would overtake the entire basement of the Superdome. Water was leaking at the bottom of the dam, and the overall floodwater height was still rising. I looked at Doug and he looked at me, and we both knew what was getting ready to happen: this dam would not last much longer. Our nonverbal communication to each other was, *Prepare for total darkness.*

As I walked out, it was also very noticeable that besides the building suffering damage, there were many people inside the Superdome who were very ill, and they were not faring too well. Those who were marginally well when they entered the building were now suffering from physical problems as well as post-traumatic stress. The effects of the conditions they'd had to endure over the past several days and the mystery of not knowing the status of their homes, family members, and friends was too much to handle under these extreme conditions. Limited food and water was adding to the pressure and stress. The lack of sanitation due to the sewer system now having backed up created such unhealthy living quarters that many were forced outside to endure the heat, humidity, and growing mosquito population just to get away from the rancid smell and filth.

However, as the hours passed, thousands more people continued to migrate to the Superdome. Many were being rescued, others walked out of the floodwaters, and some came from places outside of New Orleans. At this point we were firmly convinced that there were more than twenty-eight thousand people in the building. In addition, the I-10 interstate was full and from the sky looked like a concrete version of the Loch Ness Monster. Its look-alike humps were the only remains of the road that emerged sporadically from the waters below. People continued to make their way over to these humps; they swam, waded, or floated. If they had a car that could get them through the water, they used it. Others found boats, wooden doors, anything that floated and would get them to higher ground. The dry, elevated road was the only means of getting access to downtown and into the Superdome.

Residents of Plaquemines and St. Bernard were in some respect worse off than we were. Their areas were completely under water, and many had little to no levee protection. These groups were also being rescued and dropped off at the Superdome or airport. Like the road to Mecca, people came in a constant stream from many directions. With a super steady stream of people continuing to come our way, we needed another dry shelter, and we needed it now.

Earlier that morning I had ordered the Police Chief Compass to go to the Convention Center near the river to open its doors by any means necessary. The chief and his men were able to secure several sections of the building that were clean, dry, and spacious. We then spread the word that the Superdome would stop accepting any more evacuees and the preferred drop-off location was now the Convention Center. Within the hour, this new shelter was receiving a steady stream of people. All were looking for food, water, and a place to get out of the floodwaters and the hot, burning sun.

We once again tasked FEMA with getting food and water to this location. Sadly, it would be days before that request was fulfilled. We also worried that the Convention Center could become a much more dangerous place than what we had at the Superdome. We just didn't have the time or capacity to screen people for weapons. So we kept piling them in as we nervously continued to wait for escape buses and more federal troops to arrive.

By the time I returned back to the Hyatt hotel and the command center, it was midafternoon. The national media had somehow started to arrive in droves. In an effort to deal with the rapidly increasing requests for media interviews, we set up a morning and evening press briefing in the ballroom of the Hyatt so that we could answer reporters' questions all at once.

Every print and live TV service was either at the Hyatt with us or at the very enterprising Sheraton hotel on Canal Street. CNN, ABC, CBS, NBC, BBC, *60 minutes*, the *Miami Herald*, the *Baton Rouge Advocate*— you name it and we had them. By Thursday the international press arrived in full force. The theater grew so large so rapidly that the Hyatt atrium ledge area quickly became too small and we were forced to find a larger location for press briefings. We ultimately ended up holding almost daily press briefings with over five hundred reporters and cameras in a separate set of Hyatt ballrooms.

This was very challenging for me as I was accustomed to dealing with only four to five local TV stations, two major radio organizations, and three to four print reporters pre–Hurricane Katrina. It took me a few days to adjust, and to be honest I don't think I ever really adjusted. The growing communication challenges became much tougher as time went on. Instead of reporting the news, some reporters resorted to creating news as competition for the latest unique angle to this tragedy suddenly heated up.

At this point FEMA was now in the groove of regularly over promising and under delivering or not delivering at all. Earlier that morning they sent in an emergency response medical crew of only four to help treat thousands and thousands of stressed-out, wet, and sick rescued people. They had not provided a single National Guardsman or military police to assist us with security at the Convention Center. At times I wondered if someone was playing a heartless joke on us.

The funny thing is the FEMA guys all looked and sounded sharp. They were clean-shaven, freshly pressed, and full of smiling faces. They generally had very positive attitudes and spoke in calming, monotone voices that made you want to take a nap after meeting with them. When they first greeted you, they would almost behave as if you were their long-lost friend. After a day or so I caught on and became very frustrated at the lack of meaningful follow-through. It was also very hard to get specifics as they tried hard to get you to pretend with them that everything was moving faster than it really was.

I remember one FEMA person who was a heavyset smooth talker who always smelled like he had just eaten a Big Mac from McDonald's. My standard line was, "Where are the buses?" and every time I would get a different response. He would just smile and then immediately say with a straight face, "They are on their way. They will be here tomorrow." Of course, tomorrow always turned into the next day and then the next.

The other big operation that FEMA was simultaneously managing was with the Army Corps of Engineers. This involved the closing of the levee breaches so the floodwaters would stop flowing into the city. In meetings they briefed us that the plan was to initially drop three-thousand-pound sandbags via helicopters into the breaches to halt water flow. Once that was completed, temporary pumps would be installed for draining floodwater out of the city and back into the lake. I was repeatedly assured that this process had started at the Seventeenth Street Canal so water would stop flowing downtown.

The next day I flew up in a Black Hawk and was flabbergasted that this operation was nowhere to be seen. Once my flyover was complete, I immediately confronted the FEMA representatives and demanded to know why this critical project was not progressing toward completion. The answer was that there was some phantom technical problem with the latch that released the sandbags. Marcia St. Martin later told me that the Army Corps of Engineers had in fact commandeered some sandbags from them and tried to drop them into the breach. They used up the board's filter media, a gravel used for water treatment to fill fifty three-thousand-pound bags. The Corps used these bags and had Black Hawk helicopters drop them into the canal. Unfortunately, they underestimated how many bags would be needed and were feebly scrambling around for much-needed resources.

The new FEMA promise was of course that this was being worked out. The plugging of the breaches was supposed to resume before the day was out. Well, the next day I went up to inspect progress and was once again disappointed. The excuse this time was the governor allegedly diverted helicopters to pick up a politically connected pastor and some of his congregation who were stranded but high and dry.

It got to the point that after a couple of these false-hearted meetings with FEMA, I gave up believing anything that was not independently verified. I decided from that point on that I would trust but verify. So I went up every day for a helicopter inspection ride so I could see for myself what was really happening. I found this to be incredibly ironic as during my initial run for mayor my opponents tried to spin me as "Ray Reagan" to the African American voters. Now here I was in a major disaster following a phrase that he made famous: "Trust but verify." I had no choice as time was working against us.

The next crisis to be thrown my way was when Marcia St. Martin with the Sewerage and Water Board called me again to frantically state that the power station that generated all the backup power for the entire water, sewer, and drainage systems was almost to the point of shutting down as it was going under water. Her staff had been working for days building and reinforcing temporary dams to try and keep floodwaters out of this essential operation. I could hear in Marcia's voice that she was panicked. She was trying to get me to just focus on this particular problem, but I couldn't as there were way too many crises happening simultaneously. My initial thought was, "It's basically another pumping station going off line." Her elevated, almost frantic response was, "No, when this one goes down, everything stops. There will be no fresh water, sewer, or drainage. It all goes dormant!"

Located in the Carrollton area not far from the Seventeenth Street Canal, this station was the heartbeat of the entire system. It was developed in 1903 because the commercial power from the electricity company was not dependable. So the Sewerage and Water Board built its own power generation plant that can produce about sixty-one thousand cubic kilowatt hours, which is enough power to power the city of Lafayette, Louisiana. It's a very inefficient and expensive way of generating power, but it's reliable.

Right before Katrina hit, Entergy had pretty much shut down shop, so we activated this power plant so that critical operations could continue. I asked Marcia, "If things do not improve, how much time do we have?"

She paused for a moment as I could hear her take a very deep breath and said, "Twelve to twenty four hours, max!"

I said, "Are you kidding me?"

Her immediate response was, "I wish I were." I asked her to keep me posted as things developed. This disaster had just moved up several notches on the crisis scale.

The next big challenge that also required immediate attention was that the Convention Center was now rapidly filling up with people just like the Superdome. So many people were moving through the doors that the few police officers assigned there struggled with the massive crowd that outnumbered them several hundred fold. Once the sun went down, there were reports of assault, stabbings, and a few shootings as thugs no longer in their comfortable territories came face to face with enemies. Everyone there was forced to share the same space with one another. Fortunately, may fearless, innocent citizens banded together to protect themselves and others. Like the Superdome, there was little food or water available, but it was a temporary place out of the floodwaters and hot sun for individuals without any other options.

It was also at this point in time that looting mushroomed significantly. We noticed over the past day or two that some had forced entry into stores primarily in search of food and water. Most had little choice but to venture out as the first rule of nature kicked in: survival.

New Orleans, like many other urban cities, is a place full of new age urban dwellers. We primarily live a fast-food lifestyle. Many just didn't do much cooking except for special holidays and Mardi Gras. They are also not like earlier generations of parents and grandparents. For them, anytime you went to an old-school mom or grandmother's home, you would find cupboards full of canned goods and other nonperishable foods. They could sustain themselves for a full month or more.

By Tuesday morning, these new age urban people had run out of whatever meager supplies they had and were hungry and thirsty. Unfortunately, there was no Popeye's chicken, McDonald's, Burger King, or other fast-food restaurants open to satisfy their needs, so some started breaking into stores. Initially, they only took necessities. Then the opportunists and drug addicts realized no one was stopping these actions, and in pretty quick fashion survival turned to opportunity, which then turned into passionate greed.

With our rescue missions producing the highest results since we started, I ordered that all first responders maintain their focus on rescue. My hope was that we could continue these concentrated efforts for one more day, and then we would sharply pivot to shut the looting down. The key question was how long before the looting got to the point where we had to reduce our efforts to save people from floodwaters?

Our first responders were also working under extremely arduous conditions with very few supplies. Some were allowed to break into retail stores for technical equipment in an effort to get much-needed communications up and running. They even had to confiscate clothing items such as underwear and socks. Since this was a true state of emergency, we had the authority to commandeer essential items, and we did. Most of our employees followed the order, and a very small number didn't.

As it turned late into the evening, back at the Hyatt hotel, I stood on the fourth-floor ledge and looked up out of the atrium glass toward the Superdome. My mind slowly started to process the day's mind-numbing events. For the most part, it had been completely challenging and totally overwhelming. Every key moment was preoccupied with strategies and tactics on how to get us safely through this nightmare. My mind was in overdrive, and with little to no food in my body, I started to feel both physically and emotionally exhausted. I was also still amazed and extremely disappointed with the governor and crew's photo op visit and exit without resource commitments or supplies. Then there was FEMA's many broken promises, their current on the ground medical support staff of less than ten, and their unacceptable lack of progress on fixing the levee breaches. Add to that the images of water everywhere, the sights of thousands of citizens walking on the interstate for safety, and the amount of dead bodies floating in the floodwaters, and it was extremely emotional, stunning, and somewhat unbelievable.

Telephone communications were essentially still down, and we only managed to receive an occasional BlackBerry PIN or text message. I made my way back into the command center and sat down at a table with Terry Davis (our communications specialist), Sally Forman (my communications director), and Greg Meffert (the city's chief technology officer). Within a few minutes, Wondell and Louis managed to somehow secure a landline with Marcia St. Martin so that we could check on the status of our essential power station. She was past desperate. As I grabbed the phone, she immediately started talking very fast and said, "Look, we tried everything to see if we could save this, but I just received an update from our best engineers who told me that in twenty minutes the power station will shut down." Then she added, "Completely inoperable." We just went up the crisis meter ten more notches! This meant all drainage would completely stop, and water would flow faster into the city, only stopping when the lake water height leveled out with floodwaters inside the city. The whole city, even the dry areas such as St. Charles Avenue uptown, could all soon be under water.

To make matters worse (if that was possible), my attention was quickly diverted to the arrival of twenty or so men dressed in black combat outfits and adorned in bulletproof vests, rifles, and leg straps holding at least two very large handguns each. Their presence was shocking, menacing, bizarre, and surreal. As they walked into the meeting room, they announced their arrival by stating that they were taking over. The leader stood confidently at over six feet three inches tall, was probably in his early forties, and was fit enough to play linebacker for the New Orleans Saints. He barked out, "We're here to protect the mayor. Everybody else get out." At this point my two executive protection guys bravely moved closer toward me with a look in their eyes that screamed out, "Oh, hell no! Not on our watch."

I quickly stood up and firmly asked, "Who are you guys, and who sent you?" No one ever directly answered my question. They refused to say specifically who sent them or why I needed protection. They also made it clear that they had no intentions of leaving.

With all the many challenges we were facing, the last thing I needed was an invasion from mercenaries or the arrival of some secret army. I literally had to pinch myself as this scene was unfolding. Here we were in the middle of the largest man-made and natural disaster in history, and this shadow army shows up with a phony message of "we're taking over" and *wink, wink*, "we're also here to help." If they were here to protect me, I sure did not feel that as my gut told me there was another agenda in play, and it clearly did not have our best interests at heart, period.

As my brain continued to process this hallucination-like scene, it brought to mind an emergency call that I had received earlier that day from Jimmy, local businessman. He and his family had evacuated and were safe in some sunny resort area far away from New Orleans. Jimmy, a member of the Rex organization, lives on Audubon Place. This is where the city's ultra-elites live. It is a super-exclusive, gated community located uptown, across from Audubon Park and Tulane University. The houses are plantation-like in magnificence and would have been the envy of the homeowners depicted in the classic film *Gone with the Wind*. Not just anyone could live there. Before buying in this neighborhood, the neighbors had the power to approve who the purchaser was.

Jimmy was leader of the Business Council, an organization made up of most of the city's CEOs of various industries. We had worked well together during my first term in office to clean up our transit agency, so we knew each other well. He had called me the day after Katrina hit. As I picked up the phone, I was quite surprised that he had managed to get through. I was also somewhat looking forward to getting his perspective, help, and advice on how to get more resources to help rescue more citizens in need. Unfortunately, Jimmy had other things on his mind. Instead of asking how I was doing or if there was any way he could help the city, he immediately started demanding that I let a private security firm into the city to protect, get this, only Audubon Place. My instinct was to immediately hang up the phone on him, but I resisted this very strong urge. It was crystal clear that he and his neighbors wanted special protection for their precious physical assets.

I now recall that his preferred security company, Blackwater, had also been hired to work in Iraq. They received very negative international media coverage when it was revealed that their "guards" questionably killed seventeen Iraqis. They were very enterprising as hired guns throughout the country and world. After the initial shock wore off, I told Jimmy that I just could not honor his request at this time. I went on to say that my priority was to focus our limited resources to continue our rescue operations and get as many people out of harm's way as possible. I also told him it would be very problematic to have multiple security agencies, fully armed, running around New Orleans playing GI Joe. I finished my answer by saying I would also have to check with our city attorney about who would be liable in the event a Blackwater guard ended up shooting an innocent citizen.

Jimmy was definitely not happy with my response. As a matter of fact, his anger came through loud and clear on the call. His parting words to me were, "If you do not let guards in to protect our homes, and if something happens to them, if they are vandalized, then you will have made the biggest mistake of your life!" Since I had enough I hung up the phone after curtly saying goodbye. This exchange caused me to pause for a moment as I was really taken aback that he was more focused on saving inorganic items like property instead of helping to save human lives. Although Jimmy and I came from very different backgrounds, his reaction was surprising to me because we mostly had had a very good working relationship in the past. He normally came across as a sensible, pragmatic, level-headed guy. I suppose Katrina, money, and saving personal stuff brought out the worst in some, including him.

Back in the command center, we finally got out of the Blackwater guards what their other assigned mission was: to gain access to my hotel suite on the twenty-seventh floor. They really wanted access to my room to "help with communications." Another factor we surmised was that they probably wanted total control of overall security, including first responders and National Guardsmen, in order to redirect resources to certain neighborhoods. The bigger unanswered question was who really sent them? It really wasn't clear at that time from anything they said.

Wondell told me later that at one point he was talking to Louis and felt as though somebody was watching them. In the hallway, when he quickly turned around he noticed one of the Blackwater guys suddenly duck behind a column as if to evade being spotted. Then their leader kept saying, "We have to put a perimeter around the mayor's room immediately." What we didn't know was that another part of their team had already made it up to the twenty-seventh floor. They had put up all kinds of wires that ran up and down the halls and eventually made their way to the roof. They claimed it was for a satellite connection. These wires also ran all around the door to my suite. This stealth team then tried to gain access to my suite at the same time we were debating with the main group on the fourth floor.

Luckily, Greg Meffert and his high-tech crew were already in my suite working on alternative communication equipment. They were desperately trying to devise a reliable way for us to get information flow. Greg and his crew stopped the Blackwater guys cold. Interestingly, these commandos told Greg that they were the ones who were there to fix my communication problems. Now they were trying to present two different faces of Blackwater, the ones downstairs who were there to protect and the group upstairs who were technical experts.

We were not buying any of their stories. And after several rounds of going back and forth, our unwelcome visitors got the message that we were not going to allow them to take over or gain access to my room to plant bugging devices. So in true ninja style, as quickly and as quietly as they arrived they were gone.

Even after they left, my team and I were still pretty shell-shocked. All we could do at that moment was stare at each other and look out the windows. No one spoke for several minutes as we just tried to reorient ourselves back to reality. It was really hard at this point for us to distinguish what was real with so many extraordinary events happening minute by minute. It seemed impossible to anticipate the next crisis.

Over the course of the next few days and weeks, we obtained more legitimate supplemental protection from federal agencies like ATF and ICE. Thankfully, their mission was not to take over my room or the city but to provide additional supervised protection. I ended up with a team of four executive protection personnel, with my guys Wondell and Louis being in charge. All other offers of protection support were politely turned down, including more Blackwater "communications experts."

Later that evening, I went in my bedroom to lie down and hopefully take a good nap as I was totally exhausted. After about a half hour, I was suddenly interrupted as another staff member ran into the room with an urgent message that the White House had been trying to get through for the past three to four hours. She handed me the phone number, and we all proceeded to scramble around trying to get an open line. Since my BlackBerry was down and so was everyone else's, we tried a landline, then another, and finally found one that worked and got a call through. Andrew Card, the president's chief of staff, answered. "Mr. Mayor, how are you doing? Our prayers are with you. Hold on one second," he said. The next voice on the phone was the unmistakable Texan drawl of President George W. Bush. "Mr. Mayor, how's it going? What do you need? I'm working with the governor to try and get you more resources. Everything is going to be alright. Here are my numbers—keep in touch. We're trying to come and see you real soon." Before he hung up, I hit him for one very specific request: to plug the Seventeenth Street Canal and other levee breaches. He told me he was "on it."

My thinking was if he couldn't do anything else right now, we needed to stop the flooding. This would do two key things: stop further deaths by drowning and allow us to hopefully restore power desperately needed to drain the city. For some reason, Sally Forman was not happy with my single, focused request of the president. She believed I should have emphasized and requested more supplies, food, water, and medical support. My very firm response to her was, "Let him do this one damn thing, Sally, and then we'll move on to the next set of needs." The pressure was intense and I snapped, regretting the tone as soon as the words left my lips. I got up from the table, and as I walked away, I turned and said, "Look, I've got FEMA blowing smoke up my butt every day, so I just want him to deliver on this one thing for now." What we really needed at that moment was for water levels to stabilize in order to save lives.

I was also aware as one of the FEMA guys had briefed me earlier that the Corps of Engineers was struggling to plug the canal breaches supposedly because the size of the sandbags, weighing several thousand pounds, required specially designed pulleys for releasing them into the breach. Each extra-large sandbag and the entire attached steel wires had to be dropped into the water also and lost forever, each one. Therefore, a special manufacturing order had been placed for these attachments. The problem was the delivery date was several days out.

Unfortunately, we didn't have a few days to wait as water levels continued to rise. It was also true that disaster capitalism was alive and well and would grow as this tragedy continued to unfold. I am sure a special disaster rush order for these pulleys brought a government rate that was astronomical. I sensed that greed was continuing to rear its ugly head as profiting tended to overshadow recovery and rebuilding efforts. If those in power really wanted this expedited, then it would happen. Only time would tell if they cared enough. As we waited, the water continued to flow into the city with disastrous consequences.

I retreated to my hotel suite, and I was finally alone with my thoughts. I quickly slipped into quiet, deep reflection. I got up for a moment and went in to check on and feed Fishy. He was fine and happy to see the light from my flashlight. I took my shirt and shoes off and lay down on the bed. As I stared at the dark ceiling, I could hear in my mind so clearly the president's words that he had spoken to me earlier during this very full day. "Mr. Mayor, we just want you to know that everything is going to be alright." I really hoped he meant that because right now I was in a living hell, and it was getting hotter every hour.

CHAPTER SIX

JOHN WAYNE DUDE

———■———

D
uring major disasters, the director of FEMA becomes THE
key power player for the federal government of the United
States. This person is responsible for immediately mobilizing
the magnificent resources of the federal government. For New Orleans
and the Gulf Coast region, Michael Brown was the undersecretary for
FEMA when Hurricane Katrina made landfall. Unfortunately for us, Mr.
Brown lacked any meaningful emergency management experience.

As a matter of fact, the closest he got to disaster management
experience was for a brief period of time when he was the assistant
to the city manager of Edmond, Oklahoma, population fifty-eight
thousand. After Mr. Brown was hired to head up FEMA, the White
House claimed that he had "emergency oversight services" duties in
Edmond. Some people in that city disputed this claim and countered
that Brown did not have oversight over anyone and in fact was more
like an intern. Next on his résumé was an undistinguished stint at a law
firm. Right before joining FEMA, Michael Brown's big job was Judges
and Stewards Commissioner for the International Arabian Horse
Association (IAHA) from 1989 to 2001.

Next, he joined FEMA as general counsel. He was hired there by
his close friend, then FEMA director Joe Allbaugh. Joe ran President
Bush's campaign in 2000. After FEMA merged into Homeland
Security, Mr. Allbaugh left and Mr. Brown was promoted to FEMA
director in 2003.

A few days prior to Hurricane Katrina making landfall, on Saturday,
August 27, 2005, Michael Brown made a confident statement to a CNN
reporter. He proclaimed that FEMA was fully prepared to respond

and that he would do everything in his power to help all victims of Hurricane Katrina. It was now Wednesday morning, August 31, and as I looked out at the thousands of people stranded in the Superdome, who were dirty, hungry, and thirsty, waiting in sweltering heat, there was no sign of rescue or help from FEMA. Later that day President Bush would go on national TV to compliment Mr. Brown on his Katrina efforts. His infamous quote is, "Brownie, you're doing a heck of a job."

Michael Brown would later claim that he was not aware people were suffering in the Superdome until Friday, day five after the storm. It now seemed that everyone in the world knew about these conditions but Mr. Brown.

Months and years later during intense congressional hearings, e-mail transcripts and other documents were release to the public that told the real story of what Mr. Brown was actually doing during this disaster. It is now clearer that his bosses were not fully supporting him, he had very limited resources, and he was constantly spinning the truth about what was really going on. This gentleman seemed greatly overwhelmed, fearful, and more concerned about his physical appearance on TV than in rolling up his sleeves and helping thousands of fellow Americans during a catastrophic disaster of this nature.

Michael Brown would resign as FEMA director on September 12, 2005, in the wake of what was widely believed to be extremely inept federal handling of the aftermath of Hurricane Katrina. Before leaving, Mr. Brown gave initial congressional testimony where he blamed Governor Blanco and myself for all of the problems and said he should have recognized our shortcomings sooner. Interesting perspective from a guy who took five days after the storm to fully realize that 80 percent of the city was flooded and thousands of people were without adequate food and water. The rest of the world recognized after a day or two that local governments were stretched beyond their limits and desperately needed help. Somehow Michael Brown completely missed this fact.

Much later, in January 2006, he contradicted himself again once he realized that some of his bosses were figuratively throwing him under the bus. He quite frankly said he should have done things differently by immediately calling in the military. He also admitted that his earlier statements were incorrect and he now realized that this disaster was so large "it was way beyond the capacity of state and local governments, and was even beyond the capacity of FEMA."

Finally, in February of the same year, Michael Brown again testified before Congress and said the entire blame for an insufficient response to Katrina was mainly due to the Department of Homeland Security focusing too much of its attention on developing the multibillion-dollar anti-terrorism industry. He further insinuated that this benefited a few of his bosses and Vice President Dick Cheney's closest friends. He also in very convincing fashion contradicted earlier claims by the White House that they were unaware of levee breaches right after they first happened. His direct quote into the congressional record was, "For them to claim that we didn't have awareness of it is just baloney." It took six long months for the truth to finally come out from a high ranking federal official.

On the Wednesday after Katrina hit New Orleans, while Michael Brown was still in denial, we were struggling with a city rapidly descending deeper into chaos and misery. We were marooned, cut off from the rest of world by gross inaction and rising floodwaters. We were basically alone in this struggle.

The city now looked like a massive liquid landfill. The floodwaters contained trash and debris mixed in with many precious personal belongings—wedding photos, family albums, high school yearbooks, debutant dresses, Zulu paraphernalia, birth certificates, and even cash money. These items no longer had an owner except for the wind and waves. Animals left to their own devices swam for their lives or stood on any item above water, scared and disoriented.

On this day it seemed to me that there were more human remains in the floodwater, floating aimlessly or tucked snugly inside a corner. Some were respectfully covered by a blanket, while most were left completely exposed to the elements. My daily Black Hawk flyovers took in all of these inconceivable scenes. This was the most extreme "reality TV show" where masses of people were also occupying the elevated interstate system. In addition, all of this was unfolding in August, the hottest and most humid month of the year in New Orleans.

These American citizens had no choice but to endure the blazing sun on super-heated asphalt. The heat coming off the concrete interstate was so hot that it was tough to focus on any particular spot. It was as if your eyes were playing tricks on you. This heat was so thick that it created that fuzzy effect that you get at a 3-D movie when you take off the special eyeglasses in the theater and continue to stare at the movie screen. We received reports of individuals who swam out and made it to the interstate barefoot. As they walked around on the hot, coal-like concrete, the soles of their feet would burn so badly that some developed huge blisters. Their only immediate relief was if they dipped their feet back into the toxic water.

In the coming weeks as these same floodwaters were being drained, I kept asking FEMA to perform scientific testing on the water and soil in all affected areas. We were consistently told that proper sample testing would be done and we would get to see the results. Weeks later we only received a very general summary report that really did not say much.

On the day of Katrina's landfall as the storm surge was easily punching holes in the federally built levees in the Lower Ninth Ward, President Bush was busy sharing a birthday cake photo opportunity with fellow Republican Senator John McCain. On this Wednesday, Governor Blanco had put in yet another call to the president's office requesting help. She pleaded, "Send everything you've got." The Democratic governor's call went unanswered.

My telephone call with the president the day before was our first conversation as he asked me, "What do you need? I am working with the governor to try and get you more resources." He also left me with the impression that he was on the job and in Washington quickly mobilizing the awesome resources of the United States. I would later learn about the cake and ice cream party he attended as he was wrapping up a month-long vacation at his ranch in Crawford, Texas.

The growing public pressure and my conversation seemed to have resonated with the president enough for him to cut his vacation a little short. On Wednesday afternoon he took off in Air Force One on his way up to Washington DC. He ordered the plane to detour and fly over New Orleans to survey the damage from thirty-five thousand feet in the air instead of landing nearby with federal troops to survey up close and personal. It would take another two days until he actually set foot in the city or state.

When he arrived at the White House, it has been reported he instructed Donald Rumsfeld, secretary of defense, and Michael Chertoff, the secretary for homeland security, to do a full assessment and take immediate steps to deploy federal troops to the region with supplies. They both resisted, the president vacillated again and there was no immediate deployment of troops or supplies.

Later that day, Michael Chertoff publicly announced that he was extremely pleased with the response to the disaster by all factions of the federal government. This was amazing since he had not visited the area either. It was becoming crystal clear that the federal media spin was now moving into action while much-needed resources were still frozen.

My take on President Bush and his administration was that they grossly underestimated this event, and as time went on indecision ruled the day. They also bought hook, line, and sinker the initial "New Orleans dodged a bullet" media reports that were extremely inaccurate. They had the best technology known to man and didn't utilize it to verify the truth. Some of their own people, like Michael Brown, reported very bad information, and as time went on, reality set in and they tried to cover their butts but couldn't. Soon deflecting attention onto others became fashionable.

President Bush's other problem was an overreliance on updates from Baton Rouge. They either called the state EOC, FEMA personnel stationed there, or the governor's office directly. Then the governor and our U.S. senators were holding multiple press conferences, basically claiming, "Everything is okay." The truth was New Orleans had not dodged a bullet but had been almost fatally struck right near the heart.

As the days continued to unfold, this disaster took on a media life of its own. The entire nation and most of the world was totally mesmerized and appalled. They watched their TVs and saw this great American city abandoned, tormented, and practically left for dead. The awful scenes of despair were way too scandalous and gripping for most to turn their attention from. The whole world also now saw America's dirty little secret fully exposed: her inner cities had intense pockets of poverty. It was painfully clear to all that our federal government really didn't care enough to help in the past. And now their pattern of indifference, particularly in our time of severe need, was live and in living color for everyone to see.

As a result, the Bush administration was under the gun and in damage control mode, big time. The president and his administration had been caught flat-footed. His advisors did him a huge disservice by trying to pacify the public with a very tardy flyover inspection. They made matters worse by releasing a cold, insensitive looking picture of him looking down on the disaster out of one of the plane's windows. The message received by everyone was that the president of the United States did not care that much about New Orleans, a place where many of the stranded never voted for him.

On the other hand, the American people cared a whole lot about fellow Americans suffering in front of the world stage. They were horrified, disgusted, embarrassed, and started demanding action. The White House and congressional phones lines lit up, were overloaded, and almost shut down. Radio talk show lines were full, and many wrote letters to local and national newspapers expressing their outrage.

Unfortunately, just like Michael Brown didn't get it for six months, many others in the Bush administration grossly misunderstood this defining moment. Secretary of State Condoleezza Rice was roundly booed on the streets in New York City while shopping for shoes and attending a Broadway production as our nightmare was unfolding. Homeland Security Secretary Michael Chertoff was spinning, running for cover, and virtually frozen in inaction. Vice President Dick Cheney was basically AWOL from assisting the needy.

The million-dollar question is why didn't they take effective action immediately? Was it partisan politics? Were there racial considerations? Were there class considerations? My humble opinion is that it was all of the above.

By Wednesday afternoon, day three of the disaster, President Bush made his first major TV address on Hurricane Katrina. He was immediately criticized for this halfhearted press conference and his casual and detached demeanor regarding the minimal degree of response by the federal government to this disaster. They were now way behind the eight ball. Some say the president never recovered.

Internal strife in Washington was also growing as public pressure continued to mount. Marty Bahamonde, the lone FEMA representative who was in New Orleans when Katrina hit and was the first to alert me to the severity of the disaster, was just as frustrated with the lack of federal response as we were. He continued to send e-mails to Michael Brown and other FEMA officials, pleading for urgent assistance, much-needed supplies, and medicine.

These now public documents clearly depict that Marty, over and over again, advised FEMA officials concerning the horrific deteriorating conditions in and around the Superdome, the Convention Center, the elevated expressway, and on rooftops. He warned that many more innocent people would die within hours if immediate assistance was not provided. In painstaking detail, he repeatedly advised them that there was no running water, toilets were backed up, and food and drinking water were almost gone.

On Wednesday afternoon Marty finally received some feedback from Michael Brown's press secretary, Sharon Worthy. Ms. Worthy detailed in this e-mail that Michael Brown would need more than thirty minutes downtime so he could enjoy his dinner. Evidently restaurants in Baton Rouge were booming with business, and he would most likely arrive late for an interview and couldn't follow up with Marty at the moment.

This level of insensitivity was the last straw for Marty, and he lost his cool. His response has now become public: "OH MY GOD!!!!!!!!! NO won't go any further, too easy of a target. Just tell them that I just ate an MRE and crapped in the hallway of the Superdome along with 30,000 other close friends so I understand her concern about busy restaurants. Maybe tonight I will have time to move the pebbles on the parking garage floor so they don't stab me in the back while I try to sleep, but instead I will hope the wait at Ruth Chris Steakhouse is short. But I know she is stressed so I won't make a big deal about it and you shouldn't either." Marty had had it and clearly reached his boiling point. It would only take me another day until I went down that same animated route. The big difference is that the whole nation would in pretty short order hear my explosion real-time, very loud and clear.

At this point, all working drainage pumps stopped operating, and there was now no resistance to the waters coming in from Lake Pontchartrain. The previous day, water had been creeping into downtown. Now it was streaming in, and there was no indication of just how high the water would rise as the lake had not yet leveled off.

By Wednesday evening, the water was six to eight feet deep on Poydras and other streets surrounding the Superdome. I felt now more than ever that it was absolutely imperative that anyone else who still could should leave the city immediately. Unfortunately, the buses and other transportation that had been promised had still not arrived. We also had no idea if any other levees were also on the brink of failing.

As had been my practice since the storm hit, I gave daily morning and evening media updates. That evening I gave my update and directed the message to those who had in fact already evacuated and frankly informed them to expect that the city may not be functional for several months. I also spoke to those who were still in the city in dry areas. I told them that conditions would continue deteriorating as the floodwater continued to consume more land. I reinforced that they were ordered again to leave immediately, especially those who had stayed behind in Algiers, Uptown, and the French Quarter, our so-called high ground.

Right on cue, media reports were unified in reporting that St. Charles Avenue, the city's second most prominent boulevard, would soon meet the same flooded fate as the rest of the city. I instructed Chief Compass to assemble a team of men and women and have them go house to house in these target "dry" areas to inform any remaining citizens of the risk and instruct them that they had to leave now. And for the most part, most had had enough, followed instructions, and later that night and first thing Thursday morning they took the one and only route out.

Since there are no hills in New Orleans to hold water back, the flow continued moving down Poydras Street headed towards St. Charles Avenue at a faster and faster rate. Unless things changed quickly, New Orleans would become a true modern-day Atlantis, 100 percent flooded.

Communication with the outside world continued to fade. All phones were barely operating. We received a burst of e-mails and PIN messages generally very early in the mornings. I was also receiving a tremendous amount of voicemail messages that I could neither hear nor return. My voice mailbox stayed full.

I was being inundated with messages from businessmen frantically concerned about their homes and business locations. Somehow they got through and left a text message as I recognized their names as most of them were in my cell phone's electronic contact list.

When I did get to talk to one of them, I would relay the same thing I told the very animated local businessman Jimmy when he called earlier: my first responsibility was the safe rescue of people, not property. Mansions and business locations would have to wait in line behind a very long list of other priorities. We were clearly in nuclear crisis mode, and saving lives was all that mattered at the moment.

By Wednesday morning, the situation in the Superdome and Convention Center was way past extreme dreadfulness. The hot temperature during the day forced people to take refuge outside as conditions inside the Superdome in particular were now at subhuman levels. Power was completely out, and for the most part, people were inside in darkness with the exception of sun or moonlight that poked through a few holes in the roof.

Toilets had been backed up and overflowing for several days now. Human excrement that only a few days ago had spoiled just the semi-private hallways and stairwells was now spread over most open parts of the building. Just about any spot inside was now eligible to become part of this open toilet system. American citizens were being forced to live inside a giant sewer under a domed roof. There was no place to take a bath, shower, or just wash your face. Shamefully, the animals at our local Audubon Zoo were in better living conditions than this. This was an absolute disgrace—a national disgrace!

As I continued my daily walks around the Superdome, many people would stop to ask me the status on supplies and when the buses were coming to get them. They were also desperate to know how much more time they would have to live in this nightmare. My heart broke every time I had to look into their eyes and tell them that this would end soon and we were working on getting them all out.

Mothers held their suffering little children close, and their penetrating, heartbreaking stares would just cut through me like large, very sharp knives. Young men would come forward and just want to talk. They just could not comprehend why their mothers and grandmothers had to endure such madness. Most senior citizens just moved around very slowly with slumped shoulders as they were totally confused and humiliated by what was happening to them and around them.

For the most part, these people knew me and talked to me very sincerely in hopes that I could do something, anything to relieve their burdens. I spent most of this time trying to comfort them by first telling the truth and then trying to give them hope that somehow we would get out of this. My message was always to hang in there, look out for each other, and as soon as the floodwater stops rising, we would get everyone to a better place. They trusted me and depended on me to do whatever it took to fix this reprehensible insult. I was determined to spend every waking moment doing everything I knew how to do just to get them to a better place.

As we walked among them, it was obvious that they were starving for reliable updates. Another problem was if someone had a working radio with batteries, a lot of what they were hearing was coming from local reporters who had left the city when floodwater first started flowing downtown. The people in the Superdome and Convention Center would hear exaggerated, inaccurate news reports and become more frustrated and angrier. This lack of accurate, consistent information surely compounded many mental health issues as most were already suffering from stress and deprivation from being in dreadful isolation. Many would later tell me that the feeling of not knowing was much more terrifying than knowing what was actually happening, no matter how bad things were.

We also heard many stories of people naturally banding together inside the Superdome, especially if they knew one another before Katrina hit. New Orleans is a very parochial city, and your neighborhood is considered part of your soul and identity. There were also sections in the Superdome where neighbors, family, friends, and church members were known to hold regular prayer sessions. Many times this would lead to gospel singing and a related second line–type procession around the inside of the building that would lift the spirits of all within earshot. These familiar clans also looked out for one another, so for the most part they remained relatively safe in spite of the few predators who caused some harm.

Unfortunately, we were still receiving reports of violence and looting that was still prevalent in the dry areas of the city. Gunfire was the norm at night and many times during the day. It was truly a godsend that we had effectively screened for weapons and drugs inside the Superdome. However, it was also very unfortunate that we did not have the time or resources to similarly screen at the Convention Center. The other tragedy was that there was really no way for us to screen for pedophiles and rapists at either location.

We had been hearing stories of rapes occurring for several days now. The National Guard and NOPD investigated every rumored incident as best they could. These stories of the most violent of violations shocked us in a very different way. We heard from fairly reliable sources that this had happened to several people in the Superdome and at least one small child in the Convention Center. Another young girl was also attacked and severely beaten in a bathroom.

Much later, I had a few private conversations with several women who were in these facilities who recalled stories of horrible episodes that were never formally reported. They told me it was highly unlikely that anyone would come forward. First, what happened to some women was done in almost total darkness. The other terrifying issue was they were still confined to specific areas where their attacker roamed freely. Therefore, they never knew if they would be attacked again before being rescued. A few were indeed attacked again. The other extremely frightening thing for these victims was that when they were evacuated to other shelters in another state, there was the fear that their attacker could still be secretly among that crowd also.

The political and media spin later claimed that many of the rapes were basically the figment of our collective imagination. This ensured that anyone who was raped would not come forward to face unfair, invasive scrutiny while being forced to defend their credibility. However, a very brave, high-profile woman, the daughter of one of our world-famous musicians, courageously came out to report that she had been raped while seeking refuge during the storm in an old school building in the Lower Ninth Ward. Her brave stance was a rare event as many continued to live quietly with these violations and basically tried to move on with their lives. I pray that they are somehow healed from all of their pain, suffering, and nightmares.

It should also be noted that men were not exempt from feeling violated as some were being pushed past their limits. One sad example was a man who just couldn't take it anymore and jumped from one of the top stadium levels in the Superdome, nearly fifty feet to his death. This suicide got everyone's attention. We started watching the people at the Superdome with greater concern. Our daily prayer was for the president, FEMA, the state, and anyone else who could help to get everyone out as soon as possible.

Our unfortunate reality was that FEMA kept promising buses, and we waited and waited for them to arrive. In the mornings we were told they would arrive in the evening, and by the evenings we were then told they would arrive the next morning. The people would get wind that the buses were coming, get their hopes up, and then sink into mass depression when nothing happened. We tried to keep optimism alive by once again getting word out that according to FEMA some of the buses were right outside the city limits and they should be here in the morning. This latest bit of encouragement would kind of keep everyone calm. Then when the sun would set, the reality that they were still stranded would set in again. Rumblings would start up again, and many could be seen very visibly upset. Every day it became tougher to maintain calmness in the face of so many false starts.

I could tell that in spite of being in a constant state of hope followed by despair, most desperately wanted to believe that buses were indeed coming no matter how many times FEMA was very liberal with the truth. Most people wanted to have faith that they would soon get out of this hell. They desperately wanted to secure a seat on a bus, any bus headed north.

Just to make sure that they would not miss out, some started to migrate out onto the large elevated walkway between the Superdome and the shopping center that led to the Hyatt hotel. Once they secured a spot closest to the exit doors, they didn't move for anyone or anything. Just about all were scared that if they left their place to go sit in the shade near the Superdome doors, then they would lose their position in the front of the line behind the barricades and would risk not getting a ride out.

I would go in and out of my hotel room on the twenty-seventh floor several times per day. The windows facing the Superdome gave me a very good view of this crowd and the interstate. At least twice per day I'd look out to view the entire landscape, to see how the mass of people was doing and if buses were arriving. Unfortunately, my daily norm was to see an empty interstate and people below packed like sardines. There was also high floodwater, helicopters, and lots and lots of trash piling up among the masses. It was a very depressing scene.

The elderly continued to get weaker and weaker. Many became very ill, and some died waiting. Even after the buses arrived a week later to transport people out of the city, the dead remained in place. Some who died at the Convention Center were left on the sidewalk since the big, empty food freezers inside the building that initially doubled up as a temporary morgue were full. The smell of death was overpowering. I'll never forget that smell as at times it felt as though the city was consumed by it.

I still have flashbacks; one in particular is of a very precious little old lady who was in her wheelchair waiting at the Convention Center. She passed away right there before being rescued. Someone had written her name, age, and social security number on a piece of paper that was stuffed under her crookedly shaped arm. A blanket was all that respectfully covered her as she rested in that spot until we could arrange proper burials for poor souls like her.

As we continued to wait and wait for FEMA rescue buses, others decided they were not going to sit on the sidelines any longer to watch us suffer. State Senator Cleo Fields and his good friend Ben Jeffers were so frustrated by the lack of commitment to rescue efforts by the state that they decided to act. Mid-day Tuesday, these two brave men gassed up a couple of buses from the nonprofit they sponsored and started driving from Baton Rouge to New Orleans. They were determined to do their part.

On their first mission they came face to face with roadblocks that were manned by Louisiana State Police. Senator Fields used his credentials and authority as a state legislator to get past these barricades to continue into New Orleans. They would later tell me that they were shocked once they got to the city to see so many people still walking through water, some pushing babies in big plastic containers that they used as floating devices so that they could get to dry ground. As soon as they had dropped their first few busloads off in Baton Rouge, they immediately turned around for another mission.

After completing several runs, the word got out that Senator Fields and Mr. Jeffers were the only ones with buses helping evacuate people out of the city. Besides the standard rescue missions, they would soon be asked by the Southern University president if they could rescue Dr. Norman Francis (who would later become chairman of the LRA board) and some students who were stranded at Xavier University. The two agreed to collect them on a subsequent mission.

On Wednesday they stopped at a truck stop at LaPlace just off the interstate, an area between Baton Rouge and New Orleans, to get gas and coffee. To their dismay, they saw several hundred buses with drivers filling up the parking lot. They discovered that these resources had been sitting idle for several days. It was infuriating that these buses had been sitting so close without orders to rescue. The question is why? They surmised that with this many buses, the Superdome and Convention Center could have been emptied in just two or three full runs. Senator Fields tried to get answers once he got back to Baton Rouge, but no one there would acknowledge or take responsibility for these immobile assets.

On a later run that day, Cleo and Ben were able to convince two of the idling drivers to join them. They added them to their convoy and resumed their mission to Xavier University. As they entered the city, they stopped on an elevated bridge and set out on foot in search of Dr. Francis and his students. When they returned, a number of other stranded people in that neighborhood had been watching them drive in and were hoping to be rescued this time. When they saw Cleo and Ben loading the Xavier entourage on the buses, their anger flared up.

Many of them had pleaded for help as they watched military helicopters flying over for days rescuing other neighborhoods without stopping to help them. So they ended up making a human chain around each bus, thereby preventing them from leaving. They started shouting, "Hold up. What are you all doing? You come in here just to get certain people?" They then defiantly started chanting, "If we don't go, they don't go."

Senator Fields and Mr. Jeffers quickly noticed that the leader of the group was a strong-willed elderly gentleman. They asked him to step aside privately to talk with them. Cleo tried to reason with the leader by reminding him that they were the only people coming in with buses to do any rescuing and that they had to leave so there would be time to start another mission. They promised him that if the group let them leave, then they'd come right back for them.

The elderly gentleman thought for a minute and then turned to his group and said, "I trust these guys. They are the only ones who care as they have brought buses in to rescue people like us. Let them go. He gave me his word that they're coming back." And at that moment everyone just stepped aside and let them drive off. Cleo and Ben kept their word as their bond and came back for the elderly man and his neighbors.

Back at the Superdome, things had descended to being on the verge of blowing into a full-scale riot. Our director of health and his top assistant, who were administering medical help to the sick, were tipped off by several patients that a plot had been developed to over-power the National Guardsmen and take their weapons. From there they planned to take hostages, gain full control of the Superdome, and then storm the Hyatt hotel. They wanted control of their own destinies. These conspirators also mistakenly thought that there were in fact more buses already in the city that were first evacuating other areas, in the affluent parts of town.

FEMA's broken promises had now become ours as well as the people's disappointment and anger was also pointed toward us. With only three hundred National Guard troops at the Superdome and a handful of police officers, a coup d'état could be successful as the sheer number of people in the Superdome gave them an overwhelming advantage. If our limited security force was defeated, then a simple push through the barricades on the crosswalk from the Superdome through a set of doors would give them clear access to the third floor of the Hyatt hotel. From there, our command center was only one flight of stairs up, on the fourth floor.

The patients also revealed to Dr. Stephens that the gang had placed special markings on their caps so they could quickly and easily distinguish who was on their team when the chaos started. With this insider information of how organized this group was, we immediately alerted our entire security group to the plan.

It was now the middle of the day on Wednesday, and the sun was absolutely brutal. It felt like it was at least 110 degrees with 100 percent humidity. The Superdome crowd was excessively restless. Drinking water was very scarce, and most people used old newspaper, cardboard, or food wrappers as fans or shades for their heads.

All of a sudden, without warning, a gunshot went off in a lower parking lot area of the Superdome. We had been alerted that a diversion of some sort would start everything and as everyone was distracted then the overpowering of the National Guardsmen would occur. Chief Compass immediately ran into the command center and yelled out, "Mr. Mayor, there has been an incident at the Superdome, and we have to leave right now!" Since the elevators were not working, we all ran up twenty-three flights of stairs to the twenty-seventh floor where our rooms were. Everyone moved instinctively as we had no time to think about anything but getting out of danger.

However, this incident was very taxing on our bodies. We had all been under a huge amount of stress, and our bodies were basically running on pure adrenaline. We had gotten very little sleep and were barely eating one decent meal a day since the storm hit. By the time we reached my suite, I was exhausted, had badly twisted my right knee, and was sweating profusely. The summer heat and humidity and this race to the top was all-consuming.

As I sat on the sofa catching my breath and rubbing my swollen knee, Chief Compass gave me the latest on the rebel plan. A National Guard member had been shot in the leg, and there was still a struggle to get the situation under control. We would later learn that the attempted takeover failed as our National Guardsmen and NOPD officers were able to protect each other from being overpowered. The tips we had gotten probably allowed us to save lives and maintain control. We survived our latest threat and lived to fight another day.

Things weren't much better outside the perimeter of the shelters. With the vast majority of police, fire, and EMS occupied with search and rescue, the city was teetering on the fringe of anarchy. All hell was breaking loose simultaneously in many different areas throughout the city. We still had people on rooftops who had been stranded for several days now. They were past furious that helicopters and boats were passing them by and rescuing others. Reports came in that gunshots were being fired near helicopters in flight.

We were also starting to have very serious problems along the elevated interstate. We received reports that those who had drinking water and food up there were being robbed by bandits. We also received reports that a Good Samaritan–type man confiscated a Kentwood truck and was trying to deliver bottled water to those baking on the hot concrete. It was alleged that he was stopped by several gunmen, pulled from the truck, brutally attacked, shot in the head, and coldly pushed over the railing of the overpass into the shadowy floodwaters below. The drinking water in the truck was thoroughly ransacked and emptied as quickly as the attack itself occurred. Everything was now peaking toward mass chaos. It felt like we were witnessing the actual end of our world as we once knew it.

Looting on Canal Street, downtown, and in other dry areas was now much more than just taking food and water for survival purposes. It was basically out of control. Since the vast majority of police officers were rescuing citizens, there were not enough cops in these areas to make a difference. The forty or so cops and recruits from police headquarters who were sent downtown for reinforcements were just not enough.

The word was now out that we didn't have a jail as police were forced to release those caught stealing. The net effect was many of the same people looting over and over again. The police were also so outnumbered that there would be two or three cops together per block, and the next second about twenty to thirty people would run out of a retail store with stolen goods. It was just too much to contain. In a few instances, looters just ran out of a place and punched an officer in the face and kept going. The cops really didn't want to shoot them because most of the citizens were unarmed and mixed in with those who were only searching for food.

Unfortunately, a few police officers were caught on TV cameras taking non-emergency items. However, the vast majority of the activity generally fell into two categories of looters. There were those who were strictly in survival mode and were taking only necessities, such as food, water, and clothes. Then there were the ruthless opportunists who were looking to profit later from this lawlessness.

Mass raids were carried out on grocery stores, drugstores, gas stations, department stores, and even jewelry stores. They took TVs, electronics, bikes, clothes, hats, and mini refrigerators. Anything that could be sold later was carried away to who knows where. One famous TV report showed people breaking into a Wal-Mart store on Tchoupitoulas Street involved in mass piracy. It was like a bizarre retail smorgasbord. Shopping carts were overflowing with stolen booty as they were quickly wheeled out of the store's front doors.

In other dry areas, signs started to appear on boarded-up shop fronts and homes boldly stating, "I have a gun. I will shoot looters!" Some lawless individuals got so cocky that they even started shooting at police officers in an act of definitive defiance with a very direct message not to interfere. The shootings quickly escalated to very frequent, intense encounters. At that time Deputy Chief Riley told me that in his twenty-five years of service he had never heard over the police radio officers calling for more ammunition as they had run out during a particular gun battle. It got so bad that I really didn't think we'd make it through Wednesday night without an Armageddon-like war occurring in the total darkness.

There was one more growing challenge, and that was drugs and drug addicts. Prior to the storm, like most urban cities, drugs flowed in and out of New Orleans and the surrounding metropolitan area in ways that were extremely difficult to slow down. Drug trafficking was secret, sophisticated, and highly organized. This contributed greatly to the city's high murder rate.

When Katrina hit, she effectively put the drug dealers out of business. After a few days, drug addicts were frantically walking around looking for a fix. Soon they started breaking into drugstores looking for anything that could take the edge off. After that supply was exhausted, they started to case out the few hospitals that were still barely operational. We became aware of this hospital threat and sent some of our best officers to protect the doctors, nurses, and patients. Several times the police arrived just in time as a crazed addict was standing inside a hospital nervously pointing a knife or gun at anyone in the room who he thought could get him the drugs his body craved.

At one point on Wednesday, I announced to the media who gathered around the atrium on the fourth floor of the Hyatt daily briefings that looting had escalated to the point that we had no choice but to shift resources from rescue missions. They were also informed that drug addicts had successfully raided most pharmacies. I went on to say that these looters were now focused on hospitals and that we were going to put a stop to it right now.

I had earlier told Chief Compass that I was extremely concerned about how we were going to get through the night. I felt we needed to get very creative. I suggested that he take every police vehicle he could find and instruct officers to drive throughout the dry areas in the city with bright blue strobe lights piercing the darkness. The strategy was to give the appearance that there was a strong police presence everywhere. Of course our officers were dead-tired from several days of nonstop rescue missions, but we really did not have any other choice. This was do-or-die time. And so we redirected most of our resources from rescue operations to try to restore law and order in New Orleans. Thank God it worked that night and several subsequent nights until military reinforcements arrived.

Mind-bogglingly, we were still mostly alone in managing this multidimensional Katrina nightmare. Governor Blanco had not made a return visit and claimed that she never got confirmation that the city had descended into this unruly state. She would also say that she had heard about a "little" looting but didn't hear about shootouts and sniper attacks. However, she also claimed that she was being kept informed with solid information from the Louisiana State Police, the only law enforcement agency that was directly under her control. According to a press report, Governor Blanco said that her state police were in New Orleans working with NOPD and that none of her people could verify these major looting reports.

The facts are her state police left town and headed back to Baton Rouge right after the contraflow evacuations were concluded immediately before Katrina made landfall. So they would not be a very good source for accurate information of conditions in the city. All she had to do was check with her EOC and/or talk to my CAO, Dr. Hatfield who was in Baton Rouge desperately trying to get the governor to comprehend what was happening.

Surprisingly, later that evening in an impromptu press conference from Baton Rouge, Governor Blanco had a 180-degree change of heart on what was really going on in the city. She announced very forcefully that she was going to restore law and order in the city of New Orleans. She was sending troops "who know how to shoot and kill and they will, are more than willing to do so, if necessary. And I expect they will."

Governor Blanco obviously felt the need to try to act like a strong leader, a commander in chief. Sources who were in the OEP at Baton Rouge would later tell us that the governor and her key staff were never really focused on New Orleans. In fact, there were many law enforcement people arriving from all over the country who came to go into the city to help but were not allowed to help us. They even came with their own supplies, guns, and ammunition. Amazingly, these desperately needed law enforcement professionals were secretly assigned to other areas in the state that were not in crisis.

You have to ask yourself why these critical resources would be withheld. The state government also had emergency powers to close schools throughout the state, to commandeer school buses, and to order law enforcement and National Guardsmen to immediately go to New Orleans, and they weren't doing it. The billion-dollar question is why?

I kept hoping and praying that the governor would snap into action. Unfortunately, she never did. Very reliable sources told us that some in her staff kept stressing that she was a female governor. They emphasized that she just couldn't come across as weak and be stereo-typed as an "emotional female." A key staffer would continually affirm, "You need to be assertive and powerful." This all added to her lethar-gic decision making as she moved abruptly and very awkwardly from being her normal self to trying to act outside her comfort zone.

A couple of hours before the governor's macho-woman press con-ference; I received a message from Colonel Ebbert and FEMA that I had a meeting with an army general at the heliport. He was being sent by the president to hopefully take charge of federal and state assets with the expressed mission of accelerating rescue efforts. I was anxious to meet him. I was very hopeful because I knew we desperately needed federal military support as they had more than enough resources to deal with Hurricane Katrina's aftermath.

I also knew that a three-star general's arrival could give us a great opportunity to change the dynamics of what was going on. The cur-rent federal and state people who were in charge just did not have the juice to help us get the resources we needed. So I headed toward the heliport, updated some citizens around the Superdome, and eventu-ally walked up the heliport's administration office as helicopters took off and landed every few minutes.

I walked in and said hello to everyone, a Coast Guard officer, pilots, Colonel Ebbert, Marty, and others. I then sat down and chatted with various people about current challenges and corresponding problem-solving tactics. The general's helicopter was running late, so we all just patiently talked and drank coffee. Then his helicopter landed. The room quieted down in anticipation. What happened next was memo-rable and something that I can still vividly visualize as I write.

It was late in the afternoon on Wednesday when all of a sudden the door swung open and General Russell Honoré strutted into the building. This tall, brown-skinned, confident man marched in with an immediate impression that said he was all business. He had three other military support guys around him. Everybody in the room stood up and either saluted or greeted him with a firm handshake. Someone started to talk to try to break the ice.

The general stood tall and stoic in full army uniform and with a black beret on his head, slightly but perfectly cocked to the side. He slowly and deliberately took his dark eyeglasses from his pocket and put them on in a smooth motion. He then got a pad from one of his assistants and took an ink pen from one his many pockets on his uniform, handling it like it was a mini Samurai sword. In a strong, aggressive tone he barked out, "Alright, goddammit, what's going on? I need a full assessment."

I started the briefing him by giving him a rundown of the past few days, highlighting the ever-evolving crises. I finished up with covering my one-page action plan that I was still carrying around. General Honoré is a very good listener and took copious notes. His assistants also jotted things down just in case he missed something. Once I finished, others were given a chance to give their assessments.

Then the FEMA guys started doing what they do; they shot him a line of bull, and he reacted strongly and without hesitation. He started cussing with his booming voice and said, "Stop the bullshit. Tell me what you can really accomplish. Don't blow smoke up my ass!" They straightened up fast, real fast, and didn't speak again unless he gave them specific permission. I just smiled inside and out and watched as this very skilled brother firmly established himself. It immediately popped in my head that this was a bad man, a modern-day "John Wayne Dude"!

This was definitely a turning point as more people were now fully paying attention and moving with a greater sense of urgency. That's when I knew things were about to change for the better for us. General Honoré's presence and authoritative manner gave us all comfort that federal help had finally arrived and things would move faster.

For example, there was a Coast Guard officer/pilot who had been pacing the floor since I first arrived at the heliport. I turned to him and asked him if he had any concerns that we needed to know about. He opened up and said he had a new crew of pilots and helicopters that were not being maximized as their orders were confusing so they couldn't fly consistent rescue missions as they had previously done. He went on to say, "Somebody needs to give us the orders to go. I have a plan, we've got all these helicopters, and we just need to rescue people."

The officer then very quickly presented a detailed plan to stretch the rules by flying systematically. I looked at General Honoré and nodded, and he instinctively said to the pilot, "Soldier, get out there and do your job and save some more U.S. citizens." The pilot beamed, shouted "Yes sir," saluted, and almost ran through the door to get to his men and their flying machines. As a result, the Coast Guard officers and pilots were once again unbelievable, true heroes as they saved thousands.

The remarkable irony to this episode is that General Honoré really didn't bring a lot of resources or people with him. He mainly brought a can-do attitude that said he meant business. The other reality is that he didn't have a lot of authority at that time. He just assumed some and acted accordingly. In essence, General Honoré had just been given responsibility for coordinating military relief efforts on the Gulf Coast without the military.

He was the second highest ranked African American in the U.S. Army at the time. His military experience was extensive, having served in Korea and Germany among many other places around the world. A native of Louisiana, Honoré is of Creole descent. Born during a hurricane in 1947, it seemed that the general was destined to play a pivotal role in the biggest natural and man-made disaster in U.S. history. Like us, he was sort of on his own, but as we worked together, positive developments started to occur.

Once the meeting ended, General Honoré and I went into a small meeting room for a one-on-one chat. We immediately saw eye-to-eye and communicated well with each other. Over the course of the next few days and weeks we would meet regularly, mostly in the evenings. After a full briefing we'd leave each other to deal with the plethora of issues as they unfolded. We quickly became true partners. He could see how frustrated I was. The two of us would bounce strategies, tactics, and other ideas back and forth on how we could sustain those in the shelters as we continued to wait for evacuation buses to arrive.

Another big challenge we struggled with was the continued rescue of people from other parishes being dropped off at the Superdome and Convention Center. Although we had little to no food and water for our own citizens, we could not in good conscience turn them away. They needed a shelter of last resort, and we did our best to accommodate everyone in need.

Later that day I put in another urgent call to the governor to make sure she was aware of this enormous problem. Once again she offered nothing specific. She tried to convince me that it was probably best that everyone stayed put until the buses arrived. I asked her when she thought the buses would show up. She would only say they would be there soon. Since I was operating on so little sleep and under so much pressure, I lost my Southern gentleman manners for a moment.

I firmly stated to the governor that I really didn't believe she fully shared these problems and that I didn't get from her a real sense of urgency on meaningful solutions. I went on to say it appeared that she believed these problems were only ours to solve. I then point-blank said to her that we were going to make this problem more real for her by allowing our stranded citizens to march across the Crescent City Connection Bridge to Baton Rouge. I reminded her that most of these struggling citizens were Louisiana voters, some from surrounding parishes. I concluded by saying they would be headed to the governor's mansion, so she should make sure she had food and water when they arrived. She very nervously said she did not think that was a good idea. I hung up after emphatically stating that our constituents would be on their way in the morning if rescue buses did not show up.

What the governor didn't know is that General Honoré and I had already discussed this option. We knew citizen in the shelters were openly debating how to best pull this off. Time was not on our side as we were well beyond capacity, almost out of supplies, and the natives were extremely restless. We were running out of solutions. We knew the escape route well as it was the same route Dr. Hatfield's car used to evacuate to set up the city's offsite city hall in Baton Rouge. The general and I discussed ways that we could alert FEMA, who would hopefully drop off food and water by helicopter along the way. We were also hopeful that once this procession started, it would spark the powers that be to ensure that idle buses would pick these citizens up and bring them to a better place.

A march of this sort would also garner a lot of national and international press, and just maybe this wouldn't just be our problem anymore—the governor and president would finally be forced to do the right thing. Everything was in motion. The only way this "Freedom March" would be called off was if buses and supplies arrived by noon tomorrow. Thursday would be day four after Katrina made landfall. This was way past ridiculous.

Meanwhile, Marcia St. Martin had contacted me to update us on the challenges that the Sewerage and Water Board was facing. She had nearly three hundred Sewerage and Water Board personnel on duty during the storm. By Wednesday most had been evacuated by boat to the headquarters downtown and then to the West Bank facility. This facility was dry, had backup power, and was stocked with food, supplies, and equipment.

Marcia later told me that as they crossed the Crescent City Connection Bridge that would take them to the New Orleans plant on the West Bank, they were stopped by the Gretna police. They originally wouldn't allow them access to the West Bank but reluctantly let them through. Once they got settled in, the team started to focus on identifying and repairing major water leaks.

Surprisingly, the team stumbled upon the fact that excess water was being pumped to the city of Gretna as their water-producing system was totally shut down. In years past, the New Orleans Sewerage and Water Board had helped Gretna out when they ran into capacity issues. A couple of years earlier the valve that connected the two cities had been shut off as our water was no longer needed. So it is a great mystery why after Hurricane Katrina hit that this valve was now open and our water was flowing freely. Maybe that's one of the reasons why Gretna police wanted to restrict our employees' movements on the West Bank.

After settling in, Marcia and her husband would later again try to drive into Gretna to find a hotel room and something to eat as they didn't want to stay at the power plant overnight. They were again stopped by the Gretna police, but this time with fully loaded guns and attack dogs. Once again they were interrogated. We would later find out that this was now the practice to try to prevent people from taking the only exit route out of the city in order to protect Gretna property.

Much later that night I returned to the Hyatt exhausted, hungry, thirsty, hot, and sticky. I reflected on my telephone conversation with the governor and felt in my gut that it was very unlikely that she would deliver buses and supplies tomorrow. By this stage I was way past just blindly believing these types of promises. I went up to my very hot hotel room that did not have an open window to relax and check on Fishy. I was amazed that he was still alive in that small fishbowl that was now looking pretty funky. I changed out a third of his water, cleaned his tank a bit, and fed him some fish food by flashlight. Fishy seemed happy to see me and was now content with the fresh water. I was still quite taken aback that this little fish was surviving the heat of the day when the room temperature was well over a hundred degrees. After doing a little research later, I would learn that this species of fish actually thrives in the wild in very warm, shallow ponds.

Fishy's bowl was in the bathroom on the counter near the sink. After I finished taking care of him, I looked over at the shower that no longer worked. I would have loved a nice shower right about then, even a very cold one. That would make me feel somewhat normal. Because water and power were out, we had to resort to taking military-style baths. This consisted of filling a small bowl with water from the tub or toilet, and with a small hand towel I'd wet it in the bowl, lather up with soap, and wash off buck-naked. To rinse off I would use the same towel dipped in the bowl until all the water was just about sopped up. From there I would use a different towel to dry off water and any soap residue. After a little deodorant under the arms, I would be a bit refreshed and ready to face another day or night.

Over the past few days, the Hyatt had gotten pretty nasty just like the Superdome but on a smaller scale. You could not find a working toilet that wasn't all stuffed up. Some were forced to relieve themselves in the stairwells. We had to really watch where we walked when we went up and down the stairs.

What was surprising to all of us was how quickly we adjusted to these conditions. I quickly became accustomed to eating maybe one meal per day and taking military baths. I also adjusted to the intense heat and not having air-conditioning. Severe sweating became the norm. We basically went to sleep sweating, we woke up sweating, and we sweated throughout the day. I got used to peeling off all my clothes to get down to just my underwear for sleeping at night. The best I could do was maybe two to three hours per night on a sweat-drenched sheet. This really put things in perspective and made you appreciate what was really important. Luxuries just didn't matter anymore. It was survival of the fittest with very few resources.

After leaving Fishy, I moved over to the hotel window to look out at my city. Below me with the help of the moonlit sky I could see my poor citizens near the Superdome. Just about all of them were still in the same place they had been in all day because they were scared to lose their spot so they could have a good shot at a seat on a bus that would take them to a better place. Not far from me out in the distance, I could hear periodic gunshots from the pitch-black streets. It all was so surreal, as though we were somehow cursed to endure this fate.

I was still totally flabbergasted that by day three our federal and state governments had not pulled out all the stops to come and help us. When the tsunami hit in 2004, it took our American government only two days to deploy ship and troops around the world to help people from other countries in their time of extreme need. Did we not deserve a similar response? Why were leaders at higher levels of government not here with us, fasting and sweating like we were until the buses arrived?

Then it really hit me how very different the nighttime was. It was more eerie and uncertain. All streetlights were out. There were no lights in any homes or buildings. As the Bible says, "Darkness covered everything." On this night, somehow through the blackness, in the distance, I could see the flashing blue lights from the tops of police cars dancing through the streets like blinking Christmas lights. I watched them dance until I fell asleep around three or four a.m.

Before dozing off, I reflected on the day's critical events. We had somehow miraculously managed to put creative actions in motion that had gotten us through the day and were now getting us through a night that I'd worried about all day long. Today also felt like a major breakthrough with General Honoré's arrival. And now our amazing police force's blue light show was working to suppress stressed-out bad guys. We were positioned to see another tomorrow. It was now just a matter of time. As I laid my head down for hopefully two to three hours of sweaty nap, I felt with refreshed confidence that we would face tomorrow with unyielding determination to figure out more creative ways to survive yet another day.

CHAPTER SEVEN

RADIO CUSS OUT

—◼—

Between the extreme heat in my room, my mind racing with problem-solving thoughts, and the discomfort of sleeping in sweaty, wet sheets, I may have gotten three hours of sleep overnight. As I slowly opened my eyes that early Thursday morning, I stared up at the dark ceiling. My opening thought was thank God we had managed to make it through another night. Although the sun had not yet risen, it was undeniably daybreak for me.

I suddenly realized I had just gotten my normal amount of sleep since Hurricane Katrina first hit. It's probably not accurate to call this real sleep; it was more like mild rest with my eyes closed. My body was just so exhausted that I would intermittently fall into a mini coma of sorts only to wake up suddenly with a lightning jolt back to reality. As I peeled myself off sweat-soaked sheets that were poorly draped over the mattress, I slowly made my way over to the window.

A warm glow came over me as I looked out. Just like before I got in bed, there they were, the blue lights from the police cars piercing the darkness, still patrolling the streets. My eyes followed these movements on the horizon to the ledge below, where also like yesterday thousands of people congregated, still waiting for buses to arrive outside the Superdome. The warm glow I had immediately faded as I shook my head in disgust. I thought out loud, "Those damn buses better arrive today." I was absolutely sure my citizens could not take much more of this torture.

I stepped back from the window and checked my BlackBerry. Just like clockwork, a number of PINs, e-mails, and voice messages had come in on their normal early morning shift. I brushed my teeth, washed my face, pulled on a mildly dirty T-shirt and a pair of slacks, and ventured downstairs to the fourth-floor conference room.

Power was now completely out at city hall. And although it took Colonel Terry Ebbert and the EOC staff a few days to transfer over to the Hyatt, they had finally moved in and were finalizing setting up operations. Colonel Ebbert and Greg Meffert were working together trying to figure out how to complete the setup in the Hyatt ballroom to accommodate our command center that was growing in size. Some people who worked during the 9/11 crisis in New York had helicoptered in and were assisting in setting up this very complicated operations center. They had pretty much taken over the entire main ballroom with a number of key functions already operational. Regular daily briefings were already in process.

Unfortunately, conditions inside and around our shelters had continued to deteriorate. I received word from the National Guard and NOPD that suffering in the Superdome and Convention Center was certifiably intolerable. Pressure continued to build for evacuating these buildings, and incidents of violence were constant.

There were now some estimates that the Superdome and Convention Center collectively contained sixty thousand people. We were also still accepting rescued people from neighboring parishes who were continuously being dropped off on our doorsteps. The areas around both buildings were jam-packed with anxious, increasingly angry people. Federal and state rescue and support efforts were still pathetically slow; most of the time they seemed to be virtually nonexistent. It was as if the powers above us had decided to let us wallow in this tormented state, as if we were in a quarantined city that had an outbreak of some rare disease.

Another troubled area was our hospitals. These facilities were primarily being run by very brave, super-dedicated nurses as many doctors had evacuated. These nurses, on the other hand, were the backbone for hospitals that had no power, and most were flooded. More often than not, they singlehandedly moved patients from lower floors when floodwaters first reached downtown and carried them up several flights of stairs to where it was dry. They nursed the sick with no help from modern technology as electrical power had been out for days. Death surrounded them like a suffocating fog, with no sign of lifting. Threats of attacks by looters and drug addicts trying to steal what little medicine they had left was a constant fear and struggle, which further elevated this nightmarish experience.

Charity Hospital, also located in downtown New Orleans, was reportedly under sniper fire. Rescue operations to evacuate their sick patients were suspended several times as police scrambled to secure the area. Doctors, nurses, and other support personnel there were all scared, exhausted, and totally overwhelmed. Somehow they all found the strength to continue to do their jobs under these extremely hostile conditions.

Frustration levels continued to escalate for all, climbing higher and higher as the days passed. I was almost to the point of blowing my top, intensely livid. Meaningful help had still not arrived, just more broken promises. To make matters worse, the governor advised the media that buses had taken New Orleanians to a "refugee camp" in Houston, Texas, at the Astrodome. This was puzzling since we had not seen any buses since the storm hit other than a few that came to evacuate special needs patients and critically sick people in select hospitals. Not one bus had arrived at the Superdome or Convention Center to start evacuating sixty thousand physically and mentally exhausted people.

What was really going on behind the scenes? When State Senator Cleo Fields started his evacuation bus runs Tuesday, he called the State Department of Social Services before arriving in Baton Rouge so that they could direct him to a shelter in the area. But by Wednesday after only a couple of rescue missions he received a very clear signal that nobody in the state really wanted to help.

Senator Fields called as he was en route to Baton Rouge and asked which shelters were available. Wednesday the responses were,

"We'll get back to you," and they stopped answering their phones. Finally, someone called and told the senator to drive his buses full of evacuees to Houston, Texas, a six-hour ride one way. This would severely slow down the number of people they could rescue. If fact, Cleo believes they were really trying to put them out of the rescue business. As his bus caravans arrived in Baton Rouge, they were immediately stopped by Louisiana State Police and told they couldn't stop there.

The state also tried to make the case that all their shelters were full. This was preposterous, as Senator Fields had made very few trips to New Orleans. The number of people in his buses was just not that significant at this point. This also made no sense from the perspective that the governor under the current state of emergency had the power to open other shelters to accommodate these evacuees. But instead Cleo and Ben were repeatedly told that there was nowhere else in Baton Rouge or in the state to take homeless Louisianans, period. Next, they were told that the people they picked up were now their responsibility. It was now up to Cleo and Ben to be totally responsible for and take care of everyone on their buses, not the state.

Another irony is that most people on theses buses didn't really need to stay in a state-run shelter. They just needed to get out of New Orleans so that they could clean up a bit, get a quick bite to eat, and make a phone call to a friend or relative who would come to pick them up. Most were very capable of taking care of themselves after receiving a little assistance.

The other heartbreaking aspect of this episode was that all of these vile rejections happened right in front of the people on the buses. They heard the conversations that Cleo and Ben were having with state officials. These buses didn't contain looters; they were working people who were black, white, young, and old. The group was peaceful and basically did everything Cleo and Ben asked them to do. This was extremely heart-wrenching because they could see officials and law enforcement officers, people with authority emphatically saying that they didn't want them and couldn't care less that they had greatly suffered.

What we later concluded was that during this catastrophic disaster, the governor allowed many local government officials to decide what shelters they would open and whom they would accept. Therefore, some very conservative officials pushed back on the state, claiming that they didn't have any more room to accept "those" people from New Orleans. The additional capacity was there, but the will to be compassionate was blocked by hardened hearts.

Back at the ever-growing EOC in the Hyatt ballroom, my instincts were on red alert that we needed to get more truth out to the public. The media was reporting everything, including what the governor and others were misrepresenting. Most of the press knew we were definitely not okay—far from it. We also didn't have time to waste. Every hour was critical in saving lives.

Because communication channels were very inconsistent, we started utilizing creative text messages. Sally Forman was a BlackBerry fanatic and had been consistently sending out e-mails and texts updates. Unfortunately, she was not getting any responses. We concluded that the problem was they probably did not recognize her name and therefore blew her messages off. So we decided to send very succinct messages with my name attached to it. We devised a plan to send out SOS text messages that were powerful and concise. These messages were designed to get immediate, broad-based attention.

The first set of SOS messages that were sent out were about the Convention Center. Supplies there were definitely an issue, and we didn't know how much longer we could contain the growing unrest. Every hour it seemed that Chief Compass had another report on attacks. His most shocking claim was that several police officers were beaten back by an angry mob at the Convention Center earlier that morning.

I drafted the first message, and we all agreed on the final wording. Then Sally and Tami released it widely. Tami, our press secretary, was now safely in Houston and really helped to give this message wings. Limited to the number of words we could use in the text message, it read as follows:

This is a desperate SOS. Right now we are out of resources at the Convention Center and don't anticipate enough buses. We need buses. Currently the Convention Center is unsanitary and unsafe, and we're running out of supplies.

This worked beautifully. It was picked up and spread like wildfire. The national media ran with it, and by that afternoon, it was headlined on major newspapers and in newsrooms across the country.

Returning to my somewhat chaotic routine, I then left the Hyatt for my regular midmorning helicopter inspection flight. With the recent turn of events and the volatile nature of the situation at the Superdome, we realized it just wasn't safe to walk through the Superdome anymore to get to the heliport. Still fresh on all of our minds was the recent failed attempted plot to overpower the National Guard the day before. Wondell went about working out an alternative route in Big Daddy.

As we were walking through the shopping center of the Hyatt hotel to get to the truck, I noticed that a black puppy, a little pug, was following me. He had lost his owner. There was something in this dog's manner that touched me, and I bent down to pick her up. Cradled in my arms, I petted this dog, carrying it part of the way to the truck. I actually contemplated keeping her, but Fishy was about all I could handle in the pet department at this stage.

I realized at that moment how much of an emotional shield I had been wearing over the last few days just so that I could function and carry out my duties. If I could, I would have taken everyone and all the needy pets in, but we didn't have enough resources to accommodate them all. Over the course of the week, some tried to give me sick babies, elderly mothers, or crippled fathers. In essence, they really wanted me to take their pain, worries, and burdens. These images have never left me and sometimes haunt me now in my dreams.

Meanwhile, the little black dog made her way all the way to the heliport. One of the guys there started feeding her, so she hung around and soon became the friendly heliport dog. I petted and hugged this pup just about every day. The general manager of the heliport actually ended up adopting her. I saw him recently and he said to me, "You remember that little dog? Well, I adopted her, and she has been one of the best pets I've ever had." She turned out to be a nice Katrina rainbow on four legs.

Once we got into the truck, Wondell maneuvered Big Daddy around the barricades and the outside perimeter of the Superdome like a master at work, avoiding people and temporary tents that the National Guard and Coast Guard had set up. When we reached the heliport, I noticed that Marty and the other FEMA representatives who came to the city after the storm made landfall, were in the process of leaving. You would think that with the state of affairs that New Orleans was in, it wouldn't be a good time to remove FEMA officials whose mission was to effectively manage this disaster. However, the recent failed plot to overpower the National Guard at the Superdome the day before had caused FEMA to lose its collective nerve. The retreat order was for them to go to Baton Rouge, the state capital, about seventy-five miles northwest of New Orleans.

Michael Brown also told CNN that day that he had just found out about these dire situations, and based on this "new" information he had now authorized more supplies and resources to be sent our way. This was his day for revelation and order. He conveniently left out the fact that he had also just ordered his staff to abandon the city. By sending all FEMA representatives to Baton Rouge, they lost all connection with the city, severely weakening their ability to make good on any of these new promises.

As I flew above the city that day, I noticed the water was still getting higher. It was still shocking to see the number of dead bodies that were floating in this filthy water, some face up others face down. Roofs continued to be littered with many weary citizens still frantically waving for help. There were many on rooftops in Gentilly, New Orleans

East, and the Ninth Ward. In contrast, I noticed the roofs around the Seventeenth Street Canal were all clear.

The bottom line was that the lake had not managed to level out yet with floodwater in the city. That critical equilibrium had not yet been achieved. We really needed the breach at the Seventeenth Street Canal to be fixed so that the flow of water would stop. The threat of water continuing to rise and take over more dry areas was still a real and present danger.

From the air I inspected all the canals and breaches and noted there was still no work underway. There were no steel bars bridging the gaps as reported by the feds. I did not see a single sandbag being placed to plug the huge open hole that was at least three hundred feet wide at the Seventeenth Street Canal. It was again infuriating and frustrating, as FEMA and the Army Corps of Engineers had been claiming that they had been working on this for days now. Until these breaches were fixed, our hands were tied and we couldn't start draining the city.

This reminded me of the latest Hoey's Cut update that I had just gotten from Marcia St. Martin, who ran our Sewerage and Water Board operation. She told me Jefferson Parish officials had secretly set up temporary pumps with pipes draped over the Seventeenth Street Canal and were pumping floodwater from their side into the breached canal, which further flooded New Orleans. Marcia had confirmed these unthinkable acts firsthand and per my directive had taken pictures to document this injustice. As she was taking those pictures, one of their sheriff's patrol cars was hidden nearby and surprised Marcia and her husband by demanding they leave this public land. I still cannot understand how these elected leaders could authorize such an uncivilized plan that was so detrimental to their neighbors. We immediately alerted the Army Corps of Engineers, who wrote a very stern letter to Parish President Broussard ordering them to cease and desist.

Back at the Hyatt, I ran into Ron Forman, the head of the Audubon Nature Institute which managed the zoo and aquarium. Ron had been bunkering down with us in the hotel for the last few days. He is also the husband of my communications director, Sally Forman. It was good to see him again because after the storm his visibility was fairly intermittent. He was very focused and as concerned with saving animals as I was with saving human lives.

He reported that the aquarium, which is situated at the end of Canal Street downtown and next to the Mississippi River, was now on the verge of total shutdown. Floodwater that was in the streets was slowly heading towards this building. They also had a poorly designed aquarium system that provided filtering and aeration in the various fish tanks. This antiquated system used a lot of electrical power and massive amounts of fresh water. Unfortunately, we didn't have much of either. They had already lost over a thousand very expensive fish, and their backup generators were starting to shut down due to a lack of maintenance and fuel.

Ron had managed to convince a few police officers to help out at the aquarium, protecting the mammals and fish from potential looters and angry rioters. Many of these officers were also helping out with feeding the fish once per day, trying to keep the remaining ones alive. Ron had also somehow arranged for evacuations for the largest fish and mammals. If I ever find out these fish left on modified FEMA buses, I will go to DC and chain myself to FEMA headquarters in protest.

Audubon Zoo, on the other hand, was located uptown near the Mississippi River mostly on very high, dry land. Luckily, there was no significant damage, and it seemed to be functioning fairly unscathed. Prior to Katrina's landfall, Ron and his staff had a plan in place to euthanize predatory animals with tranquilizer guns if they were seriously injured or showed any signs of possible escape. The last thing the city needed was for lions and tigers to roam freely among our already frightened citizens.

Luckily, the storm had been very kind to the animals at the zoo. A few trees had come down right next to some elephants and rhinos, but no animals at the zoo were seriously harmed. Ron claimed to have heard threats from certain devious people wanting to set the zoo on fire and release animals into the city to create more chaos. So he was desperately trying to secure armed security. He was also packing his own gun since he was riding around solo going back and forth between the two facilities.

The days just seemed to be jam-packed with nuclear-type crisis management challenges. From one area to another there were major issues that needed to be dealt with immediately. Even with the little sleep that I was getting each night, there just weren't enough hours in the day for this type of record-setting disaster.

As I reentered the command center, I noticed that Chief Compass was clearly shaken up. Over the last few days, Chief Compass had been making claims about horrific attacks that were panning out throughout the city. He reported many women were getting raped, innocent tourists were being preyed upon, and gangs engaged in frequent shootouts with police. Now the chief was telling me he had been nearly kidnapped at the Convention Center. He went on to say an angry, hungry crowd of people surrounded him and tried to take him hostage, but he managed to break free. It was never confirmed from officers who were with him that this group was trying to take him hostage. Lack of sleep and major stress was secretly starting to take its toll on my friend, our chief. I strongly suggested to him that he go get some much-needed rest. He promised he would.

Needing to clear my head of all this madness, I made my way up to my hotel suite on the twenty-seventh floor. Terry Davis, my communications specialist, was with me along with my executive protection team. As we discussed the many unfolding events along with Chief Compass's reports, we all tried to guess what could happen next. I moved over to the windows that gave a panoramic view of the Superdome, expressway, and part of downtown. As we looked down, I noticed the crowd on the ledge below was significantly larger than usual. I could see and feel their collective anger as they of one accord started to push hard against the barricades around the Superdome. They were fed up, hot, and determined to be set free from their misery. The National Guardsmen who were patrolling the barricades had called for reinforcements, and most had a look of extreme alarm. They knew we were greatly outnumbered, and if this crowd really wanted to they could easily overrun the barricades, which would start a new, much more dangerous riot-type crisis.

The sun was at its zenith, and the temperature was sweltering like an industrial oven on full blast. It was just another incredibly hot, humid, New Orleans summer day. The sun had been beating on the people for days now who had been waiting outside fully exposed. They indeed looked like they had reached the boiling point and were ready to explode. It was quite evident that whatever control we thought we had was about to be fully tested. My heart was beating so fast and so strong that it sounded like it was outside my body. I motioned to Wondell to quickly make sure Chief Compass and Deputy Chief Riley were aware of what was transpiring.

Just the day before we had gang members who were among this same crowd trying to figure out how to take guns away from the National Guard. The people around the Superdome had heard many times that buses were on their way and had been patiently waiting amidst the harshest of conditions. The difference this time was that instead of a small group trying to take matters into their own hands, it now seemed like the entire Superdome, all thirty thousand people, were united in their push for freedom.

After fully comprehending what I was seeing outside this window, I turned to Terry and said, "We could be in big trouble. This thing looks like it is going to blow, and it will take a miracle for us to hold it together any longer." To make matters worse, most of our police force was already dispersed throughout the city trying to reclaim order. Other officers were sleeping in their cars, on the floor of the fourth floor at the Hyatt, or anywhere else they could find a dry place to rest their heads. They were almost totally exhausted, both physically and mentally.

I remember thinking that things just couldn't end this way. We needed a special blessing to stop this riot from happening. Thankfully within a few minutes, God answered our prayers. Miraculously, as if taking a heavenly cue, out of nowhere a dark cloud moved over the Superdome. Before I could close my mouth in amazement, cool rain started to fall lightly over the crowd. If Terry hadn't been next to me to confirm what was happening, I don't think I would have believed what I was actually seeing. It was like something you'd read in the Bible or see in the *Ten Commandments* movie. It was unbelievable, but reassuring. It wasn't a big thunderstorm with lightning and thunder but just a light, steady rain that was quietly saying, "Peace, be still." This amazing cloud of grace only appeared over the Superdome area, nowhere else in the city. All I could do was look in amazement and say out loud, "Lord, have mercy."

The rain shower lasted long enough to wet everything around the Superdome, cool the people and their tempers off, and allow us to exhale again. We could now see steam coming off the pavement. It was a different kind of a cleansing. It cleansed some negativity for the moment. The people stopped pushing on the barricades, and some even went back inside the Superdome. And once again we lived to fight for survival another day. Halleluiah!

Within the hour we received reports that buses that were meant for New Orleans were stopped outside the city, and we couldn't confirm why. Whether this was because the drivers were rescuing others, were afraid of looters, or water was blocking their path didn't really matter now since the urgency of evacuating people out of the city was way past critical. Maybe of these were the same buses that Governor Blanco in her hourly press conferences had been claiming had been in New Orleans for several days now. We later learned that other areas in the suburbs outside the city had indeed been receiving buses and managed to evacuate most of their people out. But New Orleans didn't have the same priority as they had.

Later that day the situation at the Convention Center seem to mimic the near riot we had at the Superdome. Supplies had nearly all but run out, angry mobs roamed freely, and others were frustrated and extremely restless. True to my word, I asked General Honoré if he could approach leaders at the Convention Center to confirm interest in a possible walkout across the Crescent City Connection, a bridge over the Mississippi River that linked New Orleans to dry land in Gretna on the West Bank. If all went well, the people could walk over it and board buses that had been idle for days in the suburbs. He and his men spoke to a number of people who had proposed this type of protest march a day or two earlier. They completely agreed that if the negative energy around them was not channeled differently, then all hell would break loose. The leaders decided to move forward, organized themselves, and started the procession.

There were many willing participants, and it wasn't long before the police assisted a very large group of nearly a thousand people towards the bridge. The initial group was made up of men, women, children, elderly, and people in wheelchairs and on crutches. So they took their time climbing the bridge's slope. It was a mixed crowd with the majority being African Americans.

As they finally reached the other side of the bridge, they were met by an array of cars with Gretna and Jefferson Parish police decals on the side. The sheriff and an intimidating lineup of armed police with shotguns and attack dogs stood in combat position. These so-called protectors of the public shouted profanity-laced warnings at the group, demanding they not come any closer as multiple shots were fired right above their heads.

This perverted welcome wagon further threatened that they would shoot to kill if the group didn't turn around immediately and walk back across the bridge. The people just stood there in disbelief, some angry, others scared and confused. A few brave ones spoke up and tried to explain the dire situation of lack of food and water at the Convention Center and that they were just trying to get to the buses to take them to safety. The Gretna police held their ground and shouted back, "Gretna won't be another New Orleans Superdome. Turn around and f@#king go back now," as they fired more rounds in their direction.

As if totally defeated, the crowd slowly turned around and headed back over the bridge to the Convention Center. Most were flabbergasted, in a further state of shock, stunned and heads hanging down as the humiliation was just too much to bear. It didn't take long for the story to spread back at the Convention Center, and tempers flared to the boiling point once more.

It didn't seem to matter that the Gretna and Jefferson Parish police officers had no legal authority to turn our folks around. The route across the bridge and where they were stopped is on the federal highway system. The marchers were not on Gretna streets, and the procession would have continued high above on an elevated federal expressway. Several lawsuits have been filed on this gross injustice. One was filed by former State Senator Cleo Fields, who rescued hundreds of people in New Orleans with his own buses.

When word got back to me about these attacks, it really hurt me deeply and took whatever wind I had left in my sail. I had to sit down for a minute just to register my disbelief in the human cruelty displayed by a neighboring community in such a time.

Since the storm hit, we had been accepting people from many different parishes at the Superdome and Convention Center even when our food and water supplies were running low. It never entered my mind that citizens in desperate need would be turned away by our so-called neighbors strictly based on their zip code or the color of their skin. After all, this was 2005 in America. Everyone who crossed that bridge that day was an American walking on a federal highway. I wondered out loud, "What is wrong with this picture?" Someone in the room responded and said, "Mr. Mayor, don't forget you are in the Deep South, and the only thing more south of New Orleans is the Gulf of Mexico." Wow, unfortunately they were right based upon what had just happened.

Many months later, Mayor Ronnie Harris of Gretna tried to justify the blockade and attacks by claiming that they were in no position to take in more people even though Gretna was not the marchers' final destination. Then he tried to say that it was New Orleans police officers at the foot of the bridge firing at people to make them go back. After the initial tales did not stand up to criticism, he later explained that their city had been isolated, cut off by the storm, and they were concerned about food and water for their own citizens. He also made claims that he'd seen the news reports of the looting and attacks on police in New Orleans and was embarrassed for our city. He just didn't want that to happen to the people of Gretna. He went on to say it was the police chief's decision to secure and protect the city, which he had fully supported.

It was revealed many months later that the march had been spoiled all along by a secret arrangement between the state and Gretna officials. As I mentioned, I'd had a tough conversation with the governor just the night before and informed her that citizens stuck in the Convention Center could start marching toward her mansion in Baton Rouge if she did not get rescue buses to us the next morning. Reliable sources told us—and this also came out in a related lawsuit—that someone at the highest level in the governor's "kitchen cabinet" had quietly snuck into Gretna either late Wednesday night or early Thursday morning and tipped off the officials about the walkout. Mayor Harris is a longtime friend of the Blancos and had graduated from the college in Louisiana where "Coach" coached. The governor also appointed him to the Louisiana Board of Commerce and Industry. When the marchers arrived at the foot of the bridge, Gretna's Police Chief Arthur Lawson Jr. and gang were forewarned, well prepared, and organized, having been waiting for hours for these poor, suffering people to arrive.

The Gretna experience combined with the lack of response from the state and federal government during these early days raised many questions that lingered for many months, even years after the event. Was this all race-related? Were we not getting the required response, the supplies, or help because we were a majority African American city? Was it more of a class issue than race, or a combination of the two?

Before the storm, 67 percent of the population of New Orleans was black. Nearly one-third lived at or below the official poverty line. One of the claims by the Gretna officials for denying access to their city was because they feared looting. But what made them view all of these struggling victims/survivors as potential criminals? Why were their physical assets more important than helping their fellow man, woman, and child?

What people like Mayor Harris failed to realize was that the people caught up in the aftermath of Katrina were victims of failed federally built levees, regardless of their race or class. To really tug at people's heartstrings, the media did an effective job of projecting images of primarily poor black people trapped in New Orleans. The real truth was Hurricane Katrina affected every single citizen in the city regardless of race, class, or gender.

Governor Blanco would once again stir the pot of indifference when she used the term "refugee camp" to describe another shelter in Texas. The media quickly picked up this demeaning term and started to consistently refer to New Orleanians as "refugees." Most use this term in the context of a foreigner who is seeking asylum in another country. New Orleanians are proud Americans and took great offense to this terminology. Being called a refugee in your own country was very insulting.

When President Bush made his first ground tour of New Orleans, he was struggling mightily with what was now a public relations mega nightmare. There was one point some ten days after Katrina had ravaged the city that he was asked by CNN whether the lack of federal response was due to racial bias. Bush responded, "My attitude is this. The storm didn't discriminate, and neither will the recovery effort." For many of us who were living the tepid federal response, this statement was a hard pill to swallow. Either it was race, class, or partisan politics. Pick one as there was some sort of discrimination happening.

I still believe that if this would have happened in Orange Country, California, or South Beach, Florida, there would have been a completely different response by our federal government. This was vividly confirmed in 2007 when massive fires burned through San Diego, California. FEMA responded immediately by establishing five-star quality shelters for those who were homeless. Not a single person was called a refugee. The shelters were relatively calm as displaced citizens entered a sanitary, welcoming environment. They were well provided for with a wide array of food to choose from, no MREs. There was even expensive makeshift play areas already set up for the children. Mothers were provided free diapers, formula, and baby wipes. To keep these individuals relaxed and comfortable, they had the option to receive a massage, acupuncture, or join a yoga or meditation class all paid for by Uncle Sam. The government even brought in live bands that provided musical performances to keep the people relaxed and entertained.

The demographics were completely difference in San Diego, and this was a complete polar opposite federal response than what happened in New Orleans. The popular rap artist Kanye West blurted out in frustration to reporters as he watched Katrina unfold, "President Bush don't like black people."

It was now late afternoon on Thursday, and as I sat at the table in my hotel suite, Terry, Sally, and my executive protection team were positioned throughout the room at various workstations. We were all still dumbfounded over the latest incident at the Gretna city line. I cranked up and turned on my windup radio so we could listen to the latest reports that were making the airwaves. Once again, the governor was leading a press conference reiterating that there were no real serious problems down here. She further stated that things were totally under control and they were doing everything in their power to further stabilize the city. Our two U.S. senators also took their turn to pontificate about how well things were going. Then one of them said the people at the Convention Center and the Superdome were all being treated well. At that point my face turned red and I fumed. I jumped up out of my seat and said, "I've had it with this bullshit. I'm calling in to set the record straight once and for all."

Terry and I tried to get through to the radio station but had trouble making the connection. We seemed to get the first few digits, and then the system would miss the last. The phone lines were spotty, and we tried various cell phones with no luck. We moved to a landline. We finally got a dial tone only for it to drop out halfway through the dialing. Then Terry managed to get a good line out in Wondell's adjourning room and we were connected. Garland Robinette, a top rated talk radio announcer for WWL radio, was just as surprised as we were that we got through. He asked me to hold on the line, and in less than ten seconds I was on the air broadcasting live to most of the country. Listed below is the transcript of that now famous conversation. It ended up being much bigger than any SOS message we could have ever sent out and ultimately ended up being played around the entire world.

> **NAGIN:** *I told him we had an incredible crisis here and that his flying over in Air Force One does not do it justice. And that I have been all around this city, and I am very frustrated because we are not able to marshal resources and we're outmanned in just about every respect.*
>
> *You know the reason why the looters got out of control? Because we had most of our resources saving people, thousands of people that were stuck in attics, man, old ladies. ... You pull off the doggone ventilator vent and you look down there and they're standing in there in water up to their freaking necks.*
>
> *And they don't have a clue what's going on down here. They flew down here one time two days after the doggone event was over with TV cameras, AP reporters, all kind of goddamn—excuse my French everybody in America, but I am pissed.*
>
> **WWL:** *Did you say to the president of the United States, "I need the military in here"?*
>
> **NAGIN:** *I said, "I need everything."*
>
> *Now, I will tell you this—and I give the president some credit on this—he sent one John Wayne dude down here that can get some stuff done, and his name is [Lt.] Gen. [Russell] Honoré.*

And he came off the doggone chopper, and he started cussing and people started moving. And he's getting some stuff done.

They ought to give that guy—if they don't want to give it to me—give him full authority to get the job done, and we can save some people.

WWL: *What do you need right now to get control of this situation?*

NAGIN: *I need reinforcements, I need troops, man. I need five hundred buses, man. We ain't talking about—you know, one of the briefings we had, they were talking about getting public school bus drivers to come down here and bus people out of here.*

I'm like, "You got to be kidding me. This is a national disaster. Get every doggone Greyhound bus line in the country and get their asses moving to New Orleans."

That's—they're thinking small, man. And this is a major, major, major deal. And I can't emphasize it enough, man. This is crazy.

I've got fifteen thousand to twenty thousand people over at the Convention Center. It's bursting at the seams. The poor people in Plaquemines Parish. … We don't have anything, and we're sharing with our brothers in Plaquemines Parish.

It's awful down here, man.

WWL: *Do you believe that the president is seeing this, holding a news conference on it but can't do anything until [Louisiana Gov.] Kathleen Blanco requested him to do it? And do you know whether or not she has made that request?*

NAGIN: *I have no idea what they're doing. But I will tell you this: You know, God is looking down on all this, and if they are not doing everything in their power to save people, they are going to pay the price. Because every day that we delay, people are dying and they're dying by the hundreds, I'm willing to bet you.*

We're getting reports and calls that are breaking my heart, from people saying, "I've been in my attic. I can't take it anymore. The water is up to my neck. I don't think I can hold out." And that's happening as we speak.

You know what really upsets me, Garland? We told everybody the importance of the Seventeenth Street Canal issue. We said, "Please, please take care of this. We don't care what you do. Figure it out."

WWL: *Who'd you say that to?*

NAGIN: *Everybody: the governor, Homeland Security, FEMA. You name it, we said it.*

And they allowed that pumping station next to Pumping Station 6 to go under water. Our Sewerage and Water Board people…stayed there and endangered their lives.

And what happened when that pumping station went down? The water started flowing again in the city, and it starting getting to levels that probably killed more people.

In addition to that, we had water flowing through the pipes in the city. That's a power station over there.

So there's no water flowing anywhere on the east bank of Orleans Parish. So our critical water supply was destroyed because of lack of action.

WWL: *Why couldn't they drop the three-thousand-pound sandbags or the containers that they were talking about earlier? Was it an engineering feat that just couldn't be done?*

NAGIN: *They said it was some pulleys that they had to manufacture. But, you know, in a state of emergency, man, you are creative, you figure out ways to get stuff done.*

Then they told me that they went overnight, and they built seventeen concrete structures and they had the pulleys on them and they were going to drop them.

I flew over that thing yesterday, and it's in the same shape that it was after the storm hit. There is nothing happening. And they're feeding the public a line of bull and they're spinning, and people are dying down here.

WWL: *If some of the public called and they're right, that there's a law that the president, that the federal government can't do anything without local or state requests, would you request martial law?*

NAGIN: *I've already called for martial law in the city of New Orleans. We did that a few days ago.*

WWL: *Did the governor do that, too?*

NAGIN: *I don't know. I don't think so.*

But we called for martial law when we realized that the looting was getting out of control. And we redirected all of our police officers back to patrolling the streets. They were dead-tired from saving people, but they worked all night because we thought this thing was going to blow wide open last night. And so we redirected all of our resources, and we held it under check.

I'm not sure if we can do that another night with the current resources.

And I am telling you right now, they're showing all these reports of people looting and doing all that weird stuff, and they are doing that, but people are desperate and they're trying to find food and water, the majority of them.

Now you got some knuckleheads out there, and they are taking advantage of this lawless—this situation where, you know, we can't really control it, and they're doing some awful, awful things. But that's a small minority of the people. Most people are looking to try and survive.

And one of the things people—nobody's talked about this. Drugs flowed in and out of New Orleans and the surrounding metropolitan area so freely it was scary to me, and that's why we were having the escalation in murders. People don't want to talk about this, but I'm going to talk about it.

You have drug addicts that are now walking around this city looking for a fix, and that's the reason why they were breaking in hospitals and drugstores. They're looking for something to take the edge off of their jones, if you will.

And right now, they don't have anything to take the edge off. And they've probably found guns. So what you're seeing is drug-starving crazy addicts, drug addicts, that are wreaking havoc. And we don't have the manpower to adequately deal with it. We can only target certain sections of the city and form a perimeter around them and hope to God that we're not overrun.

WWL: *Well, you and I must be in the minority. Because apparently there's a section of our citizenry out there that thinks because of a law that says the federal government can't come in unless requested by the proper people, that everything that's going on to this point has been done as good as it can possibly be.*

NAGIN: *Really?*

WWL: *I know you don't feel that way.*

NAGIN: *Well, did the tsunami victims request? Did it go through a formal process to request?*

You know, did the Iraqi people request that we go in there? Did they ask us to go in there? What is more important?

And I'll tell you, man, I'm probably going get in a whole bunch of trouble. I'm probably going to get in so much trouble it ain't even funny. You probably won't even want to deal with me after this interview is over.

WWL: *You and I will be in the funny place together.*

NAGIN: But we authorized $8 billion to go to Iraq lickety-quick. After 9/11, we gave the president unprecedented powers lickety-quick to take care of New York and other places.

Now, you mean to tell me that a place where most of your oil is coming through, a place that is so unique when you mention New Orleans anywhere around the world, everybody's eyes light up—you mean to tell me that a place where you probably have thousands of people that have died and thousands more that are dying every day, that we can't figure out a way to authorize the resources that we need? Come on, man.

You know, I'm not one of those drug addicts. I am thinking very clearly.

And I don't know whose problem it is. I don't know whether it's the governor's problem. I don't know whether it's the president's problem, but somebody needs to get their ass on a plane and sit down, the two of them, and figure this out right now.

WWL: What can we do here?

NAGIN: Keep talking about it.

WWL: We'll do that. What else can we do?

NAGIN: Organize people to write letters and make calls to their congressmen, to the president, to the governor. Flood their doggone offices with requests to do something. This is ridiculous.

I don't want to see anybody do anymore goddamn press conferences. Put a moratorium on press conferences. Don't do another press conference until the resources are in this city. And then come down to this city and stand with us when there are military trucks and troops that we can't even count.

Don't tell me forty thousand people are coming here. They're not here. It's too doggone late. Now get off your asses and do something, and let's fix the biggest goddamn crisis in the history of this country.

WWL: I'll say it right now, you're the only politician that's called and called for arms like this. And if—whatever it takes, the governor, president—whatever law precedent it takes, whatever it takes, I bet that the people listening to you are on your side.

NAGIN: Well, I hope so, Garland. I am just—I'm at the point now where it don't matter. People are dying. They don't have homes. They don't have jobs. The city of New Orleans will never be the same.

[moments of low sobbing by both]

WWL: We're both pretty speechless here.

NAGIN: Yeah, I don't know what to say. I got to go.

WWL: OK. Keep in touch. Keep in touch.

As I put down the phone I asked everyone to leave the room. I needed some time alone. Most people thought I was just bashing President Bush, but my mindset was as focused on Governor Blanco and Senators Landrieu and Vitter. Of course President Bush was a big part of my frustration, but he wasn't doing press conferences every couple of hours fabricating the truth.

At the end of the call Garland and I were both sobbing so much that we could not talk anymore and just hung up. It was such an emotional rollercoaster ride. This event and radio conversation had taken its toll on me, and I was totally worn down mentally and physically. I never expected to explode like that, especially not on air, and it sort of took me by surprise that all of that anger had built up inside.

As the minutes passed and the more I thought about it, the realization totally sank in of what I'd just done. I thought to myself, "I'm a dead man! I have just publicly denounced the governor, U.S. senators, FEMA, and the president of the United States." I started wondering if during the night I would be visited by specially trained CIA agents. Could they secretly shoot me with a miniature, slow-acting poison dart? As my dad often told me, "Be careful your mouth doesn't write a check your butt can't cash." I was convinced my mouth had just gotten me into a whole lot of trouble.

After calming down a bit further, we all settled down to try to get some rest. Later that night, it was so hot in my room that it was impossible to sleep. I had stripped down to only my underwear, but with no air-conditioning and no way to open a window the air on the twenty-seventh floor was stifling, stale, and so humid.

I got up and nudged my security team, who were also struggling to sleep. Terry and Sally were also up. "We have to move and find some rooms that are cooler," I said as Wondell and Louis hurried to get their shirts and shoes on. My thought was we should go over to the tower where the windows had been blown out by the tornadoes. At least there would be fresh air coming in, even if it was still terribly humid and at least ninety degrees outside.

So we left the rooms we were in, found a master key, and went searching for decent, cooler rooms to sleep in for a couple of hours. As we walked around that section of the hotel, we'd open a door, look inside the room, and make a quick damage and livability assessment.

Most of these rooms had glass everywhere and were soaking wet. We'd walk in, tiptoe through glass on the floor, shake off the mattress, and if it was wet, we'd move to another room. After a couple of hours of searching we ended up finding a couple of rooms that were barely decent.

My room was reasonably dry even though the entire window was blown out from ceiling to floor. A hot breeze was blowing in. I could also clearly hear backup generators operating at full blast. I tried my best to fall asleep but just couldn't. If I would doze off for a few minutes, I would wake up quickly from nightmares of CIA agents or Blackwater operatives with face masks swinging into this room on ropes attached somewhere on the roof. The radio interview where I had cussed and demanded action from the president and governor was still fresh on my mind. It was proving to be another rough night after a very, very tough day. They say what doesn't kill you only makes you stronger. Well, my thinking at the time was with all that I had gone through, by morning I should be stronger than Hercules.

CHAPTER EIGHT

AIR FORCE ONE

—————■—————

After another extremely restless night, it was now Friday morning, and the fifth day after Hurricane Katrina made landfall. After giving up on sleep, I made it back to my original hotel room and took a quick military-style bath to freshen up a bit. When I came out to the living room area, it quickly became apparent that there were no positive updates or other good news. The city was still teetering on anarchy. There were no rescue buses. The floodwaters were still high, and not a single levee breach had been fixed. So that morning started just like the others with the same old heartaches. I even had a pounding headache, so I was popping aspirins as I continued to receive update briefings. I was definitely not feeling much like Hercules.

Before I could finish eating a granola bar for breakfast, reports started to come in that the city had just been shaken by a huge explosion. Chemical containers on the Mississippi River in the Mandeville Street Wharf Warehouse erupted into flames. Thick black clouds stained the skyline, marking the spot as rushed to suppress the fire. This shouldn't have been that surprising since 48 percent of all the hazard materials in the country pass through the Port of New Orleans along the riverfront.

Many were now worried that the air would be polluted with ghastly toxic fumes since we were not sure what types of chemicals were actually burning. In addition, there were other exploding propane tanks going off like firecrackers that worked to fuel the intensity of the fires. The flames then started consuming the surrounding wharfs on a projected path toward the French Quarter. Firefighting helicopters took to the skies carrying huge buckets of water, up to eight hundred gallons at a time. The water was repeatedly dredged from the river and dropped on the site to help extinguish the flames. Fire boats and firefighters on the ground battled for hours, knowing all too well that if this fire spread to the closely spaced buildings in the French Quarter, it would be like a domino effect and nearly impossible to contain.

Since Katrina hit, fires had raged across the entire city. Many homes, condominiums, apartment buildings, and businesses had caught on fire. They were either victims of arsonists or the result of ruptured gas lines ignited by a spark. Some of the largest fires in the city's history were recorded during this time.

Firefighters from across the nation rushed to offer help, but they were kept just outside the city for many days by the state and FEMA. Their reasoning was that it wasn't safe for them to enter. But today, on Friday, even though conditions were at their worst, some of the out-of-town firefighters were finally given the go-ahead to help out. Their brave, dedicated work ethic and their benevolent nature were very special gifts to us all. We were fighting major battles on every front, and we were severely undermanned.

New Orleans was like a story out of the Bible with multiple plagues hitting in rapid-fire order. In one week, tornadoes, hurricane winds, floodwater, scorching sun, fires, and shortages of food and water had descended upon us. The elements were trying to bend, break, and overwhelm us at every moment, at every turn. We also had major human battles going on simultaneously with political egos, hatred, opportunism, riots, murders, and just flat-out demonic-style evil.

There were some who predicted that the city would surely tip into total chaos and started referring to us as a total loss. There was a definite sense of anarchy, but it was way too early to throw in the towel. Marcia St. Martin with the Sewerage and Water Board had been desperately trying to get me on the phone first thing that morning, but couldn't. She did manage to speak with Sally Forman, my communications director, who relayed the message that Marcia needed NOPD police support to help protect the Water Board power plant on the West Bank.

What had her concerned was that during the night, a group of men carrying guns had attempted to break in. They saw lights on inside and outside the building and believed there was food and water inside. They probably did not realize there were many chemicals at the plant such as chlorine, lime, and fluoride. Marcia felt strongly that we didn't need gunfire around the plant. If a bullet were to hit one of our chlorine tanks, it would be catastrophic as it would release a toxic green plume over the city that would suffocate many.

Marcia told Sally that if they came back tonight, she was not sure that they could hold them off again. So we sent her reinforcements as it was also the only area of the city where we had a functioning sewer and water system.

While wrapping up a meeting with my key staff members I just happened to look out the window, and to my delight and amazement there were several buses on the interstate headed our way. I called everyone over, and we all started celebrating by giving each other high fives. After we settled down, Sally told me that she had talked to the White House yesterday and the president was scheduled to visit later that afternoon. "So buses just happen to start arriving the day the president makes his first visit, how convenient," I said. Of course I had a smirk on my face as I was being facetious. Sally further explained that the president was flying in on Air Force One and that this time it would not be just a flyover, but they would be landing in New Orleans.

I went back to the window and looked down at the people who had been waiting for days on the crosswalk between the Superdome and the shopping center, and it was evident that they also saw the buses. They were now waving, hugging each other, and cheering like they were at a Saints game. However, this euphoria would be short-lived. As more people started to realize that buses were indeed coming, the crowds became even more anxious, vying harder for a position closer to the barricades. They started pushing, shoving, and positioning themselves closer and closer to each other. As word continued to spread, more people started to come out of the Superdome as they all wanted to ensure that they were not going to be left behind. The lines for people to evacuate soon wrapped like a bloated snake all the way around the Superdome.

It was now time for all hands on deck as it related to the three hundred National Guard troops and our police force, who continued to work tirelessly to maintain order. In an effort to evacuate people smoothly, they developed a system that would channel citizens through the barricades by separating families in one area, single women in another, and men in the last area. This allowed them to control the number of people moving through, fifty at a time. Once you moved into the newly barricaded area near the shopping center doors, you were funneled into another waiting area inside the shopping center that led to the second-floor lobby and then down to the ground floor. The lowest floodwater levels were just outside the doors near the ground floor of the shopping center. Severely NOPD officers were stationed near the waiting buses. They would assist the evacuees on board and keep count of how many were entering and where the bus was heading.

Unfortunately, there was still no sign of buses at the Convention Center. The other issue was that buses for the Superdome only came in sporadic bursts. Maybe a half dozen would pull up outside the Hyatt, gather a couple of hundred people, and head north. Then many hours would pass without a single bus sighting. After experiencing this erratic schedule, the crowds at the Superdome became very aggravated and disappointed again. They were also packed in place like sardines and didn't dare leave their hard-earned spot in line. If they had to go to the bathroom, they held on or let go right where they were. This was such cruel and unusual treatment for people who were just stranded and had not done anything to deserve being handled in this manner.

For the lucky few who had gotten on the initial buses, they were headed for Texas, President Bush's home state. In preparation for the evacuees, the Astrodome in Houston, Texas, had been converted into a shelter with a field hospital erected on site. Able to house up to twenty-five thousand people, the Astrodome would soon reach full capacity, and neighboring centers were opened to take the overflow of evacuees that had started to arrive late the previous evening.

Earlier that day, the media had reported that sixteen thousand evacuees from New Orleans had made it to the Astrodome and that the facility was now full. Reports claimed that these evacuees were from the Superdome, but that was grossly inaccurate. At the time of these reports, it had been only a very short time since the first few buses left us, and they wouldn't arrive in Texas for several more hours. We would later learn that many bus drivers were still directed to not venture into the city. They were ordered to only pick people up from the periphery, the surrounding suburban areas of New Orleans such as Kenner, Metairie, and Gretna. This had been going on since Thursday.

Maybe this is another reason why Gretna officials did not allow individuals from the Convention Center to cross the Crescent City Connection Bridge and continue their march further for safe pickup. Besides being mean-spirited and racially challenged, it now seemed clear that they were only interested in making sure their people got on buses first. That was easily achievable since the state and the Blancos totally controlled when and where buses came and went. We also now know about the special relationship with Mayor Ronnie Harris of Gretna. New Orleans was again last in line for rescues.

Sources inside the state told me that when the federal government finally arrived with sufficient resources to get everyone out, they immediately ran into resistance from some local governments and a few state leaders. Key federal authorities had to make the decision do we fight these state and local officials and force our authority, or do we just ignore the foolishness so we can complete critical rescues? Thankfully, the decision was made to just save fellow Americans who had suffered for far too long.

One of the best ways of getting them out was to fly in military aircraft to the New Orleans airport, which is located in Jefferson Parish. I'm told than en route to the airport buses driven by National Guardsmen, under the leadership of General Honoré, were told by a Jefferson Parish sheriff that they couldn't bring people to the airport, as the airport was in their jurisdiction. The general made it very clear at that point that he had had enough of these pathetic games and that he was exercising his authority under the Constitution. So General Honoré stood tall and told these sheriffs that nobody was going to stop his buses from going to the airport. He went on to say, "Anybody who chooses to stop my buses will have to deal with the United States military." The sheriffs quickly backed down and moved aside as the buses continued on to meet military aircraft that would take our citizens to a better place.

At this point the whole world was watching this disjointed display at rescue, mesmerized by the images they continually saw on their television sets. Ratings were off the charts. Many sympathized with our predicament, watching with total disgust and dismay as events unfolded. In the flood zone, we had no clue as to just how much love and interest the plight of New Orleanians had generated on the national and international stage. Offers of assistance came from everywhere.

The state and White House continued to be inundated with phone calls, telegrams, and e-mails. Offers of medical ships, doctors, pumps, troops, money, food, water, buses, planes, gas, and even $40 million of oil flowed in like the mightiest storm surge. Tragically, our higher levels of government, particularly our very own federal government, turned them down or dragged its feet to the point that most gave up out of frustration. Now the shoe was on the other foot and instead of the mighty United States coming to the world's rescue, the world was coming to ours.

Obviously, the Bush administration's collective ego would not allow them to realize that they desperately needed outside help. So they poked their chests out, dug in their heels, and watched us suffer some more. This point takes me back to my very first conversation with the president when he said very convincingly, "What do you need? I'm working with the governor to try and get you more resources. Everything is going to be alright." Well, we didn't have more resources, and everything was not alright. Maybe he was bringing all the help we needed later on that afternoon when he arrived on Air Force One. Only time would tell.

At some point during the day, Michael Moore, the popular American activist and moviemaker, delivered a letter to the president. It's obvious that he is not a big fan of President Bush, but his letter captured the sentiment of every single New Orleanian and many citizens of the world. I have included the letter in its entirety as every paragraph speaks loudly to our condition at the time.

Friday, September 2, 2005
Dear Mr. Bush:

Any idea where all our helicopters are? It's Day 5 of Hurricane Katrina and thousands remain stranded in New Orleans and need to be airlifted. Where on earth could you have misplaced all our military choppers? Do you need help finding them? I once lost my car in a Sears parking lot. Man, was that a drag.

Also, any idea where all our National Guard soldiers are? We could really use them right now for the type of thing they signed up to do like helping with national disasters. How come they weren't there to begin with?

Last Thursday I was in south Florida and sat outside while the eye of Hurricane Katrina passed over my head. It was only a Category 1 then, but it was pretty nasty. Eleven people died and, as of today, there were still homes without power. That night the weatherman said this storm was on its way to New Orleans. That was Thursday! Did anybody tell you? I know you didn't want to interrupt your vacation, and I know how you don't like to get bad news. Plus, you had fundraisers to go to and mothers of dead soldiers to ignore and smear. You sure showed her!

I especially like how, the day after the hurricane, instead of flying to Louisiana, you flew to San Diego to party with your business peeps. Don't let people criticize you for this—after all, the hurricane was over and what the heck could you do, put your finger in the dike?

And don't listen to those who, in the coming days, will reveal how you specifically reduced the Army Corps of Engineers' budget for New Orleans this summer for the third year in a row. You just tell them that even if you hadn't cut the money to fix those levees, there weren't going to be any Army engineers to fix them anyway because you had a much more important construction job for them—BUILDING DEMOCRACY IN IRAQ!

On Day 3, when you finally left your vacation home, I have to say I was moved by how you had your Air Force One pilot descend from the clouds as you flew over New Orleans so you could catch a quick look of the disaster. Hey, I know you couldn't stop and grab a bullhorn and stand on some rubble and act like a commander in chief. Been there done that.

There will be those who will try to politicize this tragedy and try to use it against you. Just have your people keep pointing that out. Respond to nothing. Even those pesky scientists who predicted this would happen because the water in the Gulf of Mexico is getting hotter and hotter making a storm like this inevitable. Ignore them and all their global warming Chicken Littles. There is nothing unusual about a hurricane that was so wide it would be like having one F-4 tornado that stretched from New York to Cleveland.

No, Mr. Bush, you just stay the course. It's not your fault that 30 percent of New Orleans lives in poverty or that tens of thousands had no transportation to get out of town. C'mon, they're black! I mean, it's not like this happened to Kennebunkport. Can you imagine leaving white people on their roofs for five days? Don't make me laugh! Race has nothing— NOTHING—to do with this!

You hang in there, Mr. Bush. Just try to find a few of our Army helicopters and send them there. Pretend the people of New Orleans and the Gulf Coast are near Tikrit.

Yours,
Michael Moore

Outrage, anger, and significant calls for federal action started to snowball. People from all over the country had seen and heard enough. It was now the day after my outburst and call to action on Garland Robinette's show on WWL radio. President Bush was now coming to personally meet with me later that day and tour the city firsthand.

The feds had finally authorized more resources, and we were starting to see a long-awaited buildup. We were able to verify by midday
that some federal troops had arrived in the city. Pretty soon FEMA and
the federal government were making wild claims about how many had
arrived. To no one's surprise, there were so many contradicting reports
that these two entities ended up confusing each other. The day before,
in an interview on National Public Radio, Secretary Michael Chertoff
said there were supposed to be seventy-four hundred National Guard
troops in Louisiana, and twenty-eight hundred were in New Orleans.
We were only later able to verify that approximately fourteen hundred
troops arrived very late Thursday with an additional fourteen hundred
scheduled for duty on Saturday and Sunday.

Earlier that morning, Soledad O'Brien from CNN fought hard to control her frustration when she interviewed Michael Brown. His inconsistent statements and vague responses were astounding. Mrs. O'Brien
didn't let him off the hook and continued probing for the truth. She
was sensitive to the victims, assertive, and extremely professional in
exposing to the world what was really going on. She got quite upset
with him, and it showed. I developed and continue to have a great
amount of respect for her as a journalist.

On that show Mr. Brown wildly claimed there were fourteen thousand National Guard troops in New Orleans, a flat-out fabrication. He
then went on to predict that they planned to swiftly ramp up to thirty
thousand troops by Sunday evening. He then started deflecting by
saying the limited number of National Guardsmen who had been in
the city over the past five days was because of Governor Blanco. In
other words, that was all she asked for. He failed again to mention that
the day before he had ordered all of his FEMA staff out of New Orleans
and moved them to Baton Rouge where he and the governor were.

Michael Brown continued by asserting he was only made aware
that we were using the Convention Center as a shelter on Thursday by
listening to news reports. It was astounding to hear the head of FEMA
admit publically to being so out of touch with a disaster of this magnitude. He further falsely claimed that his agency was just too busy

doing "life-saving and life-rescue efforts" to focus on any other information. This was news to everyone in the flood zone who never saw a single FEMA representative on a rescue mission.

The other excuse he used was that it was just too difficult to get food and water to the people in the center due to the flooded roads. What about using Black Hawk helicopters or Coast Guard boats as the Convention Center was right on the river? Don't forget the fact that U.S. Army trucks could have easily gotten to this facility as it was located less than five blocks from the elevated interstate that connects to Gretna on the West Bank. This was the only open road in and out of New Orleans during that time.

In another interview the night before with Ted Koppel on *Nightline*, Michael Brown tried again to deflect blame. His justification for delays of troops into the region was, "If I move rescue workers into harm's way, and they become victims themselves, it just makes the problems doubly worse." He went on to say that FEMA was ready, but when they asked Governor Blanco what she needed, she never responded. Even if his claim was true about Governor Blanco, the federal government had the ultimate responsibility to rescue Americans and should have acted decisively.

It just makes me wonder if the ultimate goal was to allow things to get so bad that it would force the governor to turn all control over so that disaster capitalists could have even more unfettered access to make billions and billions of dollars. Most of the suburbs and areas in New Orleans that voted Republican were fully evacuated. It is a fact that if you let something marinate long enough, it becomes tender enough to do what you want with it. . The word from restaurants in Baton Rouge was Michael Brown liked his steak where he could cut it with a fork.

Since we had been tenderizing for five days, a caravan of troops and supplies in large military trucks, Humvees, and eighteen-wheelers were finally moving into New Orleans. It was around two to three o'clock in the afternoon. They moved smoothly on the elevated interstate to pass in front of the Hyatt and finally arrived at the Superdome.

As I watched them from the twenty-seventh floor, the convoy made quite an effortless wake in the floodwaters as they proceeded. Word quickly spread that there was food, water, baby items, and medical supplies onboard. A certain amount of cautious optimism returned collectively to the promise-worn assembly at the Superdome.

Two helicopter battalions from Fort Hood had also come in late the night before and were co-coordinating efforts with the Coast Guard and National Guard to airlift the sick out of the city. It was still not at the volume needed, but this was a huge improvement. And as you can imagine, these actions were a tremendous relief to us all. Citizens stranded at the Superdome and Convention Center were soon distributed food and water as buses started arriving in larger numbers.

The military also brought with them refueling capabilities for our police and fire vehicles. Refueling operations were quickly established at Harrah's Casino at the end of Canal Street near the Mississippi River. It was quite clear to me that the SOS messages, the radio outburst, and the media coverage had finally gotten the right people's attention. And besides, the president's people would not allow George W. Bush to come into New Orleans without any clear signs of progress. Finally, they had "gotten their asses moving to New Orleans."

Among the hustle and bustle of buses and military conveys arriving with soldiers and supplies, General Honoré finally had the type of troop support he had been without for several days. The "advisory" work that he'd been doing with such limited military presence had been remarkable to say the least, and now he had resources to make greater strides. Honoré clearly understood the degenerative dynamics that had built up among the stranded. There was now an opportunity to instill in the people at the Superdome and Convention Center renewed hope and faith in government again.

Wearing military fatigues with his black beret, black sunglasses, and smoking his signature cigar, Honoré stopped several passing military trucks about to enter the Convention Center area. He advised them to be careful and on guard as he knew all that the people had gone through and that they were still very upset. After briefing them, he stayed around to observe this critical interaction.

Within minutes the troops had in unison jumped out of the trucks Rambo-style and had their weapons cocked and ready. The general watched in horror and instinctively started running toward the armed soldiers yelling at the top of his lungs. He ordered them all to stop pointing their guns at the people. In his most authoritative voice developed over the years, he shouted, "Put your goddamn guns down now! These are American citizens, not criminals. This is not Iraq!" The troops looked around puzzled, realized he was serious, and slowly pointed their weapons to the ground. The civilians relaxed, and things changed for the better.

It was now time for me to meet the president of the United States. I made my way with my executive protection staff, Sally Forman, Colonel Ebbert, and Terry Davis toward the heliport. I walked around the barricades and spoke with several citizens along the way. Most were still angry but were feeling better that some people had finally gotten on buses and that food and water had arrived. They all wanted assurances that enough buses were coming and they would not be left behind. I gave them those assurances and got a few skeptical stares and more than my fair share of smiles. It was good to see some of them smile again.

Within minutes I was at the heliport saying hello to my favorite puppy, the little stranded black dog. I picked her up and petted her. She was happy and gave me a couple of big wet licks of hello. According to Secret Service and presidential protocol, we needed to arrive an hour before Air Force One was scheduled to land at the New Orleans Louis Armstrong International Airport. The White House had managed to connect with Sally Forman earlier that morning and gave her most of the details on the president's visit. They also mentioned the Garland Robinette interview, which the president had heard the night before. I suspected that this was something that the president planned to discuss with me once he arrived later that day.

While on the phone, Sally had graciously taken the opportunity to warn the White House staff that I had not had a shower since Katrina hit and that I would not be attired in a business suit. They offered for me to take a shower on Air Force One right before the president arrived. I'm not sure whether this was a calculated move to relax me, or if after five days without a proper shower they wondered if my scent and appearance might offend the president.

With the president's meeting in mind, I chose to wear a clean T-shirt that had one of New Orleans' fabulous street names on it, which also emphasized my sentiments during these trying times. On a white T-shirt were the bold letters that spelled out "Desire." That's exactly what the federal and state government was up against—our unwavering desire to be rescued with dignity, our desire to have enough food and water, our desire to have buses show up in large enough numbers to take us to safety, our desire to have holes plugged in the faulty federally built levees, our desire to drain our city, our desire to clean up, and our desire for all of our citizens to come back home and rebuild better. I wore that T-shirt proudly that day on behalf of all of our citizens in and out of the Big Easy.

As our helicopter landed on a private runway at the airport, I noticed lots of activity near the main terminals. Commercial airplanes and military planes were arriving and taking off regularly. There were lines of people entering various planes to evacuate the area.

Everyone essentially had a one-way ticket out as they boarded these unmarked planes. No one but the pilot knew where their final destination was. At that time these passengers were just happy to be getting out and going somewhere more civilized. Many cities and states had generously offered to take them in, and our folks were flown to forty-four different states around the nation.

It must have been extremely unnerving to finally get up to thirty-five thousand feet cruising altitude and then realize that you did not know where you were going. Some left New Orleans in a pair of short pants and a T-shirt with temperatures near a hundred degrees and hours later arrived in Alaska. From sweating in the Superdome to cold, snow, polar bears, penguins, and Eskimos! The good news was that inhuman suffering was over for them.

One of the things that most don't realize about the evacuation efforts after Hurricane Katrina was that many New Orleanians had never left the city before, let alone the state. Some had not even ventured out from the East Bank to the West Bank of New Orleans. Now they were being evacuated to different parts of the country, completely shell-shocked, having lost everything, and now they had to deal with the culture shock of being in a new, very foreign environment. As things would progress and we moved to the actual recovery and rebuilding phase post-Katrina, our plan wouldn't be to just fix our infrastructure, buildings, and houses; we would need to focus as deeply on recovering our people and our unique culture.

There were also critically ill patients who were being evacuated. Many patients were flown to specialty hospitals around the country. In order to effectively deal with these types of sick patients, the airport dedicated an entire concourse and converted it into a makeshift hospital. Unfortunately, some had passed away either in transit or once they made it to the triage. For the latter, officials had set up a temporary morgue in another remote section of the airport. Every few minutes medical helicopter flights landed with more patients who had been retrieved from various New Orleans hospitals that were barely operational. Many had been in very crude intensive care units and were barely alive.

Charity Hospital in downtown New Orleans had over four hundred beds when Katrina hit. This was a state-run hospital where I was born, and it is not far from the Superdome and the Hyatt hotel. Unfortunately, their backup generators were poorly maintained and had long since failed. Before going to the airport, we had managed to find a route that Big Daddy could traverse, and I was able to do a personal inspection of this hospital. I had gotten reports that they were in big trouble. When I got there I was blown away as the place was an absolute mess. Windows were blown out, there was no electricity, patients were moved into dark, damp hallways, and a few doctors and nurses were working feverishly to keep people alive. After talking with a doctor and a lead nurse, they both pleaded with me to try to get their generators working again. My nontechnical assessment was that a fix may be possible. I immediately went back to the Hyatt and discussed this matter with Rod West of Entergy, and he sent over two of his best engineers, who got the generators started. Thank God this worked—maybe a little late for some, but at least power had been reinstated and burdens were lightened.

Tulane Hospital, located a block or two away from to Charity Hospital, also had many patients, staff, and family inside. Mel Largarde, who was the most senior person for HCA at Tulane at the time, did not evacuate the hospital until Friday. He wanted to make sure every-one was out before he left. They ended up evacuating over fifteen hundred people off the rooftop in private helicopters until the military came in with their Chinooks. They also assisted with the evacuation of patients from Charity Hospital, who were transported to Tulane and then airlifted out from the rooftop.

Back at the airport, we were immediately greeted by friendly Secret Service agents who were awaiting our arrival. As they quickly escorted me toward Air Force One, I turned around and noticed Colonel Terry Ebbert was asleep on the tarmac. He was totally exhausted as I don't think he'd slept much the entire week. Apparently he had just lain down on the ground in some shade on the hot concrete with his hat pulled down over his face. He'd been in actual wars before and had been operating in true Marine mode. I was happy that he was finally getting some well-deserved rest.

On the other hand, the rest of my staff and security team were directed to a holding area just off the concourse by a different set of agents. They were joined by the governor and some of her staff. Dr. Hatfield was also there as she had made the journey from Baton Rouge to meet with us this day. I later found out that my executive protection team was shuffled off to an air-conditioned RV where they were told to wait for my return. They were like kids in a candy store as they hadn't had air-conditioning for so long. The bus also had ice cold water, a TV, and all the junk food they could eat. They told me that they finally had some quality time to relax, knowing that I was in good hands. So they just kicked back and overdosed on ice water, snacks, and heavenly air-conditioning. Louis told me later that they had never realized that microwaved hotdogs could taste so good.

Air Force One was parked on the tarmac and was absolutely the most impressive airplane I had ever seen. I would later call it the "ulti-mate pimpmobile." It was absolutely spotless. The plane sparkled as every visible part of the plane had obviously been cleaned and pol-ished in anticipation of the world's eyes being upon it.

I recall looking at the strong, powerful letters that made up the words, "The United States of America" that ran along near the top of the plane. The presidential seal was also prominently displayed, and I almost had to pinch myself that the boy from inner-city New Orleans, from Tremé, was going to meet with the president. It was exceedingly exciting as this experience elevated my pride in being an American.

Former Vice President Al Gore, a Democrat, would much later com-ment to me one-on-one that the president was very calculating on this visit. He went on to say, "You know the president was managing you the day he met you on Air Force One. He was kind of worried about how you were impacting public opinion." I told the vice president that we were managing each other as my city desperately needed the president's help. A case could also be made that after my Garland Robinette radio interview, the president realized that he had to do something to calm me down, and he took it upon himself to somehow befriend me. I believe that could have been his initial plan, but as time moved on, we got to know each other better. Through trial and error we developed a very, very unique working relationship. I walked up the stairs and entered the main door to Air Force One for what I would later realize was very special, once-in-a-lifetime treatment.

The first person I met onboard was a brother from New York who was the president's chief flight attendant. His name was Reggie Dixon, and he was very professional and reassuring. He put me at ease. He quickly whisked me into the president's personal quarters. He told me he was not sure who I was, but it was very rare that someone other than the president got to use his area. This part of the plane is considered the White House and is off-limits to most people.

I asked Reggie if the president was onboard, and he told me that he was on the other Air Force One. I guess I had not paid enough attention to notice that there were actually two Air Force Ones. I would later learn the same security tactic exists with his helicopters, Marine One and Marine Two. When the president is in the air, our enemies will never know for sure which plane or helicopter he is really on. So I walked into the presidential suite and thought to myself, "Now this is the way to travel in style." It was laid out perfectly, and the presidential seal was on everything.

Reggie also gave me a full tour that was equally impressive. This plane had everything and then some. There was a full kitchen, chef, staff and a master dining room that could seat over twenty. There were several staterooms, meeting rooms, and a whole section in the back of the plane for press. Reggie told me all the latest technology was on board, and it is constantly updated. This plane had everything needed to run the country—or the world for that matter.

As I reentered the master bedroom, I couldn't help but focus on the presidential seal on the wall, and my pride swelled again. Reggie handed me a toiletry bag that had the presidential seal on the outside (I still have it to this day) and showed me to the adjoining bathroom. As he graciously exited the room, he told me that if I needed anything to let him know and he would personally take care of it. I was so looking forward to this shower that I didn't waste any time in taking off my grimy clothes.

I walked into the luxurious shower and turned on the hot water, full blast. As the water hit me, it felt as though I had died and gone to heaven. I couldn't recall ever in my lifetime going five days without taking a regular shower or bath. At first I just let the water run all over my body, starting with my head and neck areas. Then I put on so much soap that there was lather everywhere in the shower stall. I then took my time shaving and lathered up again. I started to feel purified and cleansed at a level that I am sure was a big part of my imagination.

Normally, for me, my morning shower is the place where I can reflect, pray, and get my thoughts together for the day. So here I was on Air Force One thinking about the events of Katrina and how I got here. I just let the water run, standing underneath the flow as I was thinking through how I was going to deal with the meetings I was going to and what I was going to say to the president of the United States. Where do I start? How was I going to get a president and a governor who didn't really like one another to get past their differences and party affiliations to do the right thing to save lives?

I'd only been in the shower for what seemed like less than ten minutes when I heard Reggie knock on the door. "Mr. Mayor, the president is about to arrive. It would be great if you could start wrapping up your shower," said Reggie. "Okay," was my response, but I was thinking to myself, "There's no way in hell I'm getting out of this shower right now." The warm water was just too invigorating, and I was not sure when I would have another shower like this. So I lathered up again and indulged myself some more. If we had waited for the president for several days, then he could at least wait a few minutes for me to come out sparklingly clean just like Air Force One.

This additional time also gave me the opportunity to really consider the magnitude of what was at stake. I knew the meeting that was coming up with the governor and the president would be monumental. Already, I knew there was a big rift developing between the two, particularly in the way that the media was starting to turn on Blanco. I knew that the White House spin machine was working overtime to get as much negative attention off the president as possible. My agenda was straightforward and to the point: rescue and evacuate citizens in need, repair the levee breaches, drain the city, and help us to rebuild a better city. My overall goal was to ensure that the city got what it needed to fully recover, and if I had to choose sides, I would.

My dilemma was that on the one side I had a Democrat governor who was still harboring ill feelings toward me and who had previously threatened me with "hell to pay." It was somewhat apparent by her actions and inactions of the past week that she was not really supporting the most devastated areas. We had also gotten strong signals from Governor Blanco that she was already starting to think about the post-Katrina world for Louisiana. Key members of her staff were already secretly discussing calling for a quick census count to provide rationalization for shifting political clout and recovery dollar from New Orleans to other areas around the state.

On the other side we had a president who really hadn't given any signs that he cared enough about New Orleans, especially poor and middle class black Democrats. It took President Bush three days to fly over for a peek at thirty-five thousand feet. Others in his administration were busy directing no-bid contracts to friends. So I had a city in crisis and had to figure out how to get one of these two recalcitrant leaders to care enough to help us. It was akin to dealing with Mr. Poe in the book *A Series of Unfortunate Events* and Cinderella's not-so-nurturing stepmother. I was seriously between a rock and a hard place.

As I continued to think this through, a focused perspective popped into my head. The key question is what does this city really need to rebuild? It needs money, and lots of it. Who prints money and has the biggest bank account in the world? It's the federal government. Who is the head of the federal government and signs big checks? President George W. Bush. And there was my answer. I would continue to try to work with the governor, but the one to actively engage and manage was the president.

Five more minutes must have passed when my thoughts were quickly interrupted by a louder knock on the bathroom door. "Mr. Mayor, you really have to come out now." I unenthusiastically said okay out loud and turned the shower water off. Once again, Reggie was courteous, but this time I sensed the urgency in his voice. I dried myself quickly and put on some clean clothes with my "Desire" T-shirt proudly displayed. I felt like a million dollars and was now ready for the fight for billions of recovery dollars for the city and region.

I left the president's bedroom, and Reggie escorted me to a board-room full of very important people. They were already seated. There was Governor Blanco, U.S. Senators Mary Landrieu and David Vitter, Congressmen Bill Jefferson and Bobby Jindal, General Blum the chief of the National Guard Bureau, Secretary Michael Chertoff, and FEMA director Michael Brown. I saw Karl Rove later as he was also onboard the plane but did not attend this meeting. I greeted them all and took my assigned seat at the table.

The president then entered the room, and everyone stood at attention. He was wearing his official Air Force One crew jacket that had his name in cursive writing embroidered down the left-hand side of the front of the jacket. He walked in with what I would later come to understand was his normal Bush swagger. He had this cowboy-type walk with slight bow legs where his hand swayed as if he had six-shooters on his side. He greeted me very warmly and then spoke to everyone else. Once finished, he settled down at the head of the table.

And on perfect cue, lunch was served. The meeting commenced with a briefing for the president on the latest on rescue, supplies, resources, and the overall recovery efforts. Everyone was extremely cordial as we reviewed all aspects of the disaster, particularly the priorities and needs of the city and region. We were all given the opportunity to talk as they went around the table for input. As I was sitting to the immediate left of the president, I got to go last. My adrenaline was flowing, and my pulse was a bit elevated.

Once it became my turn to speak, I got going by sharing what I knew. Within a few minutes I just couldn't hold back any longer, so I cut to the chase. I firmly but professionally stated, "Mr. President, with all due respect, if you and the governor don't get on the same page, this disaster will continue to degrade into something that is going to be a further embarrassment to the nation. There has to be a single person who has full authority to direct all critical resources. Someone like General Honoré would be great. We need a decision now!" I could tell I caught everyone off guard as the president leaned back in his seat and just said, "I hear you, Mr. Mayor." With that opening, I pushed further and said, "Mr. President, this is so critical and so time-sensitive that all of us at this table will leave right now and go to another room so that you and the governor can get down to business. Time is not on our side." The president's eyes looked at me with respect and a little annoyance, and he retorted, "No, there is no need for all of you to move. The governor and I can go into the Oval Office down the hall and have a private discussion." He winked at me, and the two left the dining and meeting area.

For those of you who are unaware, when the president is on Air Force One, it is the equivalent of the White House in the sky. Different shades of carpet signify to those on board when they are in the White House and when they are not. Only those with special clearance can walk on the tan carpet on Air Force One signifying you are officially in the White House and in the Oval Office.

After the two of them left the room, the rest of us remained in the boardroom and chatted with each other. I made a quick pit stop to a nearby restroom, and as I was returning Senator Mary Landrieu cornered me and said she needed to talk to me one-on-one. She was very animated and extremely angry with her face starting to turn red. I was totally caught off guard. She didn't offer many details but was very fired up. She continued to talk loudly and emphasized her points by wildly thrusting her pointer fingers. She would continue to behave this way behind closed doors. However, once in front of TV cameras, she'd became very calm, extremely polite, and was normally full of smiles.

My staff would later point out to me that earlier that day in a CNN interview with Anderson Cooper he curtly interrupted her in mid-sentence on live television. She was in studio in Baton Rouge and had spent several minutes of the interview thanking politicians like former presidents Clinton and Bush Sr. on their wonderful help in fundraising for the region. She then went on saying that she was particularly excited that Congress had just approved $10.5 billion to provide aid for the Gulf Coast. Ten billion dollars would go to FEMA and the other $500 million was for the Pentagon and its hurricane relief work.

As he cut her off, Anderson Cooper very forcefully called Senator Landrieu out for being enormously insensitive. He was ashamed of her comments in thanking politicians while citizens in New Orleans were struggling to survive with little to no food and water. He was clearly shaken as he described to Mary Landrieu and the viewers that he had seen many dead in the city and that just down the street was the dead body of a lady who had been lying there for days. The senator's response was that she did care for New Orleans as her family had homes that had been destroyed and her father was one of our former mayors.

It seems that I wasn't the only one frustrated and cutting to the chase by calling out these obvious political spin games. Nevertheless, whatever had set the senator off did it in a big way. She was ranting and raving to me about things that Democrats and Republicans fight about in Washington DC. She was going on and on about us not smiling if we stood beside the president during press conferences. She claimed, "They will use that against us." She told me to not trust anything the president said and that Karl Rove was evil. She went on and on about being stone-faced in front of the cameras. I looked at her like she had absolutely lost her mind. My blood was starting to boil, and I could sense that she was really starting to piss me off.

I remember very bluntly telling her, "You have got to be kidding me. We have people suffering and dying in New Orleans, and all you are concerned about is partisan politics. I don't have time for this." But she kept saying, "You really don't understand. This is big!" I thought to myself, "You're damn skippy this is big, bigger than anything ever in history." She kept going, and her face was now beet red and she was talking so loud that everyone nearby pretty much heard her. I then told her I was going back into the meeting and it would be great if she would calm down and think this through.

I then returned to the boardroom and turned to Congressman Jefferson and Senator Vitter and asked, "What is going on? You guys have issues up in DC, but this is not the time for these types of antics. I really don't understand what is going on with Mary. This partisan stuff has got to go. This is crazy. There are people counting on us to save them and get this right. I need everyone to get it together so we can move forward."

Within minutes the governor reentered the room and just took her seat without saying a word. The president followed her a minute or two later. Their meeting had ended after only fifteen minutes. We were supposed to immediately depart and tour the city on Marine One with the president, but he came over and invited me to join him in the Oval Office. He said it would be a short meeting. I followed him without delay as I needed relief from the senior senator's ranting and raving. As I entered the Oval Office, I took a seat across from the president, who sat behind his desk. The president leaned forward in his chair and plainly said to me, "Mr. Mayor, the governor and I talked. I took your advice and offered her somebody who could run this thing and have ultimate authority, and she told me she did not want to go in that direction. I offered to federalize all troops in Louisiana so that they could get in quicker and do the rescue and relief work that is needed without having an extra layer of delaying approvals. I am sorry to say we were not successful in resolving this matter."

What I didn't know at the time was there is a little-known federal law called the Posse Comitatus Act that basically restricts the president from sending federal troops into a state unless invited by the governor. Just about everyone believed that if the governor would agree to a unified command, then we would create the right conditions for a faster and smoother recovery approach. The National Guard and other military troops would then be under the command of the federal government, enabling a combined and unified rescue mission.

As the president got up from his seat he said, "I'm sad to say that before she left this office she asked for twenty-four hours to think about it." Twenty-four hours? I just couldn't believe that she could not make a critical, time-sensitive decision of this magnitude without getting approval from others. Unfortunately, we were in for another delay, and more people would suffer unnecessarily. Twenty-four more hours after five days of hell was something my brain just could not comprehend right now even if I did smell real good from my presidential shower.

The president also said he was not inclined to override her decision. I was deeply disappointed in both. The governor couldn't make another tough decision, and the president, the most powerful man in the world, was acquiescing to a small state governor while Americans continued to suffer. I pressed him again to override her, but he told me again he wouldn't. I thanked the president for trying and suggested maybe the governor would reconsider before the end of the day. He barely looked me in the eyes as it was clear that he was not at all confident this would change soon. I walked back into the boardroom, looked at the governor, and just shook my head in disbelief.

My staff determined from talking with the governor's staff that Blanco as a Democrat was overly concerned that if she allowed the recovery to be federalized, then she would look weak. Her re-election was coming up in about two years. She also believed that President Bush and his cronies would still undermine her and blame her anyway if the unified federal response failed. The feds would later blame her profusely for not making a decision.

Some on Governor Blanco's team played to her fears. They were saying, "Governor, you can't concede your power to the president because you'll look bad. The president is basically daring you by saying he is not sending you more troops until you federalize this disaster."

There is an African proverb that says when elephants dance the grass suffers. While the president of the United States and the governor of Louisiana were doing their off-the-wall dance, assets that we desperately needed had been frozen. Andy Kopplin, Blanco's chief of staff, was the one quoting and waving around the federal Posse Comitatus Act. Posse Comitatus is a Latin term that roughly translates to a temporary police force. The Posse Comitatus Act is a federal law that was passed at the end of Reconstruction. It severely limits the powers of the federal government to use the military for law enforcement purposes. In essence, it prohibits most members of the armed forces from exercising powers that maintain law and order on non-federal property. Exceptions may occur only by acts of Congress and if the governor invites federal troops in. President Bush was a Republican and Governor Blanco was a Democrat, so an invitation was not in the mail.

As I understand it, this law was passed at the same time as the insurrection law—and together, they sought to make certain that as disruptions emerged in Southern states at the end of Reconstruction, the federal government was limited in its ability to respond. The ultimate irony in this dispute during Hurricane Katrina between our governor and the president is that they were both from the South. New Orleans was simply a pawn in this ongoing game of political control and partisanship. So President Bush was very hesitant in overriding her by declaring this a catastrophe and pushing federalization. His public excuse was it would have looked bad for him to overpower a female, Democratic governor in a majority black city. So the two most powerful players in this disaster would not make a good decision for the people, and partisan politics rules.

The governor had still not deployed National Guard troops beyond the original three hundred who were there before the storm hit. This also was curious since, as I mentioned earlier, I was briefed several months earlier at Jackson Barracks in the Lower Ninth Ward by the state leader of the National Guard, Adjutant General Bennett Landreneau, about their capabilities in a disaster. He told me they had fifteen hundred troops on alert and ready to go in the event that this city had a major disaster. The governor had the power and the resources but never used it.

Now we were stuck again waiting, and she needed another twenty-four hours while more suffered. To me this was another critical defining moment in this disaster. This stymied whatever momentum that started with the president's visit. A more reasoned look at the bigger picture was warranted instead of focusing on looking good, maintaining power, and positioning for re-election.

Another sad result of this standoff as I later found out was that the USS *Bataan*, an 844-foot military ship, was on call, waiting patiently in the Gulf of Mexico for orders to go into New Orleans and provide help. This ship was designed to dispatch Marines in amphibious missions. They were not strangers to operating in watery or flooded conditions. This ship also had helicopters and an operating hospital that could handle up to six hundred patients at one time. It also had plenty of food and water available for many of those in need. Another great feature of this ship is it could make up to a hundred thousand gallons of fresh drinking water each day! They were just floating in place waiting for orders.

As a footnote, in 2006, Congress rewrote this law as President Bush proposed that in times of turmoil that the U.S. Department of Defense would be the "lead agency" in imposing martial law. He later pushed through a bill that allowed the federal government to deploy troops at the president's discretion without having to seek the approval of a state governor. I wonder if they called this the Blanco Act.

I would later lead a task force of mayors from around the country that formally proposed that in cases like Katrina, when local and state governments are overwhelmed, the federal government would automatically assume ultimate authority for no more than a month. Clear lines of authority would be quickly established to get critical resources moving. Once the area is stabilized, control would revert back to the locals. In hindsight, the governor could have done this very same thing with a limited, timed formal invitation.

Back on Air Force One, we were now ready to tour the city to survey the damage via the presidential helicopter fleet. The president led the governor and me onto the tarmac. The others followed closely behind. The three of us were supposed to fly up in the president's helicopter, Marine One. The other politicians and staff would board a different helicopter.

As we walked down the tarmac towards the helicopter, President Bush led the pack by walking a little ahead of the rest of the party. He then turned around and called out my name in his Texan drawl. As I walked up to him, he put his hand on my shoulder and asked me if I was still angry. His staff told him that I had said some strong words on the WWL radio interview the night before. I responded that it was uncharacteristic of me, but my people needed help, and if I offended him that was not my intention. I went on to say, "But consider being in my shoes. What would you have done?" He looked at me and said, "Mr. Mayor, I know we could have done a better job, and we're going to fix it. Tell me the truth and I will help you." I told him that he could count on me to always be truthful.

All the while this was going on the press was snapping pictures like excited tourists. The president and I continued to walk together with Governor Blanco trailing with the second group. My staff later told me that this drove Blanco's staff to basically lose their collective cool. They started yelling, "What's going on here? Is there some secret plot against the governor?" My staff was caught off guard by their paranoia and childish behavior. There were much bigger considerations than being worried about Blanco being left out of photo shoots with President Bush and myself.

There were three helicopters that went up on the tour of the city. I was in Marine One, the president's top helicopter, with President Bush, Governor Blanco (she tried to get her husband Coach onboard, but he was not allowed), General Honoré, Secretary Chertoff, and Admiral Thad Allen. The senators, politicians, and staff, along with Karl Rove, were in the second helicopter, which was closely followed behind by the White House Press Corps in the third helicopter.

Before I realized it, we were flying over flooded areas of the city. I still remember the president's reaction to Katrina's devastation. He seemed awestruck. He asked a lot of questions and wanted to know the truth. We talked turkey.

As we arrived at the Seventeenth Street Canal, President Bush seemed to be very well briefed on this operation. I was surprised to see so much activity. There were trucks, sandbags, and lots of people working. This was surprising since just the day before during my daily flyover there was little to no work happening.

After circling a bit, we landed close to the breach. I took this opportunity to really look around and explore the damaged areas. I was a fair distance behind when a Secret Service agent came running up to me and said, "Mr. Mayor, you need to catch up with the president and make sure you are walking together so that he can get a direct briefing from you." Apparently, the president had been calling for me. I'm sure one of their objectives was to show the nation that he was down in New Orleans walking side by side with the mayor and progress was being made.

Meanwhile, our senior senator and governor were not happy campers. The president's people kept them out of all of the key photo shoots. From that point on, they started publically pushing the theme that I was being manipulated by the president. They failed to realize that we were managing each other. The president's objective was to improve his public relations ratings, and my goal was to get resources for my city.

We ended up staying at this site for about twenty minutes. After that we boarded the helicopters to continue our journey to see a little more of the city, and then we headed straight back to the airport.

As we touched down on the tarmac, there were more members of the media waiting. This was a planned press briefing. As the president took to the podium, the governor and I gathered around right behind him as a public show of solidarity. President Bush started by saying that he would never forget what he had seen. "I understand the devastation requires more than one day's attention. It's going to require the attention of this country for a long period of time," he said in closing.

As the press conference ended, the president turned and acknowledged us as he said his parting words. As photographers, cameramen, and reporters were about to depart, Governor Blanco awkwardly stepped up to the microphone. Everything had already been turned off. During earlier briefings, my staff informed me the president normally has the last word. After a few uncomfortable minutes, someone turned the microphone back on and the governor said a few non-memorable words, and then everyone quickly dispersed.

The president left, and I was exhausted as his visit had taken up most of my day. As we flew back on a Black Hawk to return to the heliport at the Superdome, I noticed that more buses had arrived and a considerable number of people had been evacuated. It was encouraging to see that even though the president had left, evacuation momentum was still growing.

News must have traveled fast as people who had been hiding out in their homes or apartments heard that buses had arrived in big numbers. They too came out in hopes that they could also get a seat out to safety. Everyone was being accommodated as long as they were orderly. Our police officers were outstanding in getting everyone on these long-awaited rescue vehicles.

Earlier that day the Army Corps of Engineers announced that it would probably take up to eighty days to drain the city. Wow! This recovery was going to be a very long road for us. As I mentally recapped the day's often divisive events, I started asking myself a very critical question. Ever since Katrina made landfall, I had repeatedly pondered, "Why me? Why did this happen on my watch?"

Later that night, as I once again looked out of my hotel window, I noticed the major transformation below near the Superdome as a large portion of the crowd of people was now replaced by piles of trash. I felt my spirit whispering to me, as it did anytime I would raise this question of why. I always knew the answer, but up until this point I had not been willing to fully acknowledge destiny. I turned to Sally and Terry, and before they could say anything I said, "It looks like this is God's plan for me to be here at this moment to help rebuild a *new* New Orleans." They both smiled and gave me quiet looks of agreement.

CHAPTER NINE

THE BLAME GAME

———— ■ ————

Saturday morning's sunlight was peeking over the horizon as we entered day six. I woke up feeling better rested as I had finally gotten between four and five hours of sleep. Maybe it was the triple-lather shower I had taken the day before on Air Force One that made the difference. As I got up from the bed it was still very early and the sun had not fully risen yet. I quickly freshened up and moved to the living area where I spent some quality time alone thinking and writing an outline of a rebuilding strategy. I also developed the initial makeup of a commission of citizens who would direct our recovery.

After an hour or two, several people made it over to my room for our first update meeting. I had a chance to talk over this rebuilding strategy with Ron Foreman, who gave me some other things to think about. We tweaked the plan together. Ron's eyes lit up as he had built several successful large-scale projects in the city over the years, and this was the type of challenge that really got his creative juices going. Ron let me know right away that he wanted to head up this effort. I told him he would be a great choice and that I would give him first consideration.

Our staff meeting went on as we rehashed some old challenges, but we ended with good news regarding citizen evacuations. As I glanced out my hotel suite window to view the waiting crowds, it was reassuring to see that the lines for buses at the Superdome were much shorter. Throughout the night, buses had come and gone, busily transporting thousands of people eager to leave. Their destinations were various cities in Texas, Tennessee, Georgia, and a few in northern Louisiana. For those who remained below, still exhausted and dirty, they waited patiently, now confident in the fact that they would be out soon.

It was now very bright outside with crystal clear blue skies. This was such an amazing contrast to the toxic brown floodwater and piles of debris and trash that dominated the areas around the Superdome and throughout much of the city.

The scenes below of people being rescued and given much needed assistance caused me to reflect back on another conversation I'd had with State Senator Cleo Fields and Ben Jeffers. They told me that on one of their rescue missions they were joined by three great Americans who came down to help: Reverend Jesse Jackson, Congresswoman Maxine Waters, and Reverend Al Sharpton. As they were working rescue missions, they were all amazed that an organization such as the Red Cross was not present.

The Web site of the Red Cross very pointedly states their service or mission: "The American Red Cross is where people mobilize to help their neighbors—across the street, across the country and across the world—in emergencies." They have always been a visible organization during wars and disasters. A high-ranking spokesperson for the Red Cross claimed that the reason why they were not helping out was because the state OEP told them it was too dangerous for them to enter the city.

If that is the real reason, then why are they in the business of mobilizing help during wars and other emergencies? After all, the types of events they have traditionally been involved in all had certain severe degrees of danger and risk. So what was so different if the Red Cross did not hesitate to go into Iraq and offer aid and assistance in a war zone but refused to go to flooded New Orleans?

Another little known secret is they actually left well before the storm hit and headed north. Why they were missing in action throughout our most difficult times is still a mystery to me. It clearly was not too dangerous for the Red Cross to take billions and billions of dollars in donations that people from all over the world wanted suffering New Orleanians to have. I trust that independent audits will someday tell us where the money actually went since it was not used for immediate rescue assistance.

After our update meeting ended, I was leaving my room to go to the command center and ran into General Honoré and his support group, who were on their way to see me. We chatted, and he updated me on the bus evacuations. He was very confident that we had very good flow and the Superdome would be empty by the end of the day. We then discussed briefly the operation to plug the holes in the Seventeenth Street and other canals. The general was not as optimistic that progress there was moving at a good pace. We ended the conversation as he knew I was headed to another meeting, and we pledged to touch base with each other later that evening.

As I descended the stairs of the hotel to the command center, I really had to pay attention to where I placed my foot on each step. Six days without power and no working toilets had forced a number of people to take to the stairwells as it offered a little privacy so that they could relieve themselves. The air was stiflingly putrid.

Moving swiftly but cautiously, we made our way to the fourth floor where Greg Meffert and his team were busy trying to fine-tune some sort of reliable communications. It was their number one priority. The unpredictable phones, computers, and Internet were really impeding our communication with the outside world. They were working feverishly to find creative solutions to rectify the problem.

We then moved to the area where Dan Packer and Rod West from Entergy had set up their private offices. Most of the time they had the only working landline phones in the entire area. So we sat down for our regular briefing on how to begin to re-power the city. They were mostly scratching their heads as the damage reports that were coming in from around the city told them most of their power generating plants and distribution and feeder lines were either blown down or flooded. It would take a miracle to restore power to the city. I was fairly optimistic that if anyone could do it Dan and Rod could as they were some of the best in the business and had lots of experience in dealing with the aftereffects of hurricanes. Unfortunately, none of us had experienced anything like this, so all we could do was keep working and continue to be creative.

With so many people now being safely evacuated, we started thinking about the day when we would allow reentry and rebuilding. Within the command center we were discussing the best ways to get the city going again. Several key options were being explored. My initial focus areas were downtown where the hotels and businesses were situated, Algiers, which didn't flood, and any other areas where floodwaters were limited to two feet or less.

Since our economy was totally shut down, we were losing millions and millions of dollars each day. If we were going to fully recover, we would have to get key industries up and running again as soon as possible. We intuitively knew that this would be extremely difficult since 80 percent of the city was flooded and the Corps of Engineers was predicting it would take over eighty days to drain the floodwater out. Once the city was drained, then the challenge of debris removal would take center stage. All this would have to be completed before we could allow citizens back in to rebuild. Multitasking had now taken on a whole new meaning for us.

Before leaving the command center, I wanted us to focus on one big, very visible success that would signal to the world that even though we were still suffering, we had not given up. We needed a symbol that clearly said we were determined to come back bigger and better. Since Entergy couldn't start repowering the city until the floodwaters were drained, Rod suggested that a great beacon to show we were still alive was for them to put a priority on lighting up the string of lights that went across the top of the Crescent City Connection Bridge. I immediately agreed and asked Dan and Rod to make it happen. Our thought was that if people could see the bridge lit up at night, it would also speak volumes to those citizens who were forced out of here by floodwaters. This would help to eliminate doubts whether there was anything left for them to come back to.

It was midmorning and now about time to make my way to the heliport for my inspection tour. I quickly walked around the command center individually encouraging the brave warriors who were in there working almost nonstop in fighting for the survival of New Orleans. From there I left, and with less people around the Superdome, it was fairly easy for me to get to my waiting Black Hawk on foot.

As I walked past the mounds of trash—empty plastic bottles, discarded MRE packets, diapers, shoes, you name it—I noticed that many people's personal belongings had also been left behind. Our poor citizens must have been so disoriented from waiting so many days in the heat of the day that by the time they had moved to the holding area between the Hyatt and the shopping center and were finally told that their bus had arrived, they did not want to risk taking any chance to miss it, and so they left critical valuables behind. I can only imagine what it was like when someone announced their bus to freedom was outside. They most likely became so excited that they literally ran out the doors.

As I walked through this waiting area, I saw old ladies' purses, driver's licenses, other IDs, birth certificates, medical papers, eyeglasses, and house keys. I had to stop and take this in. As I continued to scan the area, I decided that I could not just leave these items to be ultimately discarded to landfills. So I told my staff that we needed to put together a team to come back later and start sifting through the trash to retrieve these very important possessions. I knew that these recovered items would be desperately needed later as many evacuees would not have any identification. Unfortunately for them, this would mean that their temporary financial and housing aid would be delayed until we could forward what we found or they could somehow order replacement documents.

As I continued my walk over to the heliport, I felt better and more confident in giving firm assurances to the remaining few in line by the barricades that they would soon be in a better place. I could also see a look of relief in the eyes of the National Guard troops who were just starting to relax a bit as the realization set in that they were no longer grossly outnumbered.

I made it to the heliport, and as we boarded the Black Hawk helicopter I informed the pilot that I was particularly interested to see the repair work around the Seventeenth Street Canal and the other breaches. I also wanted to maintain our normal flight route so that I could mentally compare what I had seen on previous flights. I wondered to myself whether the Army Corps of Engineers were still working as diligently as they were on the day of the president's visit.

As the helicopter lifted into the skies, floodwater was still everywhere and was as high as ever. I made a mental note to get in touch with Marcia St. Martin as soon as I returned so that we could firm up plans for accelerating the draining of the city. I also wanted a full assessment on the pumping stations to gauge the length of time it would take until they were all back up and running. In the short term we would need many, many temporary portable pumps to help in this massive, complicated undertaking. However, the reality was that none of these steps could start until all breaches were repaired. We still had lots of work to do and a very long, long way to go.

As we continued this particular flyover, I immediately noticed several significant, very visible changes. First, most people were now off their roofs. There seemed to be far fewer frantic individuals waving their arms or sheets begging to be rescued. I also noticed the Coast Guard pilots and boat rescuers were still working hard and continuing to perform miracles.

The water levels were still high, but I saw fewer gas leaks with flames coming out of the surface. Entergy had been very effective in remotely cutting off gas lines or sending divers in to manually stop leaks. Unfortunately, the color of the floodwater was still evolving due to the many chemical and other toxins that were churning in the heat. There were also clear signs that major new water leaks had developed. Whatever water pressure was left in the pipes was now pushing fresh water to the surface. Numerous very large bubbling waterspouts could clearly be seen from above.

It would later be calculated that these floodwaters applied billions and billions of pounds of pressure on the streets, subsurface, and sewer and water infrastructure. It was now buckling under this colossal weight. The weight of these floodwaters was also causing noticeable damage to many of our beautiful old trees that were now wilting as their roots were drowning. We ended up losing thousands and thousands of trees in our urban canopy. As we flew over our twelve-hundred-acre City Park, one of the largest urban parks in the nation, I feared that many of our majestic oaks, some over a hundred years old, would not survive. We would later get very good news on this matter as many of these tough old monuments to our history did survive.

As we got closer to the Seventeenth Street Canal, a smile came over my face as I was pleasantly surprised to see the hustle and bustle of major repair work in progress. It was great to see that multiple military helicopters were still feverishly working to drop three-thousand-pound sandbags into the Seventeenth Street Canal breach. I could even see some of these mega sandbags were careful stacked upon one another and a few were actually above the waterline. There were not a lot of them above the waterline, but very visible, encouraging progress was very evident. If President Bush's visit accomplished anything the day before, he got this operation going full steam ahead.

After the flight was completed, I immediately returned back to the Hyatt and the EOC. It was obviously apparent that media requests for interviews were escalating to the point where my communication people were being stretched beyond their limits. As I entered the fourth-floor atrium area, I was immediately accosted by another gang of reporters with yet more interview requests.

My WWL radio blast had quickly gone viral and global. All of a sudden I was being bombarded with national and international requests from every major news anchor known in the media world. We worked very hard to accommodate as many as we could since we knew our citizens were being spread out all over the country.

As I did more national and international interviews, our local media started feeling left out and got quite upset. Most if not all of them had evacuated the city when the floodwater started heading downtown. Initially, I was upset that they fled the city when the going got tough and did not show much courage to ride this thing out with us in the flood zone. So my initial attitude was if you were not willing to come into New Orleans like the other reporters, then we should not grant you an interview. At first the locals just sat back and complained, criticizing me publicly for not making special arrangements to talk to them. This is when rumors started that they could not find me for an interview. Of course, this was not true, and they quickly realized that they had to come back into the city for an interview. They realized that the more national and international interviews we did the less people went to their news shows for updates. We had the best real-time information, so they played by our rules.

By this point in time the regular morning and afternoon media briefings had grown so large that we could no longer hold them on the fourth-floor ledge in the atrium. We had to move everything into one of the main ballrooms of the Hyatt. To give you an indication of how many reporters were in the city before the week was out, that ballroom became jam-packed with hundreds of reporters and camerapersons. We were also starting to talk to international press from as far away as Japan.

At first this was all a little unsettling. I had never experienced anything like this. As the mayor of a medium-size city, I was accustomed to dealing with the local media, but this was a whole new world. Instead of talking to five to six news cameras, I now had hundreds of very hungry ones wanting to be fed. This was probably one of the biggest adjustments I had to make as everything I said now had immediate national and international reach. My growth in this area was bumpy at times as we made more than our share of mistakes. I had no choice but to adapt as the New Orleans diaspora desperately needed to know what was really going on.

As I continued to do national and international interviews, our local media continued to snipe, especially when they didn't get exclusives. Some felt that I owed them this right. My philosophy was you earned the right to exclusive interviews if you experienced what we were experiencing. To report accurately, they needed to be uncomfortable with the people, sweat twenty-four hours per day, crap in a stairwell, and take military baths just like us. Instead, some members of our local media were absurdly demanding that I leave the city and meet them in Baton Rouge, Alabama, or Mississippi for interviews. I just couldn't do it in good conscience as my total focus was still on completing evacuations, regularly updating the diaspora, and getting New Orleans back on its feet. Our local media would just have to adjust to these priorities, period, end of discussion.

While we were in the trenches, working day and night to stabilize things in the flood zone, behind the scenes there was another storm brewing that would seem just as powerful as Katrina. By midday Saturday the White House—or should I say Karl Rove's spin machine—leapt into action. It spun a web of misinformation that played into the overly eager hands of some media people who were waiting to lap it up.

Governor Blanco's twenty-four-hour wait time before she would decide whether she would invite the federal government in to provide a single chain of command for rescue had come and gone. Now back in Washington DC, in the Rose Garden at the White House, President George W. Bush addressed the nation on the Katrina disaster. His well-crafted speech had thorny edges as he attempted to place the blame for the inadequately slow response to the disaster squarely on the shoulders of the state of Louisiana and the city of New Orleans. "Despite their best efforts, the magnitude of responding to a crisis over a disaster area that is larger than the size of Great Britain has created tremendous problems that have strained state and local capabilities," he said. "The result is that many of our citizens simply are not getting the help they need, especially in New Orleans. And that is unacceptable."

The *Washington Post* quickly printed an article titled "Many Evacuated, but Thousands Still Waiting: White House Shifts Blame to State and Local Officials." The article further touted reports from a supposed "senior Bush official" who claimed among other things that

Governor Blanco had not declared a state of emergency until today and that is why the federal government could not deploy troops to the area earlier. This inaccurate statement helped fuel the fire and spun the wheels of confusion as other reporters took their cue from the *Post* and ran similar stories. It would have been very easy for a clear-thinking journalist following the events of Katrina to do a little bit of quick research to find out that Governor Blanco declared a state of emergency last Friday, August 26, three days before Katrina hit.

This was very unfortunate as the average citizen who was starving for real information got caught up in these opening salvos of political manipulation and started to wonder who was really at fault. Mr. Rove's strategy was working as some started directing their anger and frustration towards Louisiana and away from the federal government. The growing rift between the federal and state governments further stymied recovery momentum and made my job the hardest in America.

The blame game shifted into a higher gear depending on who was talking and where they were. In a subsequent Washington briefing, Secretary Michael Chertoff, ever the advocate for FEMA director Michael Brown's decisions (for if he didn't support Brown then all eyes would fall on him), blamed Governor Blanco for the delay of federal assets to the area. His reasoning was her refusal to sign the waiver to the Posse Comitatus Act. Blanco retaliated by saying that she would not be handing over control of the state to the federal government. What Secretary Chertoff did not say was that as secretary of homeland security he could have designated this disaster "catastrophic," and the case could have been made that the feds had the ultimate authority to override the governor under the existing law. Unfortunately, he was concerned that Governor Blanco would file a lawsuit against the federal government to further complicate matters. It was just easier to start blaming and deflecting.

Governor Blanco's next move was to hire a former Washington insider, James Lee Witt, who was once Clinton's FEMA director, to advise her on recovery efforts. The thinking was he knew the rules and regulations and could be very helpful. His hiring could also make President Bush think twice about federalizing the recovery.

The next federal salvo was Michael Brown would later trying his hand at political spin. He claimed it was me and not the governor who was to blame because thousands of people were stranded in the city, hungry and thirsty, and hundreds had died. He then stepped over the line of rational thinking by saying I had no right to declare a mandatory evacuation when the city didn't have the resources to evacuate the poor, elderly, and sick. He failed to mention that if a mandatory evacuation had not been called, then thousands and thousands more poor, elderly, and sick would have stayed in the city and region to wait, suffer, and possibly die. Mr. Brown never mentioned how an already overwhelmed FEMA would have supported this extra load of people when they couldn't support and evacuate the lesser number who needed his help right now.

As I was walking back into the command center, Sally came running toward me in a panic. Her husband, Ron Forman, CEO of our zoo and aquarium, was apparently stuck in the glass elevator that looked out over the atrium in the Hyatt. She said he had been there for about thirty minutes. She was very worried and asked me to see if we could do anything to get him out of there. Apparently, the portable generators the hotel used to power the elevators had suddenly broken and new parts had to be ordered from out of town.

I immediately went to the hotel management, who predicted that he'd be stuck there for a few more hours. After another half hour passed, we looked up and noticed Ron had started taking his clothes off in full view of everyone on the fourth-floor atrium ledge. He stripped down to his underwear as there was no air-conditioning or any air blowing in his elevator. He obviously got so hot in there that this was the only way he could stay somewhat cool. I have to admit that the sight of Ron in his underwear in a glass elevator twelve floors up from street level gave me and many others a good laugh that we hadn't had for days. Here was the zookeeper being observed and on full display in the flesh just like one of the animals that he was in charge of every day.

We eventually got him out after a couple of hours, and he too had a hearty laugh once he was free.

As quickly as our smiles and laughs appeared, they vanished in seconds as we were told the dreadful news about the death of one of our police officers, Paul Accardo. My mood quickly turned to extreme sorrow as Paul had been bunkering down with us at the Hyatt. The stress of Katrina must have gotten to be too much for him to handle and he took his life. His method to end it all was to take his assigned police gun and shoot himself in the head.

This was so surreal and shocking as I had just seen him very much alive just a couple of hours earlier. He seemed reserved and a bit more quiet than normal, but I never thought he was that far on the edge. My initial reaction was, "You've got to be kidding me, I just saw the guy and he was fine." Paul Accardo was very close to Police Chief Compass and Assistant Chief Marlon Defillo as I normally saw the three of them together just about every day.

The chief and assistant chief were absolutely devastated by this news, as we all were. Word of Paul's death started a shockwave that moved quickly around the hotel, through the entire police force and all emergency responders. This really shook up a lot of people and was like another big kick to the stomach. With all that we were dealing with since the storm hit, this loss was just too much for some to handle.

Most of the people who were with us had worked in the most challenging environments, lost their homes, and hadn't seen their families in days. Some had even lost family and friends in the floodwaters. Now this loss seemed to bring all of this very intense negativity into full focus. It felt like we were being smothered and all consumed in regret.

Every day it seemed that another more shocking, damaging thing was thrust upon us. We found ourselves regularly taking one step forward and three back as nothing was predictable anymore. This emotional rollercoaster ride made it feel like anything positive wouldn't last long enough to be worth remembering. Shockingly, Paul was okay one minute and dead the next. Depression covered all of us and would stay for quite some time.

When we thought we were at our lowest point, a few hours later we were advised that another police officer had committed suicide. He too shot himself in the head. We would later discover that this man had struggled for some time with family problems and Katrina had just pushed him over the edge. Two officers in the space of a day had taken their lives unnecessarily. With this news I knew we had to do something to stop more of these very dedicated personnel from giving up all hope. It was for this very reason that I decided that all the emergency personnel who had remained in the city—police, fire, and EMS—would be required to undergo both physical and psychological examinations as soon as possible. We put this in motion as we just couldn't afford to lose any more good people the way we lost these two devoted officers.

I immediately called a meeting with all my key staff. We were able to get some by Entergy's landline conference phone to inform them what had transpired and the required personnel evaluations. I also told them that because of recent unfortunate events, we would start the process of relying more on the newly arrived National Guard and U.S. Army troops to continue rescue missions and provide security. General Honoré clearly understood and was totally supportive of this very necessary transition. We then talked through a plan to start cycling out emergency personnel to allow them a much-needed break and the opportunity to reunite with their families.

I also asked each chief to conduct a personal assessment on every one of their men and women. We identified those who needed to be relieved on the first shift. We also noticed an increased number of resignations recently submitted, so it was very clear that many of our emergency personnel were past their limits of exhaustion and some were even traumatized. The chiefs quickly developed a complete list of those who had been showing signs of extreme stress. As a further precaution, we were able to discuss this matter with several psychologists who had worked with our emergency responders in the past. We were able to line up medical doctors with the goal of each person having a complete physical and psychological exam before they would go on a full week of rest and relaxation.

In order to get some sense of normalcy back into the lives of our first responders, I announced that the city had arranged for them to choose between a free five-day vacation to either Las Vegas or Atlanta. I had already called Mayor Oscar Goodman of Las Vegas and Mayor Shirley Franklin of Atlanta, and they were just outstanding. We worked as a team to secure charter flights, food vouchers, recreation tickets, and hotel rooms for these brave men and women. I was also able to get in touch with the CEO of Southwest Airlines, who provided airline vouchers for this initiative.

The first shift of officers and their families would leave the city first thing Monday. We had such dedicated men and women working for us that many felt the tug of duty and really did not want to leave. However, I insisted, and after a few bumps in getting everyone through the process, we were able to rest these weary warriors over the next three to four weeks.

Unfortunately, there was another dark side to Katrina policing that was happening around us in these early days that we would not fully understand until four and a half years later. Apparently, there are small secret sects within the New Orleans Police Department that saw Katrina's unfolding as opportunities to live out wicked fantasies. Their memberships are not published anywhere.

Many in New Orleans now believe that a relatively small group of officers evolved from "protect and serve" into something much more sinister. Several became evil opportunists who saw what was unfolding during Katrina and took it upon themselves to play out their deadly fantasies. These guys generally play in the shadows, and some have described them as modern-day Ku Klux Klan with badges. It is now coming to light that right after Katrina hit, a small group of racist cops went out on regular patrols with the boldly announced purpose of "time to go out and shoot some Negros" (cleaned up from racially offensive language). Many other good officers are now coming forward and telling stunning stories that are both mind-blowing and disheartening. We have even gotten reports that during this time several white officers requested transfers to get away from those who were practicing this demonic type of criminal behavior.

The first malicious incident happened Friday, September 2. It now appears that several of these degenerate cops were on patrol when they confronted a young black man who they claim was acting suspicious. One thing led to another, and he was beaten up and shot multiple times, and then they placed his dead body in the back of a civilian car. They were so bold as to leave him there for several hours, and an officer from a different unit took a picture of the bloody scene. This officer ended up keeping the incriminating photo and would later share it with an FBI agent. Soon the killers moved the car to a nearby levee and set it on fire in hopes of destroying critical evidence. To add further repulsion to this incident, when the body was later identified the man's head where he was shot had been cut off and was still missing. My contention is this is definitely a hate crime because who else would do something like this but a very sick serial hater.

The second tragic encounter happened two days later on the Danziger Bridge. Police were supposedly called out to investigate shootings in this area. Once they got there, something went very bad again as they opened fire on a crowd, shooting six black people; two were killed, with one being a mentally retarded young man. They even shot one lady's arm completely off.

Both of these matters were investigated by the police department's Public Integrity Division, the district attorney, and the FBI with each initially finding no fault. However, the Danziger case was pursued aggressively by several relatives of the victims. A year or two later, the case was then thrown out of state court on a technicality. It was not long after that the U.S. Attorney after prodding from the Justice Department stepped in and took a fresh look at the case. After receiving several anonymous tips, his team started to interview certain targeted police officers. He finally got one to talk, and others followed.

The U.S. Attorney started to apply more pressure, and soon brought the head of the police investigative unit before the federal grand jury. This head investigator was the absolute key as he is responsible for approving all reports regarding investigations involving police shootings. Once this investigator heard and saw the evidence that was presented to the grand jury, he immediately resigned from the police department. He would soon admit to covering up this shooting and pleaded guilty to conspiring to obstruct justice.

The irony here is he was not even on the scene at the time of the shooting. His link is that one of his close friends was one of the principal shooters. The good news is that the so-called "blue code of silence" against a fellow officer in New Orleans was finally broken. It has now come to light that this former police officer was cooperating with the feds and wore a wire for at least six months to get more evidence for the case.

This admission of cover-ups rocked the police department and the city to its core. However, this was not the first time that corrupt cops had been caught doing some hideous act. New Orleans history has several instances of gruesome rogue cops gone wild. But these latest despicable acts were particularly devastating as they were perpetrated against innocent people who were trying to escape a disaster. Hate crimes and police cover-ups during Katrina are now in the full light of day. My attitude has always been that we should continue to clean it all up, and if any officers choose to shoot citizens for sport or to cover up a serious crime, they should be prosecuted to the full extent of the law.

Many more horrible stories and instances of unfair treatment are also coming to light after this chief investigator pleaded guilty to a cover-up. We are now hearing Katrina stories from within NOPD about white officers shooting at black people who had run out of food in Algiers. It seemed as though a crowd went into a drugstore to get some much-needed food items. These shootings got so bad that other African American officers who arrived on the scene had to very forcefully confront their colleagues to get them to stop firing upon these innocent starving people.

Then there were other accounts of some officers being allowed by their supervisors to confiscate clean socks and underwear while other officers were told to just make do with what they had. Hotel rooms and hot meals were provided for some and not for others. Another African American officer asked his elderly, disabled mother to come over to his assigned police station that was high and dry because he did not want her to be alone during the crisis. The captain of the station told him to get rid of her and that he did not care where she went.

The officer had to borrow a truck with half a tank of gas from another officer to drive his mother north sixty-five miles to Gonzales, Louisiana, to try to find the home of his aunt, whom they hadn't visited for many years. The police in Gonzales ended up helping him find the house so he could leave his mother there. Because he only had limited gas and money to return to New Orleans, he had no other choice but to sleep inside the truck that night at a gas station near the interstate highway. Because he was so dedicated to his job, he wanted to be first in line to fill up in the morning and report back to work to the same boss who would have kicked his mother out on the street. I have always been amazed at how much good people can tolerate when they are really put to the test.

Discriminatory treatment by some police right after Hurricane Katrina hit was not just limited to New Orleans. Some Baton Rouge police officers also took this as their opportunity to harass Katrina evacuees. The *Baton Rouge Advocate* newspaper published an article based upon formal statements made by state troopers from New Mexico and Michigan who came down to help after the storm. They detailed how Baton Rouge officers routinely harassed black people, performed illegal searches, and used unnecessary violence. They went on to say Baton Rouge officers were extremely rude to African-American New Orleanians but were very polite to white people from the city. A local officer is quoted as saying he believed black people were "animals" that "needed to be beaten down."

A flabbergasted visiting state trooper said that, as a thank-you for his help, Baton Rouge police officers offered to let him beat down a black prisoner. "I was told that I could go ahead and beat someone down," Michigan state trooper Jeffrey Werda was quoted saying in the *Advocate*. Another Baton Rouge officer allegedly hit a black man in the head and "took him to the ground in a headlock," even though "at no time did the man pose a threat or mouth off at the officers," the trooper said. Another Baton Rouge officer tasered an already defenseless, handcuffed black man.

So not only did we have to overcome the effects of Hurricane Katrina, but we had to overcome racial biases and classism at so many different levels. We saw the very best and the absolute worst in some people with power. After five years, Katrina continues to expose, clean, and purge New Orleans and Louisiana. My prayer is that small hate groups like these will become a thing of the past once these federal investigations are concluded and evil people are properly disciplined.

By late Saturday evening, at least forty-two thousand people had been evacuated from many parts of the city and surrounding suburbs. As the last three hundred people boarded buses and left the Superdome, National Guard soldiers cheered in celebration. Home to nearly thirty thousand people for a week, the Superdome was now eerily quiet. I should now point out that over this timeframe at the Superdome, the New Orleans Police Department and the National Guard did a superhuman job of keeping security intact during the worst of times. They are all true heroes. They overcame everything imaginable. Rations were stretched, there was no power or sanitation, and good people suffered needlessly. It also helped that most of the evacuees showed tremendous compassion for their fellow man. A few acted up, but the vast majority held things together until help finally arrived. In the end, it was a horrible lesson and one that I am hopeful we will never have to learn again.

In an e-mail that was later released as part of the congressional testimony, Marty Bahamonde, my favorite FEMA rep who was in New

Orleans until he was ordered to leave on Thursday, sent a message to his coworker regarding the Superdome. It reads:

"The state told us we would run out of places; the army told us they had run out of places. The leadership from top down in our agency is unprepared and out of touch. When told that the Superdome had been evacuated and would be locked, Scott Wells said that we shouldn't lock it because people might still need it in an emergency. Myself and the general who had been there immediately spoke up and told Scott that it was impossible to send anyone back in there…is that not out of touch? But while I am horrified at some of the cluelessness and self-concern that persists, I try to focus on those that have put their lives on hold to help people that they have never met and never will. And while I sometimes think that I can't work in this arena, I can't get out of my head the visions of children and babies I saw sitting there, helpless, looking at me and hoping I could make a difference and so I will and you must to [sic]."

And "I could make a difference and so I will and you must too." Well said, Marty, I just wish everyone involved during the storm's aftermath had your spirit and heart. Unfortunately, many in positions of power or influence just didn't have it in them. This hurt many people, and some died directly from hurricanes and floods while others died from human action and inaction.

CHAPTER TEN

OPRAH'S SUPERDOME

———— ■ ————

We had now come full circle as it was right before dawn on Sunday morning. This was the seventh day after Hurricane Katrina made landfall. The number seven normally represents completion. From where I stood, it seemed like we were light years from wrapping up this disaster. The drama we were dealing with was still multidimensional and constantly evolving.

If there was any good news to hang onto it was on the evacuation efforts. We were making real progress. The Superdome was finally empty, and the Convention Center had a steady line of buses arriving and picking people up. General Honoré and I had met late the night before, and he assured me that the last person would be evacuated from there before the sun went down. So far so good as he was delivering as he normally did.

Just like a hurricane storm surge, the media circus was growing exponentially by the hour. Everyone was jumping on the bandwagon. Trucks and associated reporters were everywhere trying to get the freshest angle that others may have overlooked. Canal Street around the Sheraton hotel was jammed with tents that doubled as makeshift studios where news updates were broadcast around the world. They commandeered the area in the middle of the street where our world-famous streetcars normally ran. These news organizations came into the city and were fairly self-contained with campers, satellite trucks, and backup generators.

Most of the early ones were able to capture the essence of what was transpiring with all the raw emotions and frustrations from our people freely flowing on camera. Just about all of the citizens who had endured the past six days were absolutely outraged at the anemic response and rescue. They had been on such an emotional rollercoaster ride that many were now breaking down in tears on a regular basis. And with so many media people in town, these episodes were being captured on film, radio, or in print.

The blame game was definitely picking up steam as major cracks in the federal government's arguments regarding their delayed and inadequate response started to show. The American people were pretty fed up, and calls for congressional hearings echoed from New York to California. There was now intense focus on trying to sort out truth from lies and to place responsibility and accountability on those who had turned their backs on fellow Americans during such a time of need. To counter this, the spin masters were now working overtime to deflect attention.

First thing that morning, Colonel Ebbert received a message that Secretary Chertoff of Homeland Security was requesting that I meet him at the Zephyr baseball field, which was near the Saints training facility in Metairie, a suburb next to New Orleans. Earlier on *Meet the Press*, Secretary Chertoff explained to a national TV audience that FEMA had "pre-staged a tremendous number of supplies, meals, shelter, and water" in anticipation of Hurricane Katrina. He went on to brag that even before the storm hit, dozens of Coast Guard helicopters were on standby nearby. "So the difficulty wasn't a lack of supplies," he said.

This was totally counter to what we had experienced over the past six days. We had been begging and begging for supplies. We had received much-needed resources only a day or so earlier. The Coast Guard helicopter pilots who were with us right after the storm were stuck with confusing orders for rescue missions. General Honoré and I had to give them the go-ahead to get things rolling.

It would have been very interesting if the secretary would have gone to Houston or any other shelter that same morning and told evacuees who were stranded in and around the Superdome for days on end about how well prepared he was. I'm sure they would have given him a much different account, with some very spicy New Orleans language thrown in for full effect.

Colonel Ebbert arranged for our Black Hawk helicopter to take us to meet the secretary. I cancelled my normal inspection flyover of the city for what I thought was an important meeting. As we were landing at the Zephyrs' field, I asked my staff to stay alert and mentally record what they saw. There was a beehive of activity below us, and everything looked pristine and new. Once we departed the helicopter, we walked into an administration building and asked around, but no one seemed to know where Secretary Chertoff was; he was nowhere to be found. We checked our watches and verified that we were on time as we continued to search.

As I was scanning the facility, I noticed a fireman sitting alone with a sort of detached, disturbed look on his face. I could tell he wasn't from Louisiana by the colors of his fireman shirt. So I walked up to him, said hello, and asked him where he was from. He perked up a bit and told me he was from California. I asked him what part and then started thanking him for being here to help us in our time of need. I then inquired as to what time this morning had he arrived. The disturbed look returned on his face as he proceeded to tell me that as soon as he heard that Katrina had hit, that very day he and some of his fellow firefighters left California and drove all night and most of the next day to come to help out.

The more he talked the angrier he became as he went on to explain that they had been here for nearly a week and were told by the state and FEMA that they could not enter the city. "I've been here for days, and they won't let me go in to help you guys," he said. I could clearly see his sincerity and frustration. This was another hard pill to swallow as we desperately needed more manpower, and here it was just sitting unused in the suburbs. I told him thank you again and assured him we would do everything in our power to get him in the game so his long ride here would not be wasted. He was thankful, and we shook hands as I moved on to try to locate the missing Secretary Chertoff.

As we walked around, Sally informed me that it was also very interesting that right after Secretary Chertoff completed his segment on *Meet the Press*, President Aaron Broussard of Jefferson Parish also appeared on the show. He very emphatically told story after story of how FEMA was making his life a living hell as he had responsibility for communities near New Orleans and some of the other hardest hit areas near the Gulf of Mexico. According to President Broussard, the same bureaucratic insanity that we were fighting was also his cross to bear.

During his segment of the show, he went on to mention that Wal-Mart had agreed to deliver three trucks of water, but FEMA would not let them into the area. He said, "FEMA turned them back. They said we didn't need them. This was a week ago. FEMA—we had a thousand gallons of diesel fuel on a Coast Guard vessel docked in my parish. The Coast Guard said, 'Come get the fuel right away.' When we got there with our trucks, they got a word. 'FEMA says don't give you the fuel.' Yesterday—yesterday—FEMA comes in and cuts all of our emergency communication lines. They cut them without notice. Our sheriff, Harry Lee, goes back in, he reconnects the line. He posts armed guards on our lines and says, 'No one is getting near these lines.' Sheriff Harry Lee said that if America—American government would have responded like Wal-Mart has responded, we wouldn't be in this crisis." President Broussard was extremely emotional on this show.

He was also very right. If FEMA and the federal government had all the National Guard and U.S. Army troops in the area that they were claiming were here, then where were they or why were they not fully deployed? If there were companies willing to donate critical supplies, then why were we not allowed to accept them? If we needed emergency communications lines, then why was FEMA cutting them off without notice? These questions we may never get the answers to. It's like the saying, "If a frog had wings he wouldn't bump his butt when he jumped." There is no real answer to the *if* about frogs nor the *if* concerning FEMA.

Back at the Saints/Zephyrs practice facility, we walked and walked around looking for the secretary. Finally in the distance we could see a large group of people with cameras filming their movements. We headed in that direction and discovered that in fact Secretary Chertoff was in the group submerged in a sea of reporters. FEMA director Michael Brown was also there getting face time with the cameras. I caught up with them, waded through the crowd, stood in front of the secretary, said hello, and asked him how he was doing. We shook hands, he said hello and made a few comments about being happy that so many resources were here in the area and progress was being made. Our interaction was very short and obviously designed to play in front of the many reporters and cameras. He then turned and walked away.

This all struck me as being extremely disingenuous. I just stood in place for a few minutes to process what had just happened as I watched him move around the field holding court with various reporters. It was clear to me that I had been called over to just have a photo op with the secretary. My blood pressure went up again as I now realized that he was wasting our collective time. One of his aides walked up to our group and told me that the secretary would like to see me a little later. I turned to my staff and said, "Bump this, we're out of here." We then started heading back toward our Black Hawk. We didn't have all day to wait around for him to free up his busy media schedule to meet with us to blow smoke up our butts. There were just too many critical things to do back in our tormented city.

We walked around the field toward the administration building because while we were out there we might as well get a quick bite to eat. As we walked I started to really pay attention to what was all around. All of a sudden we were all startled by how much stuff was out here. There were supplies and equipment in such abundance that we stood frozen in astonishment. There were rows and rows of high-water vehicles in the parking lots. Supply trucks full of goods were lined up right behind each other and seemed to stretch for almost a mile along a road that ran through the property. You name it, and it was there.

There were unused port-a-lets lined up side by side all the way around and behind the practice football field. There were rows and rows of portable streetlights with generators, some still with bubble wrap around them. This was particularly hurtful as we had been begging for these items for days so that we could provide some light at night to the people in and around the Superdome and the Convention Center. There were ice and water trucks everywhere.

The thought struck me—what type of person would make a decision to withhold desperately needed resources from suffering people in need? Instead of being used as media props, these desperately needed resources could have relieved suffering by cooling people down and hydrating them as day after day they were relentlessly exposed to the uncompromising heat and scorching August sun. As of that day, not one piece of ice had made it to New Orleans. I couldn't imagine a single good reason that would justify what we were seeing and why these items had not been deployed where they were needed most. These critical assets had been sitting outside of the city for God knows how long when they could have made a real difference over the past six days for many Americans.

As we entered the New Orleans Saints administration building and walked into the cafeteria, it was like walking into a high-quality, all-you-can-eat restaurant. It was overflowing with food and drinks. They had everything that we could have ever dreamed of eating. A chef was busy replenishing and stacking food wherever he could. There were crates and crates of water, food, fruit, whole watermelons, ice, soft drinks, hamburgers, sandwiches, french fries, and potato chips. You name it and it was here. We all ended up eating a sandwich and drinking a cold soft drink. It was heavenly. But since we had not been eating much over the past few days, our stomachs could not accept much more.

As we were about to leave, we stuffed some granola and candy bars in our pockets for later. Once outside, Louis picked up a football that was lying around on the field and started to kick it around. I took this opportunity to grab some privacy and headed toward the port-a-let. I finally had the urge to have my first bowel movement since Katrina hit. I think with all the stress and adrenaline that had been flowing through my body, not to mention the rations of one so-so meal a day, my system had shut down.

It wasn't until I saw all of those port-o-lets that I realized I hadn't gone in a while. Since I had my pick of hundreds of toilets, I went into one that seemed like it hadn't ever been used. I gave it a very good christening. I rejoined the group, feeling better and about five pounds lighter.

As I rejoined the group, we all drank another cold beverage, talked in amazement at all that we had seen, and took a group picture in front of a Saints sign that read, "You Gotta Have FAITH." This experience added to many others that seemed dreamlike. In a way it was a good escape for all of us as we ended up relaxing just a bit. We talked and laughed out loud and thoroughly enjoyed the air-conditioning. After what seem like an hour had passed and still no Secretary Chertoff, I decided it was time to leave as Sally was pressing me that I had a very high-profile interview to do when we got back. We walked slowly back to the Black Hawk and asked the pilot to take us home. We were soon headed back into hell surrounded by hot water, the city of New Orleans.

As we were landing Sally asked me if I remembered who I was going to interview with. I told her absolutely, the queen of talk show TV and one of the richest women in the country, Ms. Oprah Winfrey. I was very honored that she wanted to interview me, but Sally was absolutely beside herself with excitement. Ms. Winfrey's producers had prearranged this interview a few days before, and it was scheduled to take place around noon starting in the atrium of the Hyatt hotel.

At twelve o'clock sharp Oprah Winfrey entered the Hyatt with her entourage in tow. They had been escorted from the heliport by Chief Compass. Oprah saw me coming toward her and extended her hand and introduced herself. She asked how I was doing, and we chatted for a few minutes before getting started with the interview. I was so focused on the disaster and our challenges that I was not star-struck at all. Besides, Ms. Winfrey was very friendly, calming, and really down to earth. She was not at all pretentious and came across as personable, kind, and caring. She wasn't dressed up like the extremely glamorous

Oprah that everyone is accustomed to seeing on television. She had dressed for the occasion, jeans and a long-sleeve T-shirt. It was a smart move, and she fit right in as the city wasn't looking too glamorous at the moment either.

We started the interview in the atrium area and then moved to walking and talking as we made our way toward the Superdome. Oprah started out by asking me all the usual questions. How many levee breaches were there? How high were the water levels? How much of the city was damaged? I answered every question without hesitation. I told her that this was an unprecedented event and one that was such a tragedy that you could even say the dead drowned again. In New Orleans we bury our dead for the most part above ground since our water table is so high. Most of the mausoleums were totally submerged.

She then turned her questioning to the looting, asking why it got so out of control. I proceeded to tell her how the looting started and how it evolved. I very succinctly explained how things evolved.

Ms. Winfrey then asked about the Convention Center, which by now was around 75 percent evacuated. I explained to her how we opened this center out of necessity and how it did not have the same security measures as the Superdome because we did not have the time or resources to confiscate weapons.

We then talked about some of the reported violence and how some gangs were even protecting citizens at night. I tried to emphasize that we needed to get everyone out as soon as possible as we had tourists and people from other parishes all mixed up with some pretty rough characters. I pleaded with her to help us get the word out and keep up pressure on the federal and state government to continue to help us. At that moment my eyes started to well up.

In the background I could see Chief Compass moving around very anxiously. He just couldn't keep still and kept moving closer to Oprah and me. Then without warning he verbally exploded in front of the cameras. He started telling stories of multiple rapes occurring in the Convention Center and Superdome. These were the same stories he had been telling us, saying that these events were occurring every night in substantial numbers.

However, only the night before, Chief Compass told *The Guardian*, a British national daily and weekly newspaper with the second largest online readership of any English-language newspaper in the world, "We don't have any substantiated rapes. We will investigate if they come forward." But now in front of Oprah he claimed that babies were also getting raped. He then told her about the failed kidnap attempt against him at the Convention Center. Next thing I know, he was sobbing, and grabbing Oprah and holding onto her. I'd never seen him in this state before. The lack of sleep, his friend committing suicide, and all the other stress associated with this disaster was really getting to the chief.

Ms. Winfrey handled this fairly well, but I could tell that she was very uncomfortable. I intervened by asking Oprah if we could take a break. She agreed and the cameras were turned off. I pulled Chief Compass to the side, making sure we were a good distance from everyone else. I said, "Chief, you've got to calm down, and pull yourself together. You have to leave Oprah alone and let her finish this interview. This is not going to come across well for you at the rate you're going." He then sat down in a nearby chair, calmed down a bit, and then suddenly got up and quietly left the building.

The interview resumed as we moved downstairs to the entrance of the hotel and shopping center. This was the staging area where people moved from the Superdome to the streets to get on buses. Many had waited so many days in the hot sun and then waited again in here until they were told some buses were outside. Oprah and I talked on camera about how tough that must have been, particularly on our senior citizens. We rummaged through the garbage that was piled high and found several very personal belongings that had been mistakenly left behind.

As I already mentioned earlier, our distressed citizens got up quickly from where they were sitting on the floor, and some left everything, including IDs and other personal items as they boarded the buses. My staff had gone through and gotten many personal items out of the trash, but it was obvious that we needed to make another sweep. We then walked slowly through this area to the shopping center area and to the Superdome itself. Everywhere we walked it was full of trash, and it was funky. This was a big mess. We all found it hard to come to grips with the fact that this was an area where human beings, Americans, had lived and suffered for several long days.

We then moved closer to the Superdome and finally stopped by the main doors. We talked about this being the place where thirty thousand people suffered for many days. Oprah then announced that she wanted to go inside. This building had been sealed up tight by the National Guard right after all the people had been evacuated. There were big chains on the doors now. We believed that the environment inside was unsanitary and was a potential health hazard, so it was important to keep people out until it was completely cleaned and sanitized.

I told Oprah that many people had suffered unnecessarily in the building; she nodded her head in agreement. "The story that would be amazing to Americans is how did this happen? How could the richest country in the world let Americans suffer the way they did over the past week? The state of Louisiana has an $18 billion budget and allowed our people to suffer," I said. "This is a travesty; this is unbelievable; this was inhumane. That Superdome, you wait 'til you see it… if you go in there. I really do not advise that you go in there." Oprah's response was, "Yes. I've come here, and America wants to see exactly where these people spent the last week."

This would be the first time that I toured the Superdome after all the people were evacuated, and it would be with Oprah Winfrey. I was very concerned with people going back in unprotected because it could be toxic inside. Oprah thought I was being tongue in cheek about not recommending she go inside, but I was serious. So I turned to her and said, "You really want to go in?" and she said yes. I then said, "Okay, turn to this camera and repeat after me…I, Oprah Winfrey, promise not to hold the city liable financially or otherwise as a result of me going into this doggone stinky-ass Superdome." I caught her a little off guard, but she quickly recovered. She then repeated what I asked her to say, without the stinky part of course. I said one more time, "Are you sure you want to do this?" Her response was, "I do." So I turned to the National Guard and authoritatively said, "Alright, open it up."

As they were unlocking the chains, I advised Oprah and her crew that as they entered the building it would be better for their own comfort to initially breathe through their mouths and not their noses. This would help them to adjust to the foul smell much quicker.

Soon the doors were opened, and we went in. As we slowly entered the building, I realized that regardless of my advice to breathe through our mouths, I could still smell and now taste funk. We walked slower toward the stands area where the open football field was. The camera light was shining brightly on both of us as we very cautiously ventured deeper into the facility. The building was dingy, dark, and wet. It felt haunted, and I could see a light fog of some sort in the main area. There was some light coming into the facility from several nice-sized holes in the roof that had been blown open by Hurricane Katrina.

As we walked, Oprah and I talked about the people and what they must have experienced. She was in tears and choked up a few times. As I looked around and fully felt some of what my citizens went through, I became extremely mad and sad at the same time. I just couldn't image my mother or sisters being in here for any extended period of time. The other thing that jumped out at us as we surveyed this pitiful facility was that there was filth and trash everywhere. It broke our hearts to see little makeshift beds made out of cardboard boxes and piles and piles of garbage.

Pretty soon we both knew that we had seen enough, and without saying a word we started walking out of this haunted place. In fact, we really didn't stay in the Superdome very long—probably ten to fifteen minutes maximum. However, it felt like we were in there for several hours. As we were walking out it struck me how quickly I really had adjusted to the foul smell inside. Unfortunately, it did leave a very bad taste in my mouth even after I was able to get outside and breathe in fresh air.

Now that we were outside again, we took a quick break to clear our heads and then started walking around the outside of the Superdome. There were some tents that had been set up for military people. Suddenly Oprah saw one or two lost, frightened little dogs. They were seemingly frantically searching for their owners and some food.

At this point Ms. Winfrey stopped everything and became very emotional again. It was very clear that she loved animals, especially ones who were suffering. She grabbed her hands together and put them on her chest and said to me, "Oh, these poor little dogs," and then shed a few more tears as she tried to pet them. We quickly managed to get her away from these animals as we did not know if they were sick, had a serious disease, or worse, rabies.

We continue our interview as we walked closer to the heliport. The second part of the interview was getting ready to start, a helicopter ride that would allow Oprah to view the entire city from above. Everyone strapped on their seat belts as her cameraman positioned himself where he could get the best shots during our tour.

I instructed the pilot to take us on my normal flight plan that we took just about every day. We left the Superdome area and headed for the Seventeenth Street Canal levee breach. On the way there we could see the water levels were still high and that work at the breaches was ongoing at a very busy pace. We next flew over Gentilly and saw the flooded stadiums and then headed toward the Lower Ninth Ward where we came across a few people who were amazingly still stranded. They were mostly in the apartment buildings as there were very few people on top of single-family homes.

I asked the pilot to circle and get closer so we could hopefully drop them some food and water. I was very concerned how after seven days they were still able to survive in these conditions. As the helicopter tried to get lower and lower for us to make the drops, the whirling helicopter blades started to push loose debris from roofs and in the water up toward the people as they quickly made their way back inside. With all our good intentions of delivering them food and water, the wind from the helicopter blades made it nearly impossible for us to properly position the drop. The supplies were not getting close enough for any citizen to retrieve them. After several failed drops we gave up, and the pilot radioed the Coast Guard their location for future rescue missions.

We continued to fly over the Lower Ninth Ward and saw all the homes that had been destroyed. We saw the barge that was stuck inside of a neighborhood and large, gaping levee breaches. We left there as we headed up the river to Jackson Square in the French Quarter. The pilot stopped in front of St. Louis Cathedral so the cameraman could get a really good shot to show that our unique cultural assets had been spared.

We ended the flight by circling around the Hyatt Regency hotel where our command center was operating. The cameraman was able to get great shots of how the tornados had broken out all the windows from a major section of the facility. There was also an interesting shot of an American flag that had obviously been flying since before the storm. The edges of our flag were literally torn off by the high winds. This tattered flag spoke volumes about how our country performed during this disaster. Our reputation around the world was now just as tattered.

On the flip side, the Hyatt Regency brand received so much free publicity during this time. They loved this incredible exposure even though it was related to a disaster. Every major reporter or media star like Ms. Winfrey that we took up, we'd ended the helicopter tour by circling this now famous Hyatt hotel.

Once on the ground, Oprah looked into the camera and very seriously said, "Nothing I saw on television prepared me for what I experienced on the ground, right here in New Orleans."

Once the filming and interview was completed, Ms. Winfrey and I hugged and said our goodbyes. She told me if she could do anything to help to let her know. I replied that her being here, caring about us, and doing a show on our plight was more than enough. I later learned that when she returned to Chicago she immediately donated money to an organization that was responsible for rescuing and caring for homeless Katrina animals. She also gave money to evacuees in

Houston and even bought several of them homes. *Business Week* magazine and the *New York Beacon* newspaper reported that Ms. Winfrey donated over $10 million of her own money for various Katrina relief and recovery efforts. I guess that bad taste in her mouth from her initial breathing inside the Superdome didn't linger for New Orleans after all. She helped us in many more ways than we can ever pay back.

It was now time to get back to the real world of post-Katrina New Orleans. All during the Oprah interview I had been thinking about Chief Compass and his outbursts. I was very concerned about his well-being. We walked back to the hotel to try and find the chief, but he was nowhere to be found.

I then started to think back and try to connect the dots to his puzzle. With all the chaos that unfolded over the last week, it was now becoming clear to me that many of his reports and comments that at the time I took as gospel may have been more of his stress reaction to the pressures of Katrina and of seeing his good friend commit suicide. He would say something one day and then retract it the next. As I replayed these scenes in my head, it was painfully evident that he had been sort of unraveling right before our eyes, but we were too busy to fully understand it.

After arriving at the hotel, we looked around again inside but still could not locate him. So I started talking about the chief with my staff, and we all began to realize that all was not well with him. I had Deputy Chief Riley to come and sit down with me to discuss what he was seeing. Riley explained that Chief Compass had not been himself for several days. We then talked about Compass's claim that he was almost kidnapped at the Convention Center. Deputy Chief Riley told me he could not verify this actually happened.

Sally Forman complained that he'd started doing his own press conferences without coordinating with her. At first these were fairly innocent, but as time went on she became very concerned by his actions.

I now had a clearer picture and ordered him to cease all independent press conferences. We also started watching him closer as I did not want to risk losing my good friend and another police officer. I had to quickly figure out a way to get him some much-needed rest and relaxation so he could clear his head.

Around the same time that we were putting two and two together on Chief Compass, we started to hear that President Aaron Broussard of Jefferson Parish was not handling his stress well either. In fact, he was really losing it, starting with his toupee that he had worn for several decades. It now seemed that after seven days the pressure had become too much for most. Reports were continually coming in that people were breaking down regularly.

The governor was very emotional on and off camera and now Parish President Broussard was wailing and screaming that no one was coming to help him. During a WWL radio interview he started mimicking that he was sick of all the press conferences and shouted, "Shut up and send us somebody," as he broke down again. He would later repeat this behavior during national television interviews.

Then he stopped shaving and grew a beard. The first time we saw him in person was several days later at a press conference with the governor. Halfway through the session I looked over his way and was shocked to see he did not have his hairpiece on. No one wanted to be rude and stare, but we had just seen him with hair right a few days earlier. He would later publically say that Jefferson Parish needed a different head of government, and he was determined to give them one.

We all were struggling, but he was sliding fast. Some would later tell me that during that time Broussard was getting calls from constituents and other political types who told him he needed to do something to reposition Jefferson Parish as it was getting lost behind all the New Orleans attention. They insisted that he needed to somehow grab the media's attention.

He was already taking heavy criticism for ordering his pump station operators to leave their posts before the storm hit, so in essence Jefferson Parish had little to no pumping capacity when they needed it most. This led to major flooding, particularly in areas where very expensive homes were. President Broussard must have thought they had all their bases covered by implementing their so-called "doomsday plan." His big miscalculation was sending their pump operators home before Katrina hit. As a result, they had no one to make corrections to start up their pumps as water flowed on both sides of the parish line.

Mr. Broussard astonishingly closed his national TV appearance on *Meet the Press* by announcing that because of a serious lack of support from the federal government, he was taking the necessary steps for his parish to secede from the United States of America. It was reported that he announced he was creating his own country and declaring it "Jeffatonia."

Midafternoon, Sally reminded me that I had another national TV interview scheduled. I looked at her without saying a word, but my expression was saying, "You have to be kidding me, right?" She told me it was with John Donvan from ABC's *Nightline*. Like everyone else, today was also an extreme emotional day for me, and I was more than mentally and physically drained. However, duty called as I was determined to get the truth out and keep our citizens and the nation informed on what was really going on in our city.

I met Mr. Donvan in the lobby of the hotel, and we decided to immediately take a helicopter tour before the sun went down. We followed the exact same route that I had taken Oprah and her team several hours earlier. He too was blown away at how destructive these levee breaches were to the city as the view from above exposed the entire magnitude of our challenge. Once we landed, we went back to the Hyatt atrium area to complete the interview. Mr. Donvan of course mentioned the radio interview where I'd used a few choice cuss words. We rehashed one more time all that had happened and what was happening now.

It must have been divine intervention that got me on the Garland Robinette show that particular day. Looking back, it is clear that that was a key turning point with the whole response to rescue and aid from the federal and state governments. The media attention we were getting was putting such intense pressure on them that they were now literally forced by public will to do something substantial and fast.

The other sticky question that Mr. Donvan and others continued to raise was did I believe the lack of response was based on race? Jesse Jackson apparently was interviewed a couple of days earlier and had said that some of the imagery of people stranded on the highways confined by barricades looked like scenes from slave trafficking ships. Donvan asked me my thoughts, and I responded, "I will tell you this. I think it could be, but it's also a class issue. Because I don't think this type of response would have happened if this was Orange County, California. This response definitely wouldn't have happened if it were Manhattan, New York. And I don't know if it's color or class or both." I then made reference to the Gretna attacks that happened the previous Thursday when our people were trying to walk out of the drowned city to safety and were fired upon and told to turn back immediately. We concluded the interview, and it was broadcast around the nation. The question of race and disasters continued during those early days and is still appropriately being discussed today.

This very dominant issue of race was being seeded from many different angles and players. Three days after the storm hit New Orleans, on September 1, 2005, Republican House Speaker Dennis Hastert from Illinois proclaimed to the nation that from his perspective, "It isn't sensible to rebuild the city. It doesn't make any sense to me." He went on to say that he questioned the wisdom of rebuilding a city below sea level that will continue to be in the path of powerful hurricanes. A day earlier a Connecticut newspaper wrote an editorial entitled, "Is New Orleans Worth Reclaiming?" It went on to write, "If the people of New Orleans insist on living in harm's way, they ought to accept responsibility for what happens to them and their properties."

Since New Orleans was a 67 percent African American city, then it is not a far reach to conclude that many of these comments had racial bents to them. Would they have said the same thing about Los Angeles or San Francisco if they had suffered a major earthquake? Would the same comments be made in American's heartland if a major tornado had devastated several cities in "tornado alley"? Would they say the same things if New York or Chicago was hit with an once-in-a-lifetime blizzard that shut down these two great cities for many weeks? I would think not, but for whatever reason our right to exist and rebuild was being put out there for a one-way debate where we were not allowed much of a voice.

To add further fuel to this racial firestorm, HUD secretary Alphonso Jackson, a black Republican in the Bush administration, told the *Houston Chronicle* newspaper several weeks later that in his opinion New Orleans might not ever again be predominantly black. He was also quoted as saying, "Whether we like it or not, New Orleans is not going to be five hundred thousand people for a very long time." He then went on to say, "New Orleans is not going to be as black as it was for a long time, if ever again." Mr. Jackson further opined that he wasn't sure the Ninth Ward, a predominantly black and low-income community, should be rebuilt at all. He kept going by predicting that New Orleans would very slowly grow back but only 35 to 40 percent of the post-Katrina population would be black. This very powerful man would be in charge of how federal recovery dollars would be spent in the city.

In addition, a University of New Orleans professor revealed that he had full renderings for a fancy new private golf course to be built in the Lower Ninth Ward. This is land that has belonged to many African American families for multiple generations.

In spite of all this tactless rhetoric and forecasting, five years after Hurricane Katrina hit New Orleans, the population has rebounded above his prediction, we are the fastest growing city in America, and 62 percent of our citizens are African American. The Lower Ninth Ward is also steadily being rebuilt higher and better. I guess we can conclude that Secretary Jackson's future career will not be as a fortune teller in Jackson Square in the French Quarter.

Back at the Hyatt, I had one more national interview to do with *60 Minutes* before my public day concluded. To put things in perspective, we were wrapping up a full week of post-Katrina rescue and recovery activities. We had performed monumental miracles by getting the city through its darkest hours. We had also stabilized her with very limited resources. The twenty-four hundred emergency preparedness workers—police officers, firefighters, and the National Guard—held the city intact before any other help arrived. It was touch and go many times, but we somehow pulled through with the grace of God.

By Sunday evening, Deputy Chief Riley announced that there were now more than twenty-nine hundred National Guard troops operating in the city. There were also twenty-two hundred troops from the Eighty-second Airborne Division that had finally arrived. We expected more troops would be arriving over the next few days.

By day's end we had successfully evacuated the remaining twenty thousand people out of the Convention Center. This work was done all in one day. As the sun had set over a contaminated and fairly ruined New Orleans, we were preparing ourselves for the monumental task ahead of draining the city, respecting the dead, and repopulating the dryer, least flooded areas. We would have to be patient and take one step at a time as we gradually got back on our feet again.

As we wrapped up a *60 Minutes* interview, I told Scott Pelley, "My heart is broken. When you see a city that you love so much and you see it devastated and almost dead, you wonder what the future looks like." Later that night in the solitude of my super-heated hotel room I came to realize maybe this was a new beginning. The good news was that the future was now ours to shape, and we had a whole lot of shaping to do.

CHAPTER ELEVEN

SHADOW GOVERNMENT

———————■———————

W e were moving into week two, and there was clear evidence of positive momentum on many fronts. Update meetings highlighted significant progress on citizen evacuation and other critical matters. The Superdome, Convention Center, and interstates were all empty of people. Massive amounts of trash were all that was left at these locations.

Electrical power was slowly being restored in the least flooded areas of the city. By midmorning, Entergy had managed to repair key substations, and power was on in a few buildings in the CBD and French Quarter. Dan Packer, CEO of Entergy New Orleans, advised me he was expecting power to be fully restored in these two areas within two weeks.

Other encouraging news was that the Army Corps of Engineers, utilizing Chinook and Black Hawk helicopters, had been working around the clock dropping large sandbags to plug the Seventeenth Street Canal breach. Around noon I went up on my daily helicopter tour, and I could now see the tops of many sandbags poking out of the water like golden seals basking in the sun. Working side by side, a local contractor with several Bobcats was bridging the gap by slowly building a dirt and rock road across the top of these sandbags.

In addition to powering buildings, Entergy, Sewerage and Water Board engineers, and the Army Corps of Engineers were working feverishly to get all the Sewerage and Water Board's pumping stations back up and running. They were particularly focused on Pump Station Number 6 near the Seventeenth Street Canal. This was our largest and most powerful station, and it could pump almost ten thousand cubic feet of water per second. The other critical job that was well underway was the repairing of breaches on the London Avenue Canal. This canal drains water from the Seventh Ward up to Gentilly and the Lakefront area. Once these two canals were plugged, then widespread pumping and dewatering would commence.

Our plan was to start pumping floodwater out slowly so we wouldn't put too much pressure on the newly secured levee walls. Then if all went well, we would ramp up to capacity so water would flow quickly into Lake Pontchartrain and ultimately back to where it came from. This was very encouraging news, and by Tuesday, the plan was working well enough for us to notice that water levels in some parts of the city were subsiding. Last week 80 percent of the city was under water. By this week's end only 60 percent was still submerged.

Help and expertise was coming from many sources as international experts were also involved. They brought temporary pumps to move water out quicker. We only experienced one minor hiccup when Pumping Station 6 became operational and sucked in some storm debris. After being temporarily shut down, repairs were quickly made, and full-strength dewatering resumed once again. With all of this progress, a rainbow of hope formed for all involved.

As the Corps of Engineers continued to focus on closing the levee breaches, the Sewerage and Water Board worked feverishly to remove and repair all of the other flooded pumps. Most of them had been invaded by saltwater and had to be individually treated, cleaned, and baked dry to avoid future damage. Over 150 permanent pumps were being worked on locally and in Texas. Marcia St. Martin expedited this process via my emergency authority and spent almost $60 million over a two-week period. As repairs were completed, we were able to accelerate dewatering efforts. The Corps of Engineers originally estimated it would take eighty days, but our team was very confident we would have the city totally drained much faster.

I spent the better part of Monday and Tuesday on the phone and in meetings, staying on top of things. We were also coordinating downtime flights for our first responders. I knew that these disaster warriors needed time off to rest, recuperate, and reconnect with their families.

For example, a day or two earlier about a hundred of our firefighters were performing house-to-house search missions in the Lower Ninth Ward. They were stunned by what they discovered in one location. They encountered so many dead bodies that the scene overwhelmed most of them to the point where they broke down, either sick to their stomachs or sobbing in tears.

This tipping point was the culmination of seeing so much carnage over the course of the week and sheer exhaustion from working so many hours under the most stressful conditions. I knew they had reached their limit, and we just couldn't afford to lose another person to suicide or to making a life-threatening mistake. So we were all busy arranging relief. This was an enormous undertaking as locating their families was very challenging. The final piece to this puzzle was the extensive physical and psychological examinations I mentioned earlier that had been set up in Baton Rouge, the state capital.

Help came in from everywhere, from regular Joe Blow citizen to the chairman of Southwest Airlines. It was so heartwarming and very much appreciated. Many good-hearted people also sent clothes, shoes, sheets, pots and pans, toiletries, and any other item they thought our people needed. New Orleanians were also welcomed with open arms all across the country. This was truly a blessing.

Although progress was evident in many areas, we still faced challenges. One big one was a concern that there could still be five thousand to ten thousand people hiding out in their homes, still not wanting to evacuate. This was problematic on several fronts. Many abandoned wooden buildings throughout the city were regularly bursting into flames. There were also unknown chemicals and open gas leaks still catching fire in the floodwater. This created the potential for large-scale explosions. The stagnant toxic water included a mixture of sewerage and decomposing cadavers, which also compounded fears that diseases were present and could spread quickly. I along with others concluded it just wasn't safe for people to remain in the city while it was in this state.

My next order was to direct the National Guard, police, and fire-fighters to strongly encouraging everyone to immediately leave the city. We now had over four thousand National Guard troops and about the same number of paratroopers from the U.S. Army's Eighty-second Airborne Division in the city primarily focused on rescue and dead body retrievals. The FEMA morgue team was also in place for the actual extraction of corpses. Resources were plentiful and coming from everywhere.

On many of these search and rescue missions, emergency workers and the military were able to provide food and water to those who had been hiding out. Citizens were also updated on the city's very danger-ous conditions. They were offered assistance in evacuating. Most took the offers, but some did not. For those who elected to stay, we made it very clear that they were totally on their own. This additional bit of real-ity worked to get others to leave, but there were still some stubborn holdouts. A day or two later the U.S. Army would do a much stronger follow-up. Since martial law was not an option in our state, their firm power of persuasion was their best weapon to get these remaining recalcitrant homeowners to leave. The rules of engagement for federal troops at this point were rifles down, rhetoric up, so to speak.

In order to ensure a disciplined, comprehensive sweep of the entire city, Deputy Chief Warren Riley, who knew the city best, worked with General Honoré in coordinating a plan for detailed systematic sweeps that utilized search and rescue teams from every discipline. To document their work and to leave a clear trail of what was done, they devised a unique marking pattern for each inspected structure. A cross inside of a circle was sprayed on the outside of the building to indicate the initials of the emergency crew who visited the residence, and another marking detailed any fatalities that were found. Animals were also included in their counts.

Many times these markers would have a big "0" indicating no dead bodies inside, other times there would be "1" or "2." They also noted where bodies were found: "1 dead inside," "2 dead in the attic," or "1 dead dog under house." Years later, some of these markings can still be found in New Orleans. They stand out as reminders that we should never forget what happened to this city when Katrina turned us upside down.

The process of searching for and retrieving the dead was complicated, exhausting, and extremely emotional. Because of high water and storm debris, many times emergency personnel were forced to wade through chest-high water while clearing piles and piles of debris just to make a path into a house. There they would have to climb and crawl over trash, old furniture, partially collapsed walls, and people's personal belongings to find remains. Specially trained dogs worked closely with these rescue crews. Their keen sense of smell became a prized tool to help narrow down the searches.

Every house and every building in the city would be searched and marked. By Monday afternoon, with the vast manpower now onboard, we managed to go through 20 percent of the city's structures in one full day. When we did come across a home where there was a living, breathing person, they were usually elderly and/or sick. They had been holding on for dear life without much food and water, and most had been without medicines for several days. This was all the more reason to push harder to get them out of harm's way.

On Wednesday, September 7, 2005, I announced a follow-up to my original mandatory evacuation order. This one did not give residents any options. Everyone had to leave, and I wanted to put maximum pressure on anyone remaining in the city. But before I put the order into effect, I had to debate with FEMA officials that this was not a license for them to cut off supplies again. They started quoting a bizarre interpretation of an obscure section of the Stafford Act. FEMA officials claimed that if I ordered this type of mandatory evacuation, they would be required to cease all food and water supplies coming into the city, even for first responders.

Fortunately, I had spoken with Secretary Chertoff about this a day or two before, and he told me not worry about it, that he would

personally waive this unique interpretation. Surprisingly, he followed up and got his people to back down without having to sign an
actual waiver. Score one win for the big guy at the top of the federal
bureaucracy.

In the press conference to announce this updated evacuation
order, I emphasized that I was not in any way suggesting we were
giving up on New Orleans. I explained that we were in a very volatile situation, with lots of chemicals in the floodwater and multiple gas
leaks bubbling up with fires igniting. There was just no way to know
what was going to happen next. This updated order essentially closed
the city to anyone not identified as law enforcement, military, public
safety, health officials, utility workers, and recovery contractors. This
order would remain in effect until utilities were restored and the city
was completely dewatered.

At this point I was also feeling much better about the level of support we were receiving from federal and state officials. During our
last conference call with the president and governor it was confirmed
that final evacuations were almost complete, federal troops were now
present in significant numbers, and the Seventeenth Street and other
canals were being repaired. I emphasized on the call that we now
needed to turn our focus to totally dewatering the city. The president
assured me he'd get all the resources we needed to get this completed
quickly.

After the press conference, General Honoré asked me and a few
on my executive staff to follow him. "I'm taking all of ya'll to dinner.
And I've arranged warm showers also," he barked. Things were indeed
looking up. I would get the opportunity to have two decent showers
in the course of four days. Life was getting much better.

General Honoré took us on the USS *Iwo Jima*, an extremely large
amphibious assault ship with a helicopter landing pad that had recently
docked near the Convention Center. The ship served as a flagship for
the president and acted as the central command center for all federal
disaster recovery operations. We very willingly followed the assertive
general and went aboard.

As we walked past the entrance plank, Honoré turned and proudly announced, "And you can watch Monday night football as well." We all smiled as if we were getting ready to slip back to the future, at least for a few hours anyway. After we were assigned rooms, it was announced that after we settled in, I would be given a physical examination and inoculations by the ship's medical staff.

I initially thought it was odd that all of a sudden there was this keen concern about my health that led to this "order" for inoculations. Since I had not had much sleep and had endured over a week of disaster madness, I was still a bit on edge and my sense of trust, rightly so, was not in a good place.

Soon I heard a knock on my door, and it was General Honoré. The general came into my room and said, "Don't worry about this. We're going to hook you up." He smiled slyly. I was then escorted to the infirmary and presented to two medical personnel. They repeated that they had orders to examine me and give me shots.

I inquired what type of shots they were prescribing before having had the chance to exam me yet. I was still a little paranoid and again started imaging a secret CIA plot where in six months I would be gone. After thinking for a minute, I said to them, "Okay, you can give me shots, but I want you to do the same for my two security guys." My thinking was it would have been easier to spin that stress ultimately took me out, but it would be much harder to explain all three of us suddenly dying mysteriously.

A few months later Wondell would confide in me that at that moment he turned to Terry before he got his inoculations and whispered, "We'll all be dead in less than three years." So I was not the only one feeling a bit uneasy about these sudden acts of kindness.

As we continued into week two post-Katrina, the local, national, and international media became more competitive and tenacious about getting the best news story. This was quite a contrast as immediately after the storm hit the media at all levels presented very balanced, accurate journalism. They clearly understood this unprecedented event and were equally disappointed in the slow response by various levels of governments. As time went on and more reporters came in, things rather quickly evolved from them strictly reporting the facts to some creating their own versions of the news.

The various images and stories captured that first week yielded amazingly high viewer, listener, and readership ratings. Now that the Superdome and Convention Center were closed, the interstates were empty, and most citizens were off of their roofs, there was a real struggle to find and cover similar types of sensational stories that previously flowed effortlessly.

My staff was now bombarded with requests for exclusive interviews. There were not enough hours in the day to accommodate them all. As my days were already so full, we were forced to schedule media appointments throughout the day from early morning to late into the night. This was a particularly challenging time for me as I was also simultaneously managing so many different aspects of this recovery. Therefore, I was constantly making mental shifts from real-time problem solving to media interviews.

On several occasions an enterprising reporter would twist my words or edit a half-hour interview to the twenty seconds that could be sensationalized. This would put me in the unfortunate position of having to spend precious energy clarifying the truth. Don't get me wrong—I made my share of mistakes. I was privileged to be interviewed by all the top people in media, and to this day I am still amazed that I did not stumble more or get more facts crossed.

What I didn't fully understand during that time was that the more this incredible Katrina story continued to unfold and the more I stayed in the public view, the more President Bush's approval ratings dropped. As a matter of fact, many experts concluded that the president never recovered from his administration's mishandling of Katrina. The good news for us was that our continuing struggles prompted additional presidential visits, which led to more federal resources. The overwhelming media attention was definitely a double-edged sword that cut both ways.

In response, the White House once again secretly unleashed its own version of a mega storm—Cyclone Karl, Rove that is. After a full week of Katrina, the master of spin came out of his mad scientist laboratory and was on a mission to take some heat off of the president. I call him Cyclone Karl because there is a real cold-core polar cyclone phenomenon that has inward spiraling winds where it strengthens in the winter and weakens in the summer, just opposite of a normal hurricane. It was now fall, and Karl Rove was just getting cranked up.

Almost five years later Mr. Rove published his memoir and devoted a good portion of it to Hurricane Katrina. Of course, he once again blamed state and local governments for the federal government's struggles. This is the same guy who now admits he orchestrated the insensitive picture of President Bush flying over a flooded New Orleans.

This man also now admits that President Bush never could have gotten congressional support for invading Iraq without the false threat of weapons of mass destruction. He was also the architect of "Mission Accomplished" and is a master at taking words out of context and hammering them over and over again. Joe Klein of *Time* magazine sums up Cyclone Karl best by writing, "When you make a political consultant your senior policy adviser, spin supplants substance, opposition research rules, and winning the news cycle becomes more important than winning the war." Joe Klein forgot to add to the list, or saving Americans after federally built levees failed after the storm of the century.

On Monday, I was on set and interviewed by Matt Lauer from the *Today Show*. His very first question was on the projected death toll in New Orleans. My response was, "I really don't know, but what I'm hearing is that there are some LSU scientists who are saying it could be as high as ten thousand." This figure had come from a computer model that the scientists had developed. Matt asked me again if I agreed with that assessment. I attempted to approach this logically by stating, "If you look at the New Orleans population, we had five hundred thousand before the storm. We evacuated most, but there may be another fifty thousand out there. You pick a percentage, 10, 20, or 30 percent— so it wouldn't be unthinkable to have ten thousand." From that point on reporters started saying the mayor of New Orleans is estimating that ten thousand people died after Katrina hit.

Early Tuesday morning, Katie Couric from the same network asked me the same death toll estimate. However, she left out the fact that the ten thousand number cane from the LSU scientists' prediction. She presented it as something I dreamed up. My response did not change as I responded, "I've heard that number. I don't know how many it's going to be. All I can tell you is that I've flown over the city just about every day. There are many bodies in the water. I've gotten reports from firefighters when they went to rescue people that they saw many more bodies in homes. It's going to be awful, and it's going to wake the nation up again."

Fortunately, much later, after we drained the city and searched every structure, it would be revealed that our losses were less than a tenth of that figure. Since we were debating fatalities, it didn't matter to me whether it was one, a thousand, or ten thousand. They were all human lives, and it was heartbreaking regardless of how high or how low the actual number was. By way of comparison, right after the horrific attack in New York on 9/11, the original estimates there were also around ten thousand dead. Here again the final results were fortunately a fraction of what was originally thought, but elected officials in New York's credibility was not challenged as mine was. This was only the opening salvo.

In a follow-up TV interview, Matt Lauer asked me who was ultimately responsible for the people in the city. He noted my criticism of the president and the governor's lack of response on my now famous radio interview. It was a fair issue to debate, but it now seemed as though the White House's list of preferred questions had made it to the top of many reporters' lists. The fact that local government was overwhelmed by a monster storm and a federally built levee system failed was now irrelevant as blame was being pushed away from those with the resources to minimize suffering.

During this same interview, Matt dug a little deeper, asking me who was responsible for the Convention Center. I stated that we all were responsible. I pointed out that the Superdome was full, we were in crisis, and people were being evacuated there from outside the city as well. The city was almost totally flooded, undermanned, and out of resources. I went on to say it is logical to believe that higher levels of government would step in to help us as they had the capacity to do so.

He went on to point out that both Secretary Chertoff and FEMA director Michael Brown claimed ignorance about knowing that we were using it as another shelter of last resort. I responded by telling him that everyone else in the world seemed to have known. Once again I reminded him that the Superdome was filled to capacity, and the Convention Center was our only other option for housing more rescued citizens. I also pointed out that FEMA had people in the Superdome who sent e-mails to their top people clearly stating that we were opening another facility.

In a follow up with Katie Couric, she also asked me about the Convention Center and demanded to know why supplies weren't on hand. As mayor of the city, she went on to say, this responsibility was solely mine. I respectfully disagreed with her and explained the Superdome situation again where we had provisions for needy evacuees for two to three days. I also explained how deceptive Hurricane Katrina was and that no one could have predicted that the levees would fail. I closed by reminding her that we successfully evacuated most of our citizens prior to the storm hitting, and no other city had accomplished this feat.

What I forgot to tell her then was that before the storm hit we pre-ordered 360,000 MREs and fifteen truckloads of water from FEMA. They only delivered 40,000 meals and five truckloads of water. If they had fulfilled our original order, no one would have gone without at the Superdome or Convention Center.

Not long afterwards I was interviewed by Stone Phillips from NBC's *Dateline*. He asked if Secretary Chertoff was right in his claim that the only way to avoid this catastrophe was with better evacuation, which fell on the state and local officials' jurisdiction. I said that is generally true for normal disasters. Mr. Phillips overlooked the fact that this was a once in a lifetime event. If the federal government had properly funded and built adequate levees, then a total evacuation would not have been necessary. It was at that point that I could no longer hold back at these attempts at public manipulation any longer.

I went on to say, "I think the spin meisters are in full effect. The nation has realized that this was a big problem. I don't know who said what. I don't care if it's the secretary or state officials. They're all running for cover. I will tell you, we as a nation failed a group of people that needed it the most. Everybody failed them. I could have done things better. I could have screamed louder. But this should never happen again. I don't give a rat's hoot about who has to ask whom to get stuff done when people are suffering."

With high-level government officials now going back and forth, the New Orleans Katrina media story maintained its momentum. We continued to be engulfed in the biggest media frenzy ever. With over a thousand media personnel in town, a few CBD hotels were like homing stations for them all. Big media trucks with generators attached lined Canal Street as they transmitted the volleys via satellite to the rest of the world.

The first Katie Couric interview was before daybreak Tuesday morning. As I was sitting on set getting ready to start, Sally Forman informed me that the governor was on the phone and urgently requested to speak with me. I reminded Sally that this live TV interview was set to start in a few minutes, so I really didn't have time to take her call. Her surprising response was, "But she is in tears!" I was speechless and stunned seconds before Katie started asking me very tough questions.

It was clear at this point that Karl Rove and Secretary Chertoff's pressure tactics were having an effect on the governor. They had been publically pounding her on the lack of response after she requested twenty-four hours to make a decision on federalizing the recovery and temporarily waiving the federal Posse Comitatus Act. Since she was still not willing to temporarily relinquish some control and power, many more people continued to suffer. Mr. Rove and Secretary Chertoff knew this and exploited her indecisiveness.

The intense media scrutiny and public scuffles with both President Bush and me were really getting to her. As a result, more and more people were now very forcefully challenging her. It had also come to light that she had been recorded—after being on live TV where she forgot she was miked—became extremely emotional and openly questioning herself on whether she had failed the people.

She was calling that morning because I was very upset about reports that she had diverted helicopters from plugging levee breaches to perform political favors. All I was concerned with was saving lives and getting my city back on its feet. So it was probably a blessing that I was not in a position to take the governor's call as I was still pretty fed up with her actions or lack thereof.

The next set of media surprises came from CNN. It was also around this time that we noticed a change in their reporting style. We started wondering whether the White House had a direct link to several CNN reporters as they became very aggressive.

Earlier interviews with them had been factual, cordial, and generally sympathetic to our plight. Now it seemed as though everything we had done was being questioned and challenged. The White House influence had them convinced them that state and local governments were basically the same entity. So the governor's shortcomings and recent breakdowns were now blended in with my very high profile. This resulted in a herd-like mentality from most other major news organizations. I now had a very large bull's-eye on my back.

Next, someone released a satellite photo of a hundred school board buses that had flooded in the city. This photo was accompanied with questions about how this could have happened and claims that we had enough transportation in the city all along. They conveniently left out the fact that there were over fifty thousand people stuck in the

Superdome and Convention Center, which meant we really needed around a thousand buses. They also failed to mention that these buses were not under my authority but were part of a state-chartered public school system.

This was classic Karl Rove. The plans was very simple—throw controversial things out there where there was some truth that could be easily twisted. Then present the topic significantly out of context and hammer your opponent from as many directions as possible. This forces you to react and spend energy clearing things up. So the truth about what really happened during the disaster and recovery becomes secondary. Well, this is another one where he probably claimed, "Mission Accomplished!"

Later that week Sally scheduled a five a.m. interview with *Meet the Press*. I asked her what the topics for discussion were as I knew this was going to be a very serious interview. Unfortunately, she did not have much information and somewhat naïvely thought that I should just go on and tell the nation what was really going on. I knew this one would not be that simple since the interviewer was Tim Russert, one of the smartest and toughest in the business. At this point I was very concerned that the White House spin machine was working every angle and probably had also worked the producers of this show.

I was also starting to sense that Sally and my communications team were struggling with scheduling and pushing back on these big-time celebrities. My lack of sleep and nonstop activities was unquestionably taking its toll. I was concerned about my ability to continue to stay sharp debating so many top news personalities.

I reluctantly relented and approved the interview. True to form, the first comment out of Mr. Russert's mouth was to accuse me of not taking responsibility for evacuating the thousands of people stranded in the city before the storm hit. I immediately shot back that this was an unprecedented event, and we evacuated more people than ever before in the city and nation's history.

The game was on, and there was no turning back as we continued to trade verbal body blows. Mr. Russert went on to blame the city government for not utilizing the RTA and school buses to evacuate those stranded before the water hit. He quoted an article that appeared in the *Houston Chronicle* on Friday, September 9, where a civil engineer from LSU, an expert in transportation planning, suggested that we could have utilized several hundred municipal buses that were supposedly available before the storm hit. So not only did we have Karl Rove firing shots at us, but now one of the governor's state agencies had jumped into the finger-pointing fray.

I explained to him how we put the city-controlled RTA buses to good use before the storm by helping needy citizens get to the Superdome. I also pointed out again that the school buses were not under my control as the public education system was a separate state agency.

I was then asked why I didn't call the mandatory evacuation a day earlier to coincide with the president's emergency declaration so that we could have moved more people out of the city. My response was as follows: "You know, Tim, that's one of the things that will be debated. There has never been a catastrophe in the history of New Orleans like this. There has never been a Category 5 storm of this magnitude that has hit New Orleans directly. We did the things that we thought were best based upon the information that we had. Sure, there were buses out there. But guess what? You can't find drivers that would stay behind with a Category 5 hurricane bearing down on New Orleans. We barely had enough drivers to move people on Saturday and Sunday, to the Superdome. So sure, we had some assets, but the drivers just weren't available." Since I didn't come across as rattled, he moved on to another topic.

The next thing he brought up was that the city government's comprehensive emergency plan states that the responsibility falls on the mayor to evacuate people out of harm's way. I told him he was technically correct, but we had essentially done the best we could with the resources we had. Not only did we get an unprecedented number of people to leave, but we also executed vertical evacuations to high-rise hotels and got many needy people to higher, dry areas like the

Superdome. I went on to say our reasonable assumption was that if things went very wrong and we were overwhelmed, then after two or three days the cavalry, i.e., the federal government, would arrive to rescue fellow Americans. Unfortunately, the cavalry didn't show up for almost a full week.

Mr. Russert continued by claiming he heard that Amtrak had offered to evacuate people on the Saturday evening before Katrina hit and the city government declined their offer. Karl Rove is good, real good. Fortunately, I had one of my staff members call Amtrak before the storm hit, and they basically informed us every train was totally booked and the earliest we could get anyone else out was late September. So this was not a viable option for us. I went on to say that I was never contacted by Amtrak, nor could anyone on my staff confirm this claim. To this date no one has produced a letter, fax, e-mail, or any other document that proves this phantom offer was ever made.

The next phase of the interview seems to focus on trying to get me to make negative comments about the president and the governor. Mr. Russert asked me to rate the president's performance. I responded, "I think he was probably getting advice from some of his key advisers or some low-level personnel that had not been on the ground that this was serious, but not as serious as it ended up being. My interactions with the president were anytime I talked with him and gave him what the real deal was and told him the truth, he acted and made things happen."

He then asked me to rate the governor's performance. I said, "Well, you know, I don't know about that one. We fought and held that city together with only three hundred state National Guard. That was it. We did not get a lot of other support for three or four days of pure hell on earth. There were resources that were sitting right outside the city. I just don't know. When her group did come down to review what was happening in New Orleans, it was just a big media event. It was followed with cameras and AP reporters, a little helicopter flyover, and then they had a press conference and were gone. So I don't have much else to say."

However, I went on to add, "And there was this incredible dance between the governor and the president about who had final authority, whether this was going to be federalized, who was going to be in charge at the end of the day, and I just don't appreciate that kind of stuff happening when people were dying in my city."

We concluded the interview, and off camera Tim told me he thought I did a nice job. I thanked him and said that was the toughest interview I had ever done. He smiled, and we said goodbye to each other.

Shortly thereafter, *Time* magazine published a national poll. The American public was asked whether they felt that the state and local officials were right to point the blame towards the federal government. The results were 39 percent agreed while 55 percent thought it was wrong. The White House strategy was having some impact.

The next day Sally arranged an interview with Ted Koppel. The interview began well, but then he suddenly started asking probing questions about Louisiana congressman William Jefferson. Apparently a few days after the storm hit, the congressman used his position of authority to get the National Guard to take him to his home in New Orleans via a high-water military truck to retrieve his personal belongings. After an hour of searching his home solo, he returned with a laptop, a large suitcase, and several stuffed boxes.

The congressman then requested a helicopter ride out. A rescue helicopter soon arrived, but Mr. Jefferson declined twice to be lifted out. All in all, the helicopter was delayed about an hour and left without the congressman onboard.

Unbeknownst to me at the time of this interview, this story was just breaking and highlighted that Jefferson was being investigated by the FBI. This was the beginning of a secret smear campaign, implying that since the congressman was apparently corrupt, then every other New Orleans political leader must be corrupt also.

This coincided with the reality that the federal government was about to embark on granting the state of Louisiana and the city billions of federal recovery dollars. This corruption theme was an easy target as the congressman had apparently been under investigation by the feds for quite some time—it just happened to conveniently come out then. The obvious intention was to build up public thinking that Louisiana officials could not be trusted considering the state's history of corruption. At issue here was who would make decisions about how and where we would rebuild, how recovery dollars would be distributed, and whether local companies would get a fair share of rebuilding contracts.

In an effort to get ahead of more criticism, on Tuesday, September 6, President Bush announced that he would be launching an investigation into what went wrong with the federal response to Hurricane Katrina. The president positioned himself to oversee the investigation with an announced intention of ensuring that lessons were learned in preparation for future disasters or attacks on U.S. soil.

Next, Dick Cheney was scheduled to visit the Gulf Coast region on Thursday to determine if there was anything more that the federal government should be doing. "We still live in an unsettled world. We want to make sure we can respond properly if there is a WMD [weapons of mass destruction] attack or another major storm," the president told reporters as he announced these new initiatives. But as far as I can recall, the vice president only made a very brief pit stop in New Orleans for a couple of photo ops and left.

The fact that the White House was doing an investigation of itself did not impress many people. Many started calling for an independent commission and/or Congress to take a hard look into what we could do better in the future. It was obvious that the White House was still in damage control mode.

Now it was Michael Brown's time to be in the federal spin machine. With all the negative attention he had generated, President Bush announced on Friday, September 9, that Mr. Brown would be immediately stripped of his duties overseeing the relief effort in the Gulf Coast region. This press conference was called only a few hours after *Time* magazine released a report on their Web site revealing that Mr. Brown's résumé was completely inflated and astonishingly inconsistent. This was the final nail in the coffin for him and was a way for the White House to have a fall guy to hopefully dispel some of the criticism they'd received.

Coast Guard Admiral Thad W. Allen was named as Brown's replacement. Surprisingly, right before the president's press conference Secretary Michael Chertoff was seen talking to reporters with Michael Brown at his side. He was claiming that Michael Brown had "done everything he possibly could to coordinate the federal response to this unprecedented challenge." When asked by the media if Mr. Brown was going to resign based on the *Time* magazine findings regarding his fabricated credentials, Secretary Chertoff quickly responded for him, "Here are the ground rules. I'm going to answer the questions…Next question."

As the end of the second week in September came to a close, amidst all the media and political games, we had succeeded in cycling out the initial group of first responders for rest, recuperation, and reuniting with their families. The city was also still on track on dewatering, and many of our breached levees were being repaired and reinforced.

During this time I would regularly check in with Deputy Police Chief Riley to make sure I was up to speed on what our first responders needed most. One day he confided in me that what was needed most right now was good housing for everyone to clean up and rest at night. He requested that I look into getting cruise ships to dock here so that the men and women could have their own place to get a decent night's sleep. He reminded me that 85 percent of them had lost their homes.

My initial reaction was that this was a huge, very creative request. I was not sure we could deliver, but I authorized Colonel Ebbert to contact FEMA. Surprisingly, in a little more than a week's time two cruise ships arrived and docked downtown on the Mississippi River. This would become home for our emergency workers who had been sleeping in hot office buildings, on hotel room floors, in cars, or anywhere else that provided cover over their heads. Now everyone would have a nice place to eat, sleep, and clean up. These ships afforded us hot showers, privacy, a clean bed, and three hot meals a day. This made a tremendous positive difference on morale.

For the first time in weeks, I felt fairly comfortable with the progress the city was making. Just about all of our first responders were being processed for physical and psychological evaluations. I now believed the time was right for me to reconnect with my family. With so many very visible improvements and significant military reinforcements, I made arrangements to fly to Dallas to spend a few days with my wife and children. I was also very much in need of rest and recuperation, some normalcy.

The morning I was to leave I was having second thoughts, but Sally and Terry insisted that I take the time off to clear my head. My plan was to leave midday Thursday and return the same time Sunday. I packed a small soft suitcase as I didn't have many clothes and headed to the heliport for a ride to the airport. As I put my bag on the helicopter, it suddenly hit me like a lightning bolt that I had forgotten something very important—Fishy!

After keeping this fish alive through the darkest days after Katrina hit, I was not going break my promise to my daughter. I held up the helicopter for twenty minutes or so while Wondell went back to the Hyatt and retrieved Fishy and his food. Once he got back we all had a good laugh, loaded up in the chopper, and headed to the airport. Once there I was soon on an airplane headed to Dallas, Texas.

My family met me at the airport. Seletha, my wife, looked absolutely beautiful. Tianna was happy to see me, but she was happier to see Fishy. My sons, Jeremy and Jarin, were all hugs and smiles. Seletha started crying at the sight of me as I had lost a lot of weight and must have looked totally exhausted. All I could do to respond was to give her a weary smile. We hugged and kissed each other and had a wonderful family reunion right there at the airport. It was such a blessing to reconnect with my family again.

I immediately realized how much I had missed them and the awesome weight and pressure I had experienced. It is amazing that I was able to function, keep track of critical events, and lead and manage the plethora of once-in-a-lifetime challenges that were hitting us every minute of every day. It would take many months and years to fully digest and understand all that we had experienced and overcome in that first horrendous week after Hurricane Katrina almost destroyed our way of life.

Since I had not seen television in quite some time, I really didn't understand that I would be recognizable outside of New Orleans. I had no real insight that most of the world had been watching us on a daily basis, awestruck by our predicament.

So before we left New Orleans, I informed my executive protection staff that I wouldn't need them in Dallas. I also thought it was important that they spend time with their families. Wondell flew separately to Houston, and Louis went to his family in another part of Dallas. Before we separated, they instinctively contacted the Dallas Police Department, who graciously assigned two police officers for my protection. The lead officer, Dwayne Bishop, met me at the airport. He was absolutely great and told me how proud he was of what we had done and that I had reached celebrity status in Texas and around the country. This was something that I originally blew off as him just being nice.

Then it started. I was instantly recognized in the airport, and people started coming up asking questions, wanting my autograph and to take pictures. I can remember later that day walking in a shopping mall and wondering why so many people were staring at me. Then they started approaching and asking me how the city was doing. It wouldn't be long before the picture taking started and I would be stuck there for twenty minutes or better. I turned to Seletha with a puzzled look, and she very patiently pulled me aside and in a soft voice said, "You really don't understand, do you? You have been on TV constantly for the past week, and everybody has been watching. Unfortunately, you may have to get use to this." I moved around as best I could, but every fifty feet or so I would be stopped for another twenty minutes of conversations and picture taking. We ended up picking up a few clothes as I didn't have anything other than the stuff I'd been wearing for the past week. Before long we had enough and decided to leave the mall.

One very nice benefit to all this attention was when we went to a restaurant to eat. No one would allow us to pay for anything. Either the manager would pick up the tab or somebody else who was dining would cover the bill. It made us feel very good that so many people really cared about us. Everyone there treated us like family. This was not only happening to us in Dallas, but it was also happening to our citizens all over the country. Americans were basically saying, "We know our federal government screwed up, but we want you guys to know that we love you and we want to make this right." It made me even prouder to be an American.

I devoted the next few days to nothing but quality time with my family. We shopped for clothes, visited schools for my daughter, and looked for more permanent housing for them to spend at least the next six months. We met a great man, Rich Horton, who is a major homebuilder in Texas. He set us up in a brand-new townhome that we ended up purchasing. I will never forget his kindness. Another key goal for me going to Dallas was to make sure that they were comfortable so I could go back and fully concentrate on rebuilding New Orleans.

On a related note, Seletha was very interested in how I was really doing. After I had a chance to settle down that first evening, she and I talked privately. She asked how I was doing. I told her I felt fine, but that she should observe me over the next few days and let me know if she noticed anything different about my behavior. She then joked that I had melted away in the floodwater and had lost a lot of weight. She was somewhat correct because when I weighed myself it confirmed that I had lost twenty pounds. I would spend these precious few days relaxing, clearing my head, and thinking about how to rebuild New Orleans into a model city.

There was another very interesting side story to this visit to Dallas. Right before leaving New Orleans, I was contacted by the chairman of the New Orleans Business Council, who requested an urgent meeting with me. I informed him that I would be in Dallas over the weekend, and he and his colleagues could meet me there in a downtown hotel on Saturday. I had mixed emotions about this meeting as it was taking me away from precious quality time with my family. On the other hand, I was looking forward to some serious dialogue with our captains of industry on how we could rebuild our city better than ever before. I was convinced that this was our greatest opportunity to fairly erase the legacy of economic inequities in our city. If we all worked together, we could very quickly get all the water out, start the repopulation process, and rebuild a much smarter, better, and larger city.

On Saturday morning I started driving to the hotel as I was looking forward to a high-level discussion of how to turn this disaster into a unifying moment in our city's history. Unfortunately, on the way over I started receiving several panicked phone calls from evacuated New Orleanians who were reading in national publications that I was going to meet with a select group of businesspeople. These articles highlighted that this group was very vocal about their desire to keep certain residents out and to shut down parts of New Orleans forever. Most of the calls were from African American community and business leaders. David White, one of my best friends, joined me at this meeting and also confirmed that he had read these articles. It then hit me like a bolt of lightning that the true purpose of this meeting was most likely very different from what I had earlier hoped.

Some of the businessmen who were going to be in this meeting had been giving national media interviews expressing another more washed-out vision of what they thought the future of New Orleans should look like. The word I got was they were saying that they believed this was a unique opportunity to in effect socially reengineer New Orleans and shrink its footprint. Their leader was no other than Jimmy Reiss.

He and others were quoted in the *Wall Street Journal* saying, "Those who want to see this city rebuilt want to see it done in a completely different way: demographically, geographically, and politically." He also threatened that if New Orleans didn't change for the better, with less poor people and better services, that he and a number of his colleagues would leave the city for good.

As I entered the conference room, I was taken aback by the large number of people who were obviously party to this insensitive purge. It also seemed like I had been invited to a private, secret meeting of the Rex and Comus organizations. Present and accounted for were just about every uptown New Orleans businessperson of the highest social standing. The group was so large that I do not recall everyone who was there, but the lineup included Jimmy, a couple of Bills, several Jims, Gary, Bob, Ralph, a few Toms, and Tommie just to mention a few. There must have been between fifty and seventy-five people there.

The meeting attendees were primarily men with two or three wives and female business executives sprinkled in. Not too surprisingly, there was only one other African American in the room who did not come with my party. He worked for a local oil baron. I showed up with David White, Dan Packer, and Mel Lagarde.

Somehow State Senator Derrick Shepherd, an African American, found out about the meeting and crashed in and pulled up a chair. He acted like I invited him, but I believe he was there as a double spy to report back to the African American leadership community and other state legislators. Derrick's sponsors were all fired up by this group's arrogant comments that had been made to the national press. The question now was could I somehow make lemonade out of exceedingly tart lemons.

The meeting started off with a general discussion about the disaster and the current status of the city. It didn't take much longer for them to cut to the chase about how this group wanted to see the city rebuilt. It was very clear to me that this group was intent on engineering a very different New Orleans than what we had before, and crime wasn't their only target. I stopped the one-way conversations, took a deep breath, and said, "Look, I am aware of what some of you have been saying to the national media. I don't know what you guys are thinking, but if you're talking about rebuilding the New Orleans of

1850, then I'm definitely not interested in doing that. Now if you want to discuss building the New Orleans of 2050, one that's new and better and inclusive, then I am your guy."

The room went silent for a few minutes. Someone spoke up and said that maybe I had misunderstood their intentions. He went on to say that all they wanted was a better New Orleans. I then pressed on and pointed out that comments in national newspapers clearly pointed out what the group's true intentions were. I made it very clear that we could rebuild a better city where economic opportunities were plentiful and that every citizen would have the right to return home to the city of their ancestors. As I looked around the room, I could tell that I had hit a nerve, and most were very disappointed in my firm position.

We somehow very awkwardly transitioned and started to discuss several issues where we could find some agreement—dewatering, debris removal, dead body removals, and repopulation strategies. We then discussed proposed timelines and next steps. The meeting ended with it being very clear that I was not in good standing with this group.

Taking the social reengineering play off the table meant I would have troubles with these very powerful, shadowy figures in the future. From that point on everything changed, especially local media treatment. I had a target on my back as the guy who stood in the way of their vision of a *new* New Orleans where mint juleps would once again be the drink of choice in a bleached, adult Disney World–like city.

I am sure there was a meeting after the meeting that put in motion a plan for achieving their objectives regardless. We received word that an intense search had started for a candidate to run against me. Elections were supposed to take place early the next year. As I rode back to rejoin my family, I couldn't help but be further amazed that there was an element like this that wanted to go backwards instead of moving forward. It was more than certain that my job as mayor, which was already the hardest job in America, had just gotten harder.

On the final day of this trip, I was scheduled to meet with Minister Louis Farrakhan, who is the leader of the Nation of Islam. Minister Farrakhan had visited the city several months before Katrina hit to give a major speech. We treated him well during his visit, and he was very appreciative. He also called and requested a meeting before I left Dallas. We agreed to meet Sunday at the Dallas airport about two hours before I would fly back to New Orleans.

I arrived at the airport on time and moved to the meeting room. I couldn't help but notice the extreme contrast of this meeting and the one I had the day before. Minister Farrakhan's group was very interesting in its own right. It included singer Erykah Badu, some high-profile black nationalists, his son, and the Fruits of Islam, their extremely disciplined bodyguards. The minister greeted me warmly and said, "Peace be with you" in Arabic, and I answered in Arabic, "Peace be unto you as well, sir," something I learned while attending Tuskegee University.

Minister Farrakhan was sincerely concerned about the people of New Orleans and their well-being. I explained everything we had gone through and how just about every citizen had been evacuated out of the city. He was also very, very interested in the levees, particularly in how they had been breached. He had a very serious, sincere look in his eyes and asked me point blank, "What really happened in New Orleans? Did they bomb the levees?" I understood exactly where he was coming from. I too had heard the conspiracy theories surrounding the breaches in the Lower Ninth Ward levee at the Industrial Canal.

The reason he was asking me this question was because many residents in the Lower Ninth complained of hearing a loud bang just before a barge burst through the wall of the levee. This was immediately followed by a twenty-foot-high surge of water that consumed many homes and people in its path. The Lower Ninth Ward is a predominantly African American community. The Army Corps of Engineer was accused of supposedly bombing the Industrial Canal to save the French Quarter, CBD, and uptown. Unfortunately, levee dynamiting of this sort has been used several times in New Orleans' colorful history.

For example, in 1927 a storm and heavy rains caused the Mississippi River to overflow, creating fears of flooding several cities, New Orleans in particular. Officials ended up dynamiting parts of the levee at Caernarvon to release the pressure of the rising river. This was also documented to have been done again during Hurricane Betsy in 1965. During Betsy, most of the New Orleans region was saved with the exception of the Lower Ninth Ward and neighboring parishes of St. Bernard and Plaquemines. Hundreds of people were killed as a result of these ill-advised decisions.

Minister Farrakhan wanted to know if anyone had bombed the levees and put people at risk to save others' property. I looked him in the eye and firmly said, "No, I haven't seen evidence of any bombings." I did explain the Hoey's Cut incident and the fact that I had fairly reliable reports of a loosely moored barge that had crashed on its own through the levee wall and caused one of the breaches in the Lower Ninth Ward. We talked for about an hour before we both had to catch our flights.

We shook hands, and he thanked me for the personal briefing. He advised me to be very careful as there were forces out there that would try to either discredit me or take me out because I was so high profile. He asked me promise to do what was best for the people, particularly the elderly and poor. I accepted his challenge. As we parted ways, he offered the full support of the Nation of Islam for New Orleans and me. I left and went to say goodbye for now to my family, boarded my plane, and headed back to the still waterlogged Big Easy.

As I landed in New Orleans, my relaxed mood immediately left as my pace of activity quickened. Within a few hours, President Bush was scheduled to arrive back in New Orleans for another official visit to the hurricane-damaged region. This Sunday was incredibly memorable for me as I recall going through some extreme mental gymnastics. That morning I met with Minister Louis Farrakhan, and in the evening I would be having a formal dinner meeting with President Bush. These two gentlemen were very strong, fairly polarizing leaders who were so very different but in many respects very similar. They were both very

conservative, strong on defense, dedicated family men, and passionately committed to their constituents.

After attending a few quick meetings to get the latest updates, we
received word that Air Force One had landed at the airport and the
president would soon be in Marine One, the presidential helicopter,
headed into the city. The agenda called for me to greet the president
as he landed on the USS *Iwo Jima*, have a dinner meeting, and spend
the next morning with him. The governor and other officials would
join us the next morning for a briefing aboard the USS *Iwo Jima* in her
command center. This would be followed by a tour of the city with the
president in a military truck.

The last time we had gone on this ship was nearly a week ago. At
that time we boarded at nighttime. This time we arrived in the daylight
hours and could clearly see how impressive this ship really was. We
had the opportunity to walk around as the naval officers allowed us
to explore this magnificent war machine. An entire section of the deck
was closed off in anticipation of Marine One's arrival, which would
be any moment now. As Marine One came into sight, officials moved
my party into another area, and I was left to meet the president as he
exited the chopper. We greeted each other warmly and immediately
moved to a conference room below for a quick briefing on the recovery. Once the meeting ended, the president and I were shown to our
quarters.

I took this opportunity to take a warm shower and freshen up a
bit. We reconvened not long afterwards for dinner. Admiral Allen, who
by now was leading the federal recovery efforts and General Honoré
were also in attendance. After finishing a wonderful dinner, we continue to chat about various issues as we enjoyed great dessert and coffee. The president was much more relaxed than I had previously seen
him. My bet was it was because there were many very visible signs of
progress that everyone could point to.

Next thing I knew we were headed to get some fresh air by climbing stairs to the top of the ship where we had a unique view of the
city and region. As we stood on the very top deck of the USS *Iwo Jima*,

the president offered us Dominican cigars and nonalcoholic beer. I just looked at the president and smiled without saying a word. He knew he was working a brother. First I get to take a shower on the ultimate pimpmobile, Air Force One, and now I was smoking a cigar and sipping a cold beer in the mild night air under the stars. Everyone really relaxed that night. We just talked about life, and we all formed an interesting bond. It seemed like everyone was now realizing were in the same boat trying to right an incredible wrong. It really didn't matter that the beer was nonalcoholic. It was cold, and for that moment we were celebrating some recovery successes. The conversations continued for at least an hour or two.

At some point my mind drifted to the city that lay before us in panoramic view. As I looked out over the Mississippi River towards Algiers on the West Bank, which was dry and fairly intact, I could see signs of life returning as many lights were twinkling in the distance. Whereas on the other side of the ship, behind us on the East Bank, most of the city remained flooded and in total darkness. There was the future and the past, the light and the darkness, very similar to what created the best rainbow analogy for New Orleans. There would be many very difficult choices that would have to be sorted through to restore and rebuild this wonderful city. As I stood there and looked out, I mentally renewed my personal vow that each and every one of my decisions would be made for the greater good, in the best interests of all citizens of New Orleans. This was my city, a city definitely worth saving, and no one could persuade me otherwise, not even the president of the United States.

CHAPTER TWELVE

DISNEY LIGHTS SPEECH

———— ■ ————

It was now week three, and we were still making progress, but the challenges were still daunting, expanding, and increasingly complex. Citizen evacuations were practically complete, levees repairs were extensive, floodwater was rapidly receding, and looting was well under control. Our search and rescue teams were focused and making great progress. Sadly, their work was bringing the kind of reports that we were not excited to hear about, the discovery of many dead bodies.

The official body count in New Orleans jumped to over two hundred and fifty. At the pace we were on, many more casualties were expected to be found in the coming days. The National Guard and emergency responders were doing what they called quick searches, basically taking the bodies out of the water or removing them from sidewalks so that FEMA's morgue teams could handle identification by family members. The teams also continued their searches of all buildings with the diminishing hope of finding someone alive.

Of the two hundred and fifty found dead so far, forty-five bodies had been discovered in one flooded hospital. This was the unfortunate incident where those on duty had coldly abandoned their patients, many of them senior citizens. Those in authority were rightly asking question about how something like this could have happened. The attorney general would later file thirty-four civil and criminal counts against the owners of this facility. It is still hard to understand how anyone could be responsible for the health, safety, and ultimate care of the elderly and just turn their backs on them in a life-and-death situation. Unfortunately, the aftermath of Hurricane Katrina created so much panic and stress that for some self-preservation was all that mattered.

Among the joys and pain of recovery, there were also comforting signs of a city slowly coming back to life. The cleanup of city streets was underway as work crews cleared fallen trees and houses that had moved from their foundations. We were also resurrecting downed telephone and utility poles up and down major thoroughfares. Debris removal crews were working diligently to accelerate this massive cleanup process.

The federal government controlled these essential cleanup functions through four separate $400 million no-bid contracts that were released right after the storm hit. The beneficiaries were several giant engineering firms like KBR, one of Dick Cheney's Halliburton subsidiaries, and the Shaw Group, a Baton Rouge firm that was very close to the Blancos. Shaw also employed the services of Joe Allbaugh, who was the former FEMA director, Bush's 2000 campaign manager, and Michael Brown's former boss. These firms knew better than most that there was big money to be made after this disaster.

They both were awarded debris removal contracts that the Bush administration agreed to pay forty-four dollars per cubic yard for debris removed from areas affected by Hurricane Katrina. These companies would then subcontract the work for twenty-seven dollars per cubic yard. At this point neither Shaw nor its first sub had pushed a broom. Their subcontractor would then contract with someone local or a hungry out-of-town firm at around seven dollars per cubic yard. Sadly, the seven-dollar firm is the only one who actually did any real work. The other two firms just pushed paper and waited for big checks to arrive in the mail. Tragically, the profits of companies at the bottom of this distorted recovery food chain were later squeezed financially with slow or no payments, and as a result, most either filed for bankruptcy or just went out of business.

Since the Davis-Bacon requirement to pay a decent wage was suspended by President Bush's executive order, these firms were free to hire immigrant workers who were sometimes paid below minimum wage or not at all. To survive, small firms were put in the terrible position of doing the work and screwing their employees because of the tactics of the big boys at the top. This was disaster capitalism at its worst, resulting in bad business and legalized robbery of taxpayer dollars.

In addition, the top-end brokers also performed other disaster-related functions. For example, Shaw was also paid $175 per square foot to install tarps on storm-damaged roofs in and around New Orleans. The actual installers who did the work earned as little as four to five dollars per square foot, and the tarps were provided to Shaw by FEMA at no cost. Just about every level of the recovery contracting food chain was so overfed with the exception of the bottom rung where the work was actually done. This gave a very different meaning to the saying, "Pigs get fat and hogs get slaughtered." Unfortunately, after Katrina the pigs got killed and the hogs got fatter.

On the lighter side, substantial improvements were being made to the levee system. Dutch and German specialists had been brought in to work with and advise the Army Corps of Engineers on the best techniques in repairing and strengthening our hurricane protection system so that the levees could withstand greater impacts. The Germans also brought pumps that were particularly helpful in completing the drainage in the Lower Ninth Ward. These pumps were of a size that made them extremely effective after the deep floodwater was pumped out. In addition the canals, lake, and river were being cleared of debris, and the overall floodwater levels had dropped considerably as more permanent pumping stations and temporary pumps became operational.

Another very interesting challenge was that the winds and storm surge had blown all sorts of wildlife into our now enhanced urban jungle. Alligators were found swimming in the remaining floodwaters and in some residential swimming pools. There were snakes in very surprising places. Wild boars lived and breed in our twelve-hundred-acre City Park for several years after the storm. A rooster and a hen even took up permanent residence in my neighborhood. It would be many months later when I'd move back home and this bird, which

I named "Big K," would continue to wake me up every morning at five a.m. I recently saw both birds walking near my lawn with eight new baby chicks closely following behind in perfect second line formation.

During week three after the storm hit, less than 50 percent of the city remained flooded. In the recently drained areas, there was now a thick layer of putrid, gut-wrenching smudge in the streets, on the sidewalks, and on private property. This residue also covered fallen trees, power lines, garbage, shattered housing material, and an occasional dead animal. The other interesting sight was as you looked at the homes, buildings, utility poles, and trees still standing, you could clearly see how high the floodwaters had gotten and where it had settled. Several yellow and/or black water lines very similar to a stained ring in a dirty bathtub remained as unwanted tattoos. Like the search markings on homes, these watermarks would remain very visual reminders of Katrina's effect for many years.

One of the quiet heroes on my staff was Reggie Zeno, our chief financial officer. Since I had an accounting background, he and I clicked from the very first day we started working together. He and his financial team were spectacular throughout the aftermath of Katrina. When we first took office back in 2002, the city government only had two days of cash in the bank, and now with Hurricane Katrina it seemed like déjà vu. Our finances had taken as harsh a beating as our levees. If we were not careful and extremely creative, the City of New Orleans could have easily gone into bankruptcy. Our economy totally shut down for months, and we didn't have any tax revenue coming in. So we desperately needed the federal government's help in sustaining the city until we got back on our feet.

Federal law basically says that once a state of emergency is declared, FEMA is supposed to reimburse us for money we spent on any officially declared disaster. Unfortunately, this turned out to be a nightmare as there were two layers of processing before we received a check. The federal reimbursements had to first be approved by FEMA and then the state. The problem was FEMA was totally overwhelmed, and the state's approval process took equally as long. Essentially, these dollars took several months to hit our bank accounts, and when they did, the amounts were normally much less than what we really needed because of consistent low-ball damage estimates by FEMA. We were never able to get anywhere close to full reimbursement for our losses.

The other major challenge was that the Federal Stafford Act only allowed municipalities to borrow up to $5 million in Community Disaster Loans for post-disaster operating costs. Since our annual operating budget was in excess of $500 million per year, this maximum loan amount was totally insufficient. Since we were desperate, we applied for it anyway.

Right after the storm hit, I made the decision that all of our employees would get their paychecks for at least ninety days. Most were scattered across the country, and some had lost everything, so the last thing I wanted was for them to be in a welfare line. It was extremely difficult, but during those first three months not a single employee missed a paycheck. Reggie and his finance team were incredible in that they set up a 1-800 number for employees to call in and let us know where they were. Another plus for us was that prior to Katrina we had migrated over 95 percent of our employees to direct deposit, so it was easy for us to wire money directly into their bank accounts. For those who did not have direct deposit, we located them and mailed debit cards so that on pay day they had access to cash.

But it wasn't long before we realized that we couldn't continue this generous gesture of goodwill. We had to slow our cash outflow as the lack of tax revenue and the slow pay on reimbursements caused me to make one of the toughest decisions I have ever had to make in my lifetime. We ended up laying off thousands of workers who were still devastated, disoriented, and displaced. We sent notices to over three thousand workers telling them their services were no longer required by the City of New Orleans. The only groups that were exempt from layoffs were our first responders. These layoffs cut our workforce virtually in half. All of our remaining employees would now have to take on more tasks and do the jobs of two and three people along with their own to get us through this tragedy.

Since floodwater had visibly receded and most had not seen their homes in over three weeks, pressure was building for citizens to return to assess how their properties had fared in the storm. I was continually managing these expectations. Businesspeople were also desperate to come in to get critical files and computer data. Just about everyone was really missing New Orleans and desperately wanted to see for themselves what shape the city was in. The challenge was to balance these desires with overall citizen safety and well-being. I was still not comfortable that we knew factually whether there were poisonous toxins around.

In relatively short order we came up with a great plan that was called "Look and Leave." This process would allow citizens the opportunity to come in from dawn to dusk to inspect their property. We were hopeful this would satisfy their need to know while not allowing major distractions from critical recovery work. This plan was zip code specific and allowed us to control the volume of people coming in so they would not overrun our very limited resources.

Back aboard the USS *Iwo Jima*, I attended an early morning briefing in the command center. The newly appointed federal recovery chief, Admiral Thad Allen, did his best to assure President Bush and Secretary Chertoff that he had the recovery efforts moving and under control. Once this meeting concluded, the next part of the agenda was for all of us to embark on a ground tour of the city in a high-water military truck. The president ended up behaving like an army general inspecting the front lines. This had been prearranged, and the media was there to cover it all. I understood what President Bush was trying to do. He had been so heavily criticized for his handling of Katrina that his approval ratings were still plummeting and seemed to be on a permanent downward slide.

The president's leadership ratings never recovered. According to a *Time* magazine poll taken around that time, Bush's overall approval rating dropped to an all-time low of below 42 percent. So I am sure his staff thought it was extremely important for him to portray to the rest of the nation that he was in the city again, on a military truck, getting down and dirty in the trenches and making things happen. He even rolled up his shirtsleeves in time for the media cameras to snap away freely.

The ground tour members on the lead truck consisted of President Bush, Secretary Chertoff, General Honoré, Admiral Thad Allen, Governor Blanco, and me. We all boarded the back of an open-air military truck and proceeded to explore the streets guided by the Secret Service and National Guard troops. We maneuvered through the debris and stagnant water effortlessly as an advance team had combed every inch of this route. The president got to see the search and seek missions underway and the spray-painted markings on homes and businesses that looked more like graffiti than body count coding. It was the fatality numbers in very bold print that got everyone's attention.

We made our way to Charity Hospital, near the Superdome. We then rode through a number of neighborhoods that included parts of Mid-City, Claiborne Avenue, and the Lafitte Public Housing Project on Orleans Avenue. The president asked questions as I pointed out certain key items so he would be better educated on our many challenges. After half an hour or so, I saw in the distance a very large crowd of people standing in an area underneath the overpass. As we got closer, it became clear that they were a gang of reporters waiting for our arrival. The trucks parked about half a block from where the pre-scheduled press conference was to take place. Cameras were snapping away as we all walked briskly up to the podium.

The president assertively stepped up to address the media with the rest of us flanking him on both sides. The very first question dealt with whether race had anything to do with the federal government's slow response to the Katrina recovery. President Bush's response was, "The storm didn't discriminate, and neither will the recovery effort. When those Coast Guard choppers—many of whom were first on the scene—were pulling people off roofs, they didn't check the color of a person's skin, they wanted to save lives." I am sure he was not briefed about the coincidence that the first roofs to be cleared were around the

Seventeenth Street Canal, a predominantly republican area. Everyone else was rescued after.

Before closing the interview, President Bush made this point: "It's very important for the folks in New Orleans to understand that, at least as far as I'm concerned, this great city has got ample talent and ample genius to set the strategy and the vision. Our role at the federal government is, you know, obviously within the law, to help them realize that vision. And that's what I wanted to assure the mayor."

Later a reporter asked me about how I felt after my meeting with the president and how I thought he viewed me. I responded, "The meeting was fine. If anything, he told me he appreciated my frankness, my bluntness." We wrapped up the press conference, got back on the truck, and returned to the USS *Iwo Jima*. The president said goodbye and immediately left in Marine One, destined for Mississippi. I was later informed that he planned to return to New Orleans later that week to address the nation from Jackson Square in the French Quarter.

Meanwhile, in Washington DC, Michael Brown officially resigned his post as director of FEMA. It appeared he no longer wanted to be the designated scapegoat for the federal government's slow response. A few days later in the hearings of the commission that the president had established on Katrina, Mr. Brown took one last stab at the governor and me before exiting as a federal official. He also surprisingly complained that FEMA lacked desperately needed resources during his stint, an apparent jab at budget cuts made by the Department of Homeland Security.

He went on to blame the coordination failures on the state and city, claiming that all mistakes were a result of our collective decisions. Mr. Brown continued by saying, "I very strongly personally regret that I was unable to persuade Governor Blanco and Mayor Nagin to sit down, get over their differences, and work together. I just couldn't pull that off." In his not so humble opinion, it was the dysfunctional nature of "the Louisiana politicians" in our preparations before the storm hit that made his job so difficult. Blanco's press secretary fired out a response that I totally agreed with. It said, "Mike Brown wasn't engaged then, and he surely isn't now. He should have been watching CNN instead of the Disney Channel."

In presenting some balance on Mr. Brown, he was somewhat correct in that his agency was not a first responder; that does fall primarily on the local and state governments. However, if an event is so devastating that it practically wipes out an entire U.S. city, then the federal government has a duty to come in and provide assistance to an overwhelmed community. Katrina was such an event.

Instead of everyone going back and forth trying to justify what they did or did not do, there should have been honest dialogue on a sensible analysis on the fundamental things we could learn from this disaster. We were obviously missing a unique opportunity to debate the outdated Stafford Act as well as which agencies should sit at the table as equal partners with FEMA to solve severe disaster-related problems. The reality of the situation was we really had a process problem—legal, regulatory, and system—with how catastrophic events are handled.

The current law and FEMA as the lead agency are just not modern enough and did not have the capacity to effectively deal with a crisis of this magnitude. FEMA is a disaster response agency created in the late 1970s. After the 9/11 attacks on American soil, billions of dollars were invested in homeland security and preparing communities against potential terrorist attacks. That was the Bush administration's main fear and focus.

The president came into office and found FEMA as a stand-alone department, and in 2003 he merged it with twenty-two other federal agencies to create the Department of Homeland Security. FEMA was originally intended for disaster response on our home soil. This soon became a distant afterthought. Reporting to Homeland Security along with an antiquated Stafford Act law severely hindered their independence and financial resources. This essentially tied their hands when we needed them to move quickly after the federal levees broke.

The other faulty decision the president made was he did not hire a FEMA director who was qualified and really cared about effective disaster response. FEMA e-mails that were subsequently released to the public shockingly reveal just how unprepared, disconnected, and unconcerned Mr. Brown was after Katrina hit. These documents are part of the congressional House committee's investigation into the federal mishandling of Katrina and paint a rather damaging picture of how Michael Brown prioritized his duties.

As Katrina devastated the Gulf Coast region, Michael Brown was more concerned with the business suit he wore than the storm damages, citizens' struggles, and related casualties. He wrote a colleague after a press conference who commented on his suit selection, "I got it at Nordstrom's...are you proud of me?" He fired off another one where he proclaimed, "If you'll look at my FEMA attire, you'll really vomit. I am a fashion god."

Now to really get a sense of his evasive mindset, the morning Katrina hit, Mr. Brown sent an e-mail to the deputy director of public affairs asking if he could quit now and go home. A few days later he would write to an acquaintance, "I'm trapped now, please rescue me."

Time magazine reported that some White House staffers took it upon themselves to educate President Bush on the severity of the catastrophe since they knew the FEMA director never got up to speed. They compiled a number of television reports that featured chilling images that were coming out of New Orleans to get the president to finally grasp the severity of what was happening.

Even though Brown left the agency in early September, he was still kept on the federal payroll for several months after. Secretary Chertoff claimed that his expertise was still needed as the investigations continued. Congress was not as impressed and out of frustration passed a law a year later restricting the president to only nominating a FEMA director if he or she had sufficient experience in emergency management and/or had no less than five years executive leadership on his or her résumé. President Bush promised to ignore this legislation, claiming that as the head of the executive branch he had sole discretion on whom he appointed to this office.

As Michael Brown was exiting FEMA, President Bush's approval rating continued to suffer. On Tuesday, September 13, 2005, the president announced to the nation that he somewhat accepted responsibility for Katrina's failings, attempting to shift the tone and defiant feel of the White House spin machine. He went on to claim that Katrina had "exposed serious problems in our response capability at all levels of government. And to the extent that the federal government didn't fully do its job right, I take responsibility." Although this was refreshing, we would later learn that more blame for state or local government had now gone underground.

In an attempt to keep step with the president and not let him steal the high ground, Governor Blanco also addressed the public and accepted her share of responsibility. She announced, "There were failures at every level of government, state, federal, and local, and at the state level we must take a careful look at what went wrong and make sure it never happens again." She said, "The buck stops here, and as your governor, I take full responsibility."

All three main players had come clean and admitted they could have done better. At least a week prior I endured many tough interviews on national TV where I point-blank said I could have done some things better now that we had the benefit of hindsight. Now that everyone was out of nuclear crisis mode, introspection was in order. As leaders, we were accountable for every decision we made. We had taken our lumps, admitted some mistakes, and pledged to do better, and it was time to move on. So you would think. Only time would tell if others were ready to put the past behind.

Not surprisingly, the Senate and the House of Representatives announced their own investigations independent of what the president was doing. Pretty soon there would be more formal hearings than we could attend. I participated in as many as I could since it was important to get the truth on the record, but they tended to take me away from my primary objective, which was getting the city back on its feet. New York Senator Hillary Clinton, a friend of mine, called for an independent national commission to review these events. She also announced that she would be seeking to introduce new legislation that would remove FEMA from the shadow of the Department of Homeland Security. Her logic was the agency should be independent again and its head person should report directly to the White House. She was and still is correct in her assessment on both fronts.

Several months later in January 2006, another round of congressional hearings started, and a very different Michael Brown showed up to testify. It seemed that with a few months of hindsight under his belt, Mr. Brown in his strongest public stance finally took responsibility for FEMA's desultory response. However, he wasn't going down alone. He charged the Bush administration with zealous obsession regarding terrorism on American soil. He was resolute that this was a severe distraction and impediment to effectively managing the disaster that had occurred. He also saw Michael Chertoff as a huge obstacle in the communication chain and admitted he had to take it upon himself to liaise directly with the White House. He stated he couldn't rely on the secretary to communicate accurately or in a timely fashion. The White House was once again caught flat-footed, and their spin machine went to work double overtime.

One of the big questions I have always pondered is that after Michael Brown was stripped of his duties and resigned, why didn't President Bush replace him with General Honoré? It would have been the logical choice since General Honoré came on the scene first, got recovery effort going with very few resources, and was very effective. He was extremely intelligent, an independent thinker, had great presence, communicated well, respected local elected officials' authority, and systematically knew how to manage multiple resources. I had been pushing hard for a clearer chain of command and for someone to have ultimate authority and accountability for the response. He seemed to be the right man for the job.

This would soon be a moot point as Admiral Thad Allen of the Coast Guard was appointed as the federal head for Gulf Coast recovery. He came across as a very nice man but was initially not very hands-on or engaging. Part of the issue could have been because he took over late and was going through a speed course of on-the-job disaster training. It became crystal clear that he was sent to carry out strict orders from the White House. He did not come in and perform an independent evaluation of the situation from the ground up. Whatever orders came down from above was exactly what he'd try to do. Key local concerns got lost in the shuffle as those who were very far away were driving and hampering our recovery.

It was also blaringly obvious that Admiral Allen's orders purely coincided with economic benefits that drove the nation's GDP with little regard to immediate local needs. He had four main focus areas, and everything else was a distant secondary priority. First, the oil refineries had to be cleaned up, repaired, and production restarted. Second, the river needed to be cleared of debris, the shipping lanes opened, and cargo was to again flow to and from our port. Third, offshore oil and gas rigs damaged after the storm needed to be assessed and repaired as soon as possible. Finally, the airport should be opened as soon as possible for commercial passenger flights and air cargo traffic.

Not too surprisingly, by Tuesday, September 13, 2005, Louis Armstrong International Airport officially reopened to limited commercial flights. Down from 174 departures and arrivals a day, the airport started with thirty flights and quickly ramped up to sixty each day by the end of October. Around the same time, damaged wharfs and container terminals were repaired at the Port of New Orleans. These reopenings were portrayed nationally as significant accomplishments. Within a relatively short period of time, before all the water was drained out of the city, Admiral Allen had completed his primary assignments, the four national economic drivers.

This was very encouraging progress, but once completed the admiral essentially pulled his foot off the gas pedal on other critical local recovery challenges. It now seemed that there was little else to offer our area and there was very little interest in pushing anything of any substance to completion. I kept pressing for urgency to complete the dewatering, remove debris, and to start the process of bringing our citizens back. I knew New Orleans needed to start breathing again, and the way to make that happen was to bring back the heartbeats of our city, our citizens, to reestablish our natural rhythms.

It was crystal clear after our second or third meeting that Admiral Allen was just giving me the good old FEMA two-step. Since I had been there, done that, this is where we got cross and our testosterone started flying. I was just not going to stand by and continue to watch the federal government award no-bid disaster contracts, open up macroeconomic engines, and then go on siesta while I had citizens stranded in forty-four different states. I was going to make sure that they cared as much about people as they seemed to care about economics and profits.

A month later Admiral Thad Allen would be promoted again with responsibility for the entire Coast Guard, and General Honoré, the guy on the ground who first got federal assets moving and had worked so hard to help people in harm's way, was virtually overlooked. This was another unfortunate dark side of this incredible odyssey we were on. Four months later, I heard and was not very surprised that General Honoré retired and entered the private sector. I wish him much success in the future as he deserves it.

On Wednesday morning after the president's latest visit, I received a call from the governor saying that she would be meeting with New Orleans state legislators after her State of the State address that afternoon and that she would like for me to attend both events. I sensed a setup as many local legislators were extremely upset that they had not been in the spotlight of the recovery efforts. They were camped out in comfortable Baton Rouge, which pretty much rendered them irrelevant relative to the disaster. They desperately wanted more say and input in the recovery process. In hindsight, they should have been more involved, and I should have been more inviting. However, I would soon learn that they were much more comfortable in air-conditioned Baton Rouge and really didn't want to come to New Orleans to roll up their sleeve.

Another major issue up there was members of the legislative black caucus were absolutely furious with the inconsiderate remarks in national newspapers by several businessmen about so-called "socially reengineering" New Orleans. They also read these statements as some powerful local elites were trying to orchestrate conditions where most black people would not be allowed to return home. Overall, the entire legislative group wanted to vent and also get directly from me a detailed update on what was really going on in the city. So I decided to go to Baton Rouge and meet them face to face.

I walked into the meeting fully prepared; confidently expecting to hear them out and then hopefully obtain their help in getting more assistance from state government. My initial apprehensions were confirmed as I immediately found most of them to be anxious, scared, and fairly combative. The published comments by local businessman Jimmy Reiss were first on the agenda. I told them any comments on gentrifying the city were indefensible and not in any way supported by my administration. Many of them insisted on his resignation as chairman of the Regional Transit Authority (RTA). At times the meeting became very hostile, and of course the media was present, so some of the legislators took this as an opportunity to get some sorely missed air time.

I was able to maintain my cool as I had been through the worst of Katrina, so nothing they could do could intimidate or overly excite me. I also sensed more than anything they were just all scared of the unknown. Just like the rest of us, they too had suffered much loss, be it their homes, cars, jobs, or income.

There were one or two who were quite upset and stressed. For example, a state representative who represented New Orleans East, one of the most devastated areas, was clearly shaken and one of the most vocal ones there. In the end, I did not bow to the pressure and calmly but firmly made my points. Most of them were hearing the truth for the first time as I comprehensively presented what was really going on in the city.

I tried to convey to them my overriding sense that we would need everyone in the city working together to get through this crisis and rebuild better. My somewhat naïve outlook was we would need even the Jimmys of the world to put aside any predisposition they had to work for the greater good of the entire city. Besides, I had worked with Jimmy for several years now, and I thought under his tough, old-school thinking that he was somehow driven out of character by this event just like Cedric was. Unfortunately, Katrina was bringing out some of the worst in a few people. I concluded this part of the discussion by saying when I got back to New Orleans I'd take Jimmy aside and talk with him before I made a final decision on his RTA chairmanship.

My closing message was very direct: "It's a very simple solution for you to plug in, just come on down to New Orleans and get to work. But before you come, get a commitment from the governor for more resources." Unfortunately, the state never did step up with any significant assistance until two and a half years later. I concluded the meeting with another call to action and a request that everyone just stop all the complaining, roll up their sleeves, get back into the city, and go to work. Unfortunately, there were those who continued to just complain and gossip. These tough times were exposing the true colors and abilities of many on several different levels.

As the meeting ended, my staff advised me that I was late for a major TV appearance. I had to rush from the legislators' meeting that had run overtime and make my way to a scheduled interview with Larry King on CNN. In true King fashion, as soon as I sat down he called me out for being tardy. "Joining us now from Baton Rouge is Mayor Ray Nagin, the mayor of New Orleans. He is a little late. Usually we have people who show up like this to tell us why they're late, so we'll ask him, why are you late?" he said. I apologized and explained the reason.

Mr. King, in his usual patient and professional way, let me answer each question my way. He asked me all the usual questions, like whether the governor and I had patched up our differences and in particular what responsibility I took in the disaster response. I told him that the governor and I were working through our issues. I also said that I could have done some specific things better, but we were over-whelmed by the greatest natural and man-made disaster in history.

Mr. King then asked me about the ten thousand dead figure that was once again being presented as my estimate. I attempted one more time to explain that my original estimate was much lower and that LSU experts had originally come up with that number. It was so amazing to me how this wayward question and other related ones kept coming up over and over again. Once a news agency picked something up, whether it was the truth or not didn't matter as the only thing that really counted was ratings.

The other good news was that this Larry King interview gave me the opportunity to explain my phased repopulation plan to the nation and hopefully reassure the New Orleans diaspora that they would be welcome to return home. This plan was designed to enable people to come back and check on their businesses, homes, and personal belongings. If all went well, we would have about two hundred thousand people back in the city by the end of September. As I spoke, there was already a full-court press demanding to clean up the city, get electricity back up, and the water and sewer system restored in preparation for these eager citizens' return.

Now that communications were more reliable, Greg Meffert and his team worked on preparing a Web site to provide real-time information on the recovery progress. This site also provided the reentry schedule and areas open to let people know when they could come back and what procedures were necessary for them to follow when they did return.

Before the interview was over, Mr. King asked me my thoughts and hopes on the president's address to the nation that would be held in the French Quarter the next day, Thursday, September 15. My response was consistent with what I'd been saying all along. I wanted to hear that the federal government would continue to keep the recovery of New Orleans as a top priority. I also wanted a commitment that the resources would be there to allow us to rebuild better. I ended by saying, "I want him to basically assure the nation that whatever it takes, there will be a full analysis of this situation and this will never ever happen again in this country in another city."

The next day the White House officials advised us that President Bush's speech would take place at nine p.m. in front of St. Louis Cathedral in Jackson Square in the French Quarter. It seemed odd to us that they proposed to do this speech at night, in complete darkness. Power was not yet restored in this part of the city. There were certain buildings that were back on the grid, but for the most part the French Quarter was still in a blackout. However, as we soon came to learn, when the U.S. government puts its collective mind to something, magic happens, darkness or no darkness.

First thing that morning the military and other technicians arrived and were everywhere making preparations for the press conference. By nightfall, St. Louis Cathedral looked better than Cinderella's castle at Disney World. All we needed was a spectacular fireworks display, and Mickey Mouse would have been all smiles. When I tell you that that place was well lit, I wouldn't be surprised if moths burst into flames when they got within a few feet of the huge lights that were rigged up. The light and dark contrast was stunning.

As we drove from the Hyatt, the streets were pitch black except for the headlights on our vehicles. Then as we got closer to Jackson Square we could see what looked like a brilliantly lit outdoor movie studio. Everything else around it was in complete darkness except for one barroom in the French Quarter that never closed throughout the whole episode, serving warm beer by candlelight.

The feds had brought all kinds of fancy, expensive equipment as if they were lighting up Times Square in New York. It was clear the intent was to try to portray to the world that the city was already back on its feet. The dark side, the mass deception part of this recovery was now taking things to a new level. This basically confirmed for me what I had been sensing all along. The federal government most likely purposely held back resources in those crucial first days after the storm in a very intense power struggle with the governor. It was now fully illustrated that when they put their mind to it they could do anything, including making a dead city look magically alive. With the president's approval ratings in such bad shape, this was their moment to pull out all the stops, regardless of the cost or effort required. If they would have had similar convictions the day after the storm hit us, the city would not be in the predicament that we were in now, that's for sure.

I just happened to see the president several minutes before show-time, and he was very confident, and said, "Mr. Mayor, you're going to like my speech. This is going to be good." I just nodded and said, "Sounds good, Mr. President, I can't wait to hear it." I then moved to a reserved seating section that was just off to the side from the presidential podium. Some of my staff sat with me along with the governor, Coach, and her key advisors. We took our seats, and soon it was announced over a loud speaker, "Ladies and Gentlemen, the President of the United States." It sounded like the same voice who announces professional boxing matches by shouting in rhythm, "Let's get ready to rumble!"

President Bush took a confident walk into the camera shot from about twenty feet back from the podium. He was casually dressed and appeared relaxed and focused. He immediately started to read the teleprompter and progressively came to the speech's climax: "We will do what it takes. We will stay as long as it takes to help citizens rebuild their communities and their lives. There is no way to imagine America without New Orleans, and this great city will rise again." These comments rebounded off the historic buildings that stood as the backdrop for the dramatic lighting and staging. They helped to emphasize his words perfectly. His speech was indeed good, very good, and it covered all the right areas.

This also gave the president the chance to announce the recently approved Gulf Opportunity Zone that would span across the entire disaster areas of Louisiana, Mississippi, and Alabama. "Within this zone, we should provide immediate incentives for job-creating investment: tax relief for small businesses, incentives to companies that create jobs, and loan guarantees for small businesses, including minority-owned enterprises, to get them up and running again," he said.

The passing of this GO zone legislation was very good news to me as I had worked directly with HUD secretary Alphonso Jackson, Karl Rove, Congressman Bill Jefferson, and Congressman Jim McCrery to develop its framework. The genesis for this legislation started several days after Katrina hit as this group would fax each other ideas that would come through to me only in the wee hours of the morning.

Once the president's speech was over, within minutes it was semi-dark again as though someone had flicked a switch that turned off the sun. The president immediately exited the stage, and the military technicians packed up their stuff. Within a few hours the place was in total darkness again. They even took the temporary lights and generators that were used to light up Jackson Square. We were not even offered these valuable pieces of equipment so we could better see key areas of the city at night. The show was over, and it was now time to get back to reality. The Disney-like magic left almost as quickly as it had arrived. Once it was clear that the show was over, we headed back to the command center to discuss further what we had just heard. The general consensus was the speech sounded too good to be true and we would just have to wait and see what really happened.

After a short break it was time to immediately refocus on the repopulation plan that we had been working on for over a week. Pressure was still building from citizens who wanted to see for themselves what had happened to their homes and neighborhoods. Comments that were being regularly repeated in the local press that the city's footprint should be much smaller and the very strong inference that African Americans were not welcome back contributed to feed severe mistrust and uneasiness.

During this time I felt strongly that I needed to send out a strong counter-message to the New Orleans diaspora. I planned to immediately meet with as many displaced citizens as I could to let them know that they may be out of the city, but they weren't forgotten. My overarching theme was that in spite of what you may be hearing, we were planning for everyone to return. Over the course of that week and weeks to come, I would travel around the country visiting key cities and shelters where New Orleanians were housed. I listened to them all as many poured out their frustrations and fears. Some told me they didn't feel welcome and weren't coming back. But for the most part the vast majority wanted to return home and help us rebuild the city. This confirmed that my number one priority was to get the city ready for their imminent return.

As we had been working on designing a plan to repopulate the city, it struck me that we needed a systematic process that coincided with the degree of damages in certain areas of the city. I asked Greg Meffert, CTO, to go back and pull up a zip code map of New Orleans when she was at peak population. From there I wanted him to overlay another map that depicted flooded areas throughout the city that had two feet of water or less. My thinking was this analysis would give us the best sense of how many people we could legitimately repopulate in the city during our initial phases. What Greg discovered provided the foundation for our recovery and gave us an initial roadmap and much-needed encouragement.

The facts showed that New Orleans' population crested in the early 1960s before integration and white flight to the suburbs at around 600,000. The areas with two feet of water or less had previously accommodated approximately 340,000 people. The lightbulb went off that the initial objective should be to create the environment where around 75 percent of our pre-Katrina population would quickly return, and then that momentum and market forces should drive the remainder back over time.

So we finalized a plan based upon this premise to start to repopulate the city in these targeted, least flooded areas by zip code. The rules of engagement would be that residents and business owners would have to show their IDs that verified that they lived or worked in a target area. Then they would be able to enter the city and move around only in their specific neighborhoods. There would be strict enforcement of a curfew. The other areas that had significant flooding or required significant debris removal would be off-limits until cleaned up and properly noticed.

We also had the foresight to arrange for big-box stores like Wal-Mart and Home Depot that specialized in rebuilding materials and other necessities to open up temporary stores in large sections of the Convention Center that had been cleaned and sterilized by General Honoré's troops. We also convinced other retailers and drugstores to set up temporary retail outlets in and around this area.

So everything was in place with the exception of one more major challenge. We would need to restart and recertify good, drinkable running water before we got too far down the road with implementing this repopulation plan. This water hurdle should have been a very straightforward, relatively easy process, but we ran into slow-down tactics at the state level and with Admiral Allen.

Since our water system had totally shut down after the storm, federal and state law required that it be flushed, properly tested, and certified before anyone would be allowed to drink or bathe in it again. Marcia St. Martin and her chief engineer Joe Sullivan had already been working on restarting the water purification and pumping systems to our targeted area. In fact, Mrs. St. Martin informed me that they knew what to do, and by the time I announced that citizens could return, they had already tested and gotten confirmation that the drinking water system was safe to drink in the targeted zip codes. Another advantage we had was since Algiers on the West Bank did not flood and was on a separate system from the East Bank, we were able to get that area certified very quickly.

On the other side of the river was where we ran into surprisingly strong and clandestine resistance. Marcia's staff worked around the clock and got the system flushed and good treated water flowing again. Next we performed double the testing that is required, and we were very comfortable everything met or exceeded standards. Our very aggressive testing lab worked with the state-sanctioned certification facility in Lafayette to verify that the East Bank water exceeded all requirements. In fact, their top person drove from Lafayette into New Orleans every day, collected samples, and tested and verified that everything was fine.

We even went beyond the call of duty and split up the water samples. This means one set went to the EPA's mobile lab in New Orleans, one directly to the state, and the final one to Lafayette. Regardless of what we did, the state kept dragging their feet in certifying our drinking water with excuse after excuse. First we were told it would take weeks for them to process the results. So I contacted the governor and some state legislators to push them to get things expedited. We finally received their approval after wasting over a week's time.

As we were moving forward, the next thing we knew the Louisiana State Health Department came into the city unannounced and started passing out dire warning flyers without telling us what the problem was. After a few days of going back and forth, they finally told us that we needed one more piece of paper from the Health Department that had not been signed yet. This was just another delay based upon a minor technicality as we all knew the running water was safe to drink and bathe in.

As we were finalizing everything with the state, the feds got into the act with Admiral Allen taking the water baton. He immediately went public and strongly advised citizens that they should not return to New Orleans because the drinking water was not safe. Not only was he misinformed, but he had overstepped his boundary of authority. I was not a happy camper.

Unfortunately, I had to expend precious energy in clearing up this misinformation. In a week or two we finally got everyone on the same page, but they came kicking and screaming. In retrospect, the repopulation plan was really forcing the federal and state governments to accelerate the recovery faster than they wanted to. I instinctively knew that the longer we delayed people returning, the more settled the New Orleans diaspora would become, and then the secret plan to have a smaller footprint would become a reality. I was fully prepared to continue to push anyone at any level so that my reinforcements would arrive, the wonderful people of New Orleans. Thank God they were seeing through all the smokescreens and were as determined as

I was to reclaim the Big Easy. If they had to buy bottled water to drink and take military baths in, they were still coming home.

Now that we had people flow back into the city, my next biggest hurdle was generating tax revenues for the city so we could provide key city services to our returning population. I was not comfortable that President Bush's Disney lights speech would cover everything we needed as I knew the federal Stafford Act, which dictates disaster recovery support, only allowed municipal community disaster Loans up to a maximum of $5 million. The challenge was that the annual operating budget of the City of New Orleans was around $500 million.

After some very hard and consistent lobbying, we successfully convinced Congress and the White House to adjust the loan maximum initially to 25 percent and then much later to 50 percent of our annual recurring revenues. Before this happened, our reality was a very small federal loan, a totally dead economy, and returning citizens whose expectations would soon be the same as what they had pre-Katrina. We would need something dramatic to kick-start the New Orleans economy to generate sustainable tax revenues.

Staring at the dark ceiling late one night trying to get a few hours of sleep, it dawned on me that we were sending most of our first responders to Las Vegas. It then dawned on me that the gaming industry that was based there had billions of dollars to invest, and Harrah's casino had already been operating in the city. I jumped out of my bed to take some notes as I envisioned a bold plan for a limited expansion of casinos in specific areas of downtown New Orleans. I also knew that the storm had wiped out all of the casinos along the Mississippi gulf coast, and investment dollars would soon be looking for opportunities. Since New Orleans' number one industry is tourism, this concept seemed like a perfect fit in our time of severe need.

My plan was fairly straightforward. We would expand the number of casinos to seven, and the locations would be limited to mainly Canal Street and the downtown area. The only facilities that would be eligible for these expansions were existing major hotels that had five hundred rooms or more. My calculation was the following if implemented: for every $1 billion Las Vegas would invest in the city, these facilities would generate an additional $150 million in taxes annually. I would also propose that we share some of these new tax dollars with the state.

I requested a meeting and went to talk this plan over privately with the governor and her chief of staff. They told me they both liked it as their economic development person was from Mississippi and he had also recently mentioned this might be the right time for the state to go after Mississippi's gaming business. I then discussed this concept with the head of the Hotel Association and then with executives from Harrah's. Since Harrah's had an exclusive land-based casino license, they would have to support the plan for it to move forward. The hook I pitched to them was they would be allowed to own one or two more locations. They also like the concept.

At this point every one of the key players I spoke to was in favor of the plan, but none of them wanted to go out front at this point. So I took the lead and announced the plan. The media's reaction was very negative, especially the local newspaper. Their concern was this industry could have too much muscle in exerting its will on the direction of the city and state. I did not share their concern as we were also going to diversify the economy with aerospace, medical research, construction, and port expansions.

As the media continued to whip up the citizenry's fears, the state, hotel association, and Harrah's ran for cover. I ended up abandoning the idea as I did not have time to fight this one alone. I had to keep moving to find other creative ways to generate revenue and keep my city out of bankruptcy. It is very interesting that a couple of years later many high-profile citizens in the city continued to come up to me and say not implementing my casino plan was a mistake and that the city's economy would be much stronger if we had done it. Whenever this happened I would just smile and say, "You are right, we missed it." But I also wondered where all these people were when we needed support. Unfortunately, at that time they were all probably still shell-shocked from the effects of Hurricane Katrina.

On Thursday, September 15, after the reopening of the previously flooded Pontchartrain Expressway, I officially announced to the press our phased plan to allow actual daytime access to residents and business owners by zip codes. Algiers on the West Bank of the Mississippi River had received only wind damage with zero flooding and would open that coming weekend on September 17. Uptown, which consisted of zip codes 70115 and 70118, would be reopened on September 21 and 23. The French Quarter would be available after September 26. This would allow up to 180,000 residents early access to the city. We reiterated that we were not allowing a permanent return at this point and access would be during daylight hours only.

In this announcement we advised our citizens that reentering the city wouldn't be a walk in the park. The stagnant water could be disease-ridden, and although their areas were dry, there could still be potential toxins in the air and soil. The other issue was the smell of mold now enveloped the city. So people who suffered from allergies and respiratory problems were advised not to reenter at this time. In preparation for these residents returning, I requested aerial spraying of the greater New Orleans area to minimize the potential for mass hatching of mosquitoes and flies to reduce the risk of vector-borne diseases spreading. I also wanted people to understand that we had limited hospital facilities back up and running just in case any health problems or injuries developed when they returned. Touro Infirmary and Children's Hospital, which were located uptown, were open only for emergency services.

As mentioned earlier, initially the running water had not yet been fully certified by the state, so we sent out the following advisory: "With the exception of Algiers, you are advised not to drink, bathe, or wash hands in water from your tap, and we recommend the use of bottled water for all personal use until further notice. You may flush toilets. We suggest you limit your exposure to airborne mold and use gloves, masks, and other protective materials."

The state would soon fully certify our water, and we quickly lifted this advisory. Our final warning for returning citizens was to immediately ventilate their homes and other buildings they entered by opening all windows as we were concerned about gas leaks. We further advised that if they detected a gas leak, they should immediately report it to Entergy and exit the affected structure.

Once we were ready to receive the first zip codes, the police and military set up computer systems at key entry points, and based on the citizen's ID such as social security number, date of birth, and address we tracked everyone's entry and reentry into the city. Our goal was to control access and keep looting down.

This strategy of repopulating the lesser damaged and safer areas of the city first was designed to get enough critical mass going so that economics and momentum took over. Once these initial areas were stabilized, then we would turn our attention to the most devastated areas, the Lower Ninth Ward, New Orleans East, Gentilly, and Lakeview. My fundamental premise was that everyone had a right to return to their home and be a part of the largest urban reconstruction project in the country's history.

We strictly enforced a dawn to dusk curfew. If civilians were caught on the streets after dusk, they would be escorted out of the city by military police. This was necessary to control the looters, the pirates. Our checkpoints required IDs, but many people had lost most of their identification papers in the flood, so we did our best to reasonably accommodate them all.

We set up a makeshift jail at the Union Passenger Terminal (UPT) station for thieves and other criminals. Entergy supplied generators to keep the UPT lit and power running. Unfortunately, our court system was still not operating, so it was impossible to process any charges, and many accused people just sat in jail for many months. These were truly amazing times that mandated unusual actions.

As this was going on, Admiral Thad Allen was still running around getting up to speed on the many aspects of this recovery both in Louisiana and Mississippi. He had a big job and a tremendous territory to cover. Sometimes when he returned to New Orleans and I would see him he would be somewhat shocked that we were moving things along so quickly without his direct input and approval. For some reason he and his key people thought they had more authority than they really had over critical local matters.

Several times the admiral would invite me and my key staff to their regular briefings with various agencies and military units. At first they just asked me to attend their meetings as a liaison, but when I asked a direct question they'd put a spin on it and would not give me a clear answer. I kept pushing on why things couldn't move faster. One of the admiral's key staff once said, "You don't understand, this is a very complicated process." My response was, "Please, tell me something I don't know."

What continued to bother me was if the United States could send ships and military troops to the other side of the world in a matter of hours, then why couldn't we get water drained and debris moved quicker? After a few more nonproductive meetings, we announced there was no need for us to continue to just sit and observe them go back and forth over the same issues. I also reminded them that I was still the mayor of the city, and decisions that directly affected my citizens had to be approved by me.

It wasn't long thereafter that Admiral Allen and I really started to knock heads, a lot of it publicly. He kept coming across as just another subversive person disregarding local needs. When I announced my plans to repopulate the city, the very next day the admiral publically made a point to counter-call my decision, advising citizens not to return. He would also publicly state that he was in charge of the rebuilding and the city. He was clearly stepping way out of his lane. It was almost like the White House was giving him orders to see how far he could go acting like he had the power of a duly elected mayor. I knew this was very dangerous and reckless since he didn't have a deep history and concern for our displaced citizens.

I was even more convinced at this point that three weeks after the storm hit, our displaced citizens had a right to come into the city and inspect their property. I had finally had enough and called him out publicly as "the federally appointed mayor of New Orleans." He immediately started to back off as this anti-democratic angle was something New Orleanians and Americans would not stand for. Our nation believes deeply in the people's right to choose their leaders through our election process, and not even Hurricane Katrina could change that.

I pulled him aside and asked him point-blank what was he doing consistently going against my authority as mayor. I then firmly reminded him he was not an elected official. Even General Honoré yanked his coattail and told him that he was way out of line. The general and I had been talking one-on-one, and he confided to me that he'd been trying to talk to the admiral to get him to understand how best to handle things. The general also told me the admiral was a good man who was a good soldier and normally followed orders from above.

In retrospect, I now believe the admiral was caught between two worlds, the disaster in our flood zone and the disaster in Washington. When I first announced my repopulation plan to the public, I'd met with Admiral Allen in advance, reviewed it with him, and he was fine with it. The only thing that makes sense is that he then consulted with Karl Rove and Secretary Chertoff, flipped his position, and went to the media to tell them he didn't think this was a good idea.

In Washington, the disaster capitalism thinking was working very hard to slow down the repopulation so that massive bulldozing could begin. If their plan worked, families would be forced to sell their properties for little or nothing, and corporate greed would be lavishly fed on the federal government's dime. The big problem they were having was I was not going to allow that to happen. Because I was so high profile, they couldn't ignore my position, and most New Orleanians had my back. New Orleans was going to be rebuilt even if I had to run over, under, or through Admiral Thad Allen or anyone else who got in the way of progress.

Meanwhile, the local newspaper, the *Times Picayune*, was working to put additional pressure on me to open up the French Quarter back to pre-Katrina levels of twenty-four-hour decadence. More and more contractors were coming in to work on the levees and on debris removal. The bar owners were pushing various buttons for unrestrained drinking, dancing, and partying. Out-of-town prostitutes from as far away as Russia were also being snuck in and out of town. This is the same newspaper that wrote on their opinion page that a limited expanded casino district was an outrageous idea.

They were hypocritically okay with all day and night absolute wildness, prostitution, and drugs in the French Quarter, but they were not willing to support billions of dollars of investment and substantial new tax dollars. I rejected their call as we were not quite up to dealing with a wide-open Bourbon Street. Our infrastructure was not ready, our police force was still totally exhausted, and we had another major challenge on the horizon.

Another storm had gained significant strength in the Gulf of Mexico and would be heading our way within a week. We were in the cone of probability for landfall. I now faced more tough decisions of possibly calling another mandatory evacuation, reversing our phased repopulation plan, and emptying downtown once again. Unfortunately, Mother Nature was not done with us after all as there were still many more secrets to behold in our continuing struggles to recovery...

AFTERWORD

—■—

Katrina's Secrets : Storms after the Storm is only part of my story, there is more to tell. Soon, I will release the second book in this series, Katrina's Secrets II: Rainbows after the Storm. This will continue your unique front-row seat journey through those remarkable five years after the storms. Complex phases of disaster management are further divulged, exposing more secrets as we strived toward the stabilization and recovery of New Orleans. Highlights include:

- Less than thirty days after Katrina hit, another more powerful storm headed our way. A second historic mandatory evacuation was called and the city flooded again.

- Unprecedented planning was done without a comparable playbook, model or guide to follow. Inspiration and guidance was found in the Book of Nehemiah.

- How we lobbied and were appropriated billions for the recovery. Federal dollars flowed through the state, who devised a discriminatory homeowner repair grant program.

- Controversy and distrust erupted with open talks of gentrification. This led to my infamous Chocolate City speech, insisting that everyone had the right to return.

- Elections proceeded even though most of our citizens were still displaced. Experts predicted my political death, as I was severely outspent in a historic national campaign for a local seat.

- Continual battles to wrestle control of federal recovery dollars from locals. The "Master of Disaster" was hired as recovery czar and we successfully invested in strategic target zones.

- Local media megalomaniacs' negativity toward an equitable recovery fueled skepticism, demonized certain leaders, and agitated racial tensions. I paid a heavy personal price as my family suffered silently. In spite of what we went through, the greatest comeback of all times happened as our citizens and the American public refused to let New Orleans die.

-By the storm's fifth anniversary, August 29, 2010, rainbows of recovery shone all over the city. Most empirical data confirmed New Orleans had regained her balance. To top this off, the New Orleans Saints won Super Bowl forty-four and we partied like never before.

-The greatest lesson of all is if New Orleans can come back from Katrina after all we faced, then anyone can recover from any disaster or struggle.

I would be honored if you would complete this journey with me by obtaining a copy or download of Katrina's Secrets II: Rainbows after the Storm in 2012.

CPSIA information can be obtained at www.ICGtesting.com
Printed in the USA
235619LV00008B/40/P

9 781460 959718

[15]